BRAND RESILIENCE

MANAGING RISK AND RECOVERY IN A HIGH-SPEED WORLD

Jonathan R. Copulsky

palgrave
macmillan

BRAND RESILIENCE

Copyright © Deloitte Development LLC, 2011.

All rights reserved.

First published in 2011 by
PALGRAVE MACMILLAN®
in the United States—a division of St. Martin's Press LLC,
175 Fifth Avenue, New York, NY 10010.

Where this book is distributed in the UK, Europe and the rest of the world,
this is by Palgrave Macmillan, a division of Macmillan Publishers Limited,
registered in England, company number 785998, of Houndmills,
Basingstoke, Hampshire RG21 6XS.

Palgrave Macmillan is the global academic imprint of the above companies
and has companies and representatives throughout the world.

Palgrave® and Macmillan® are registered trademarks in the United States,
the United Kingdom, Europe and other countries.

ISBN: 978–0–230–11138–7

Library of Congress Cataloging-in-Publication Data

Copulsky, Jonathan R.
    Brand resilience : managing risk and recovery in a high-speed world /
Jonathan R. Copulsky.
        p. cm.
    Includes index.
    ISBN 978–0–230–11138–7 (hardback)
    1. Branding (Marketing) 2. Brand name products. 3. Success in
business. I. Title.

HF5415.1255.C67 2011
658.8′72—dc22   2010049020

A catalogue record of the book is available from the British Library.

Design by Newgen Imaging Systems (P) Ltd., Chennai, India.

First edition: May 2011

10 9 8 7 6 5 4 3 2 1

Printed in the United States of America.

CONTENTS

ACKNOWLEDGMENTS

This is my second book.

More than thirty years have elapsed since I co-authored the first one, a guide to teaching comparative religion in high school. Much has changed since then, but one aspect of writing remains the same. Regardless of the number of authors who might appear on the title page, the book would never have come into being without the assistance and contributions of colleagues and collaborators, as well as the support and indulgence of loved ones. I have been the beneficiary of both.

Early on, I was encouraged in this endeavor by two colleagues, Anthony Downing and Bharath Oruganti. Both were tremendously excited by the book's topic and both made material contributions to the early thinking that went into the book's structure. Anthony first suggested the counterinsurgency metaphor, leading me to discover the *Counterinsurgency Field Manual*, which helped me structure the entire book.

Numerous current and former Deloitte[1] colleagues contributed to my research and writing. The list includes: Saqib Awan, Amy Booth, Bjorn Commers, Kaylin Connors, Lindsay Delgado, Sarah Drawert, Alicechandra Fritz, Gregg Geller, Chelsea Gorr, Eliot Hamlisch, Kristin Ige, Deepak Kadambi, Rahul Kannan, Nicole Lattner, Amanda Olsen, Laurie Pantages, Susanna Parry-Hoey, Adam Peter, Austin Piller, Eva Rowe, Kerri Sapp, Dietrich Schmidt, Andy Stevens, Hasim Surel, Bethanie Archbold Thomas, Charles Tsang, Veronique Valcu, and Rajeev Vijay.

Several Deloitte colleagues who have recently authored books or significant thought pieces were invaluable sources of insight and guidance, including Cathy Benko, Ed Moran, Anupam Narula, and Michael Raynor. Valarie Zeithaml, David S. Van Pelt Family Distinguished Professor of Marketing at University of North

Carolina's Kenan-Flagler Business School and a veteran author, provided me with great feedback on the book's content as well.

My thanks to John Callahan for sharing his thinking about Deloitte's plans for educating our practitioners regarding appropriate uses of social media.

I have gotten strong support for this endeavor from several of my partners who serve in firm leadership positions, including Jim Quigley, our global CEO, Punit Renjen, our US consulting CEO, Mike Canning, our strategy and operations leader, and Jonathan Trichel, the leader of our customer transformation practice. Tom Galizia and Paul Nelson merit a special shout-out. Both were working with me on client projects while I was writing this book and provided both moral support and air cover.

As I mention in chapter 7, I benefited greatly from discussions with a small team of graduate business students—Amit Gupta, Yueyuan "Tim" Li, Gopal Subramaniam—and their faculty adviser, Kapil Jain.

The professionals at Millward Brown, a subsidiary of WPP, provided me with great insights, as well as permission to refer to their research on brand value and brand trust. My thanks to Benoit Garbe, Phil Herr, Nigel Hollis, and Heather Stern.

Felicia Eth has served as my agent for this book. This is the second time that Felicia and I have ventured down the book publishing path, and she has, in both cases, been incredibly focused on "getting it done." Her encouragement was critical to my taking this book from concept to proposal to finished manuscript.

A number of years ago, I had the chance to meet Marty Neumeier, design guru and author of some of the best books that have ever been written on branding. Marty provided my colleagues and me with a great workspace as we went through an absolutely insane exercise of writing a pamphlet on customer strategy in three days. Marty and I remained in contact and I subsequently had the chance to help Marty out with his book, *Zag: The Number One Strategy of High-Performance Brands.* When I first started working on this book, I consulted with Marty and he provided me with blunt, thoughtful, specific, and highly usable feedback. Marty has provided ongoing feedback, and I was delighted when he agreed to lend his name to the book by authoring the foreword.

Emily Carleton, the Palgrave Macmillan senior editor, and Erica Warren, the production editor, have been a delight to work with on this project as we tried to push this book through at hyper-speed. Emily and Erica provided a good balance of sound advice and rapid editorial execution.

My wife of almost thirty years, Ellen Barreto, has been an indulgent supporter of almost everything that I have ever done, including writing this book. Ellen has, with mostly good humor, endured multiple weekends and evenings when I have been so focused on "my book" that I have had little time for anything else. She has been a good critic of my writing, offering great examples of powerful brands, as well as suggestions for how to make my key points in a more compelling manner.

When I speak to other authors about writing their books, most of them are glad that they have written the book, but not sure when they would be ready to tackle another one. I'm already thinking about the next one and look forward to the next army of volunteers who will help me with it.

WINNETKA, ILLINOIS
January 2011

FOREWORD

Jonathan Copulsky has written a book I've long felt was overdue. *Brand sabotage* is more than a catchy phrase; it's a growing reality. Brands are increasingly critical to business success, which makes them increasingly vulnerable to the attacks of angry customers, aggressive competitors, and a voracious, twenty-four-hour media.

The need to guard against these slings and arrows is a fairly new one. At the beginning of the Industrial Revolution, for example, a brand was merely a literal mark of ownership. If your goal was to keep your competitors at bay, you built a factory, not a brand. Why? Because the factory created a barrier to competition. Unless your competitors could match the efficiencies of your factory, you won, and they lost.

But let's look at where the history of competitive barriers has led.

In the Industrial Age, your rivals eventually built their own assembly lines, which caused the factory barrier to show some cracks. So the new barrier to competition became capital. If you could get capital—let's say to build more factories—and your competitors couldn't, you would win and they would lose.

After a while, money became easier to get, so the favored barrier to competition moved from capital to patents. If you could defend your product or process in a court of law, you could keep the copycats out of your yard for years, if not decades.

Today the speed of the market is shrinking the patent barrier. What is the value of a patent when your competitors can simply leapfrog it with a whole new product or a whole new technology platform? Twenty-first-century companies are learning that, in a marketplace roiled by relentless change and rising clutter, the most effective barrier to competition is not intellectual capital, but branding. A brand—which I define in the twenty-first century as a customer's gut feeling about a product, service, or company—is a clever way to keep competitors off your turf. By occupying a favorable position in your customers' minds, you can inspire them to defend you against the advances of your competitors. Not bad.

Now, notice something interesting about competitive barriers. Over time, they've moved from the physical (factories) to the symbolic (capital) to the intellectual (patents) and finally to the emotional (brands). And, most importantly, they've moved from within a company's control to outside it. You can't control how people feel. All you can do is manage the raw materials that customers use to build your brand: the products, services, communications, and company behaviors that make your brand meaningful to customers.

In fact, some of the world's most successful companies have managed their brands so well that their *intangible* assets—i.e., their brands—have achieved a higher market valuation than their *tangible* assets. Coca-Cola, Apple, and Google come to mind. They would be in serious trouble if they suddenly had to operate without the power boost of their brands.

Brands come under attack for any number of reasons—some justified, others not. Many years ago, for example, the car company Audi was attacked in the media (as well as in the courts) for "sudden acceleration." This was the alleged tendency of the Audi 5000 to speed up unexpectedly and crash into other cars, center dividers, and garage walls. The Audi problem turned out to be a case of mass hysteria and legal opportunism. But it didn't stop the Audi brand from plummeting to the bottom, nearly consigning the company to the scrap heap.

More recently, the airline JetBlue lost face when a massive storm caused their flights to back up, stranding thousands of passengers in scores of airports. In this case a quick, heartfelt apology from the company's president, along with a new policy designed to protect fliers from future crises, pulled JetBlue out of a tailspin.

While you *can* manage certain aspects of your brand, you can't control the weather. You can't control the media. You can't control what your competitors do. You can't even control the behavior of your own employees. Which means that the most effective barrier to competition—your trusted brand—is exposed to danger from any number of directions. Even the most loyal customer can change allegiances when the trust that underpins that loyalty is threatened.

What's your best defense? I won't steal the thunder from the pages that follow. But I will say this: Forewarned is forearmed. If you make the effort to protect your brand, if you behave as if your reputation were money, you'll earn your customers' permission to build this most valuable of assets—your brand—long, long into the future.

—MARTY NEUMEIER
author of *The Brand Gap*

Introduction

IT'S WHAT YOU DO NEXT THAT COUNTS

On November 27, 2009, at approximately 2:25 A.M., a man drove his car into a fire hydrant. Initial reports notwithstanding, the driver sustained no major injuries and was quickly released from the hospital. No significant property damage resulted. And, unlike most early-morning single-driver automobile accidents, reports indicated that the driver was not intoxicated.

Under normal circumstances, the accident might have merited a brief mention in the police blotter of the weekly community newspaper. And other than a few local kooks who, like me, still read that section after more than twenty years of suburban living, no one would have noticed.

But news of this particular accident made virtually every major newspaper, broadcast, and blog in the world, because the driver was Tiger Woods, golf's most influential player and, arguably, the most famous athlete in the world. As John Paul Newport reported in the *Wall Street Journal*, "this story—in essence the near-total takedown of a man who once held the highest popularity rating, 88%, of any figure in any field that the Gallup Poll has ever measured—was more than news. It was a seismic cultural event."[1]

If you're not convinced, try Googling "Tiger Woods car." Google will respond with millions of results, including news reports, crash photos, commentaries on Woods's actions—even a somewhat bizarre video reenactment of the accident from Chinese television. YouTube contains a whole host of videos related to the accident, ranging from two musicians singing "The Clubhouse Blues" ("Way

way misunderstood / Ran as fast as he could / Still got slugged by Mrs. Woods"[2]) to that dean of indecency Howard Stern dissecting Woods's indiscretions.[3]

Of course, Woods is neither the first nor the last well-known public figure involved in extracurricular hanky-panky. These days, politicians on both sides of the aisle, as well as a virtual army of athletes and celebrities, seem to be having a hard time avoiding reports of both minor peccadilloes and major imbroglios. So to simply interpret Woods's fall as the classic morality tale of a celebrity gone wrong misses its real meaning. The exposure of what *New York Times* columnist Frank Rich described as "the maniacally reckless life we now know [Woods] led"[4] was a major calamity in the world of marketing, triggering the meltdown of a seemingly unassailable brand and potentially undermining the value of any high-profile sponsor whose reputation (and integrity) was closely tied to his.

In the month that followed, in fact, several of the world's top brands announced that they were scaling back or completely discontinuing advertising campaigns featuring Woods, although others stood by him steadfastly. The investments that had been made in tying these top brands to the Tiger Woods image are mind-boggling. While Woods appeared in 27 percent of the ads of the watch manufacturer TAG Heuer,[5] more than 80 percent of the ads for Accenture, one of the world's most prominent professional services firms, featured Woods. During its six-year relationship with Woods, Accenture is estimated to have spent more than $280 million on ads that largely featured his image.[6]

A *New York Times* article by Ken Belson and Richard Sandomir in January 2010 notes the spate of inquiries inundating insurers from "corporations seeking to protect...their brands...when their celebrity endorsers suffer public embarrassment."[7] The same article refers to a study by Chris Knittel, a professor of economics at the University of California, Davis, indicating that the "seven publicly held companies that have or had sponsorship deals with Woods lost $12 billion in market value in the month after Woods's statement in December that he was taking a leave from golf." Meanwhile, the PGA—whose revenues went from $302.5 million in 1996 (when Woods turned pro) to $981 million in 2008—experienced difficulties attracting sponsors, selling tickets, and filling hospitality tents (already a tricky task when the economic winds are against you).[8] As Larry Dorman reports, "[television] ratings for 2010 tour events in which Woods usually would have played have taken a beating, with an average of half as many viewers—2.3 million versus 4.6 million—tuned in compared to 2007–08."[9]

Since the initial incident, Woods has publicly apologized (if you missed the press conference, you can easily find it on YouTube).[10] The apology generated another spate of press, television, and blog coverage, including speculation about whether Woods's return to the game might be imminent and whether his apology was sincere or effective. Reporters likened it to the confessions of an alcoholic who has finally been exposed. In his *Wall Street Journal* article "Maybe We All Need Rehab," Jason Gay wrote, "Using the language of a person not unfamiliar with the world of recovery, he acknowledged that his path to rehabilitation was long and incomplete. It was a Tiger Slam of regret."[11]

Woods's future is far from clear. By the time that you read this, he will be back in the hunt for his next golf title. It will probably be a long while before he can recapture his former glory and generate his previous level of sponsorship and advertising earnings. Whenever a sponsor does decide to sign Woods, they can expect another flurry of articles debating the merits of the decision. Time will tell which brands are better off: those that curtailed their marketing spend with Woods or those that stuck with him.[12]

Woods's story is the perfect case study for the threats that brands face from brand saboteurs, be they intentional or accidental. Every day, brand saboteurs are hard at work undermining the investments that organizations make in their brands. While some deliberately seek out opportunities to subvert carefully crafted brand strategies and marketing messages, many are unwitting employees who live within the organization or just outside its borders, as suppliers, channel partners, or even spokesmen. As the now-famous Tiger Woods incident demonstrates, the marketing equivalent of friendly fire may be more devastating to brands than the deliberate efforts of the most formidable competitors and critics. Frenemy, anyone?

INVESTING IN BRAND BUILDING IS NO LONGER ENOUGH

In a viral world where true (and not so true) news spreads like wild-fire, protecting brands from sabotage can be an all-consuming task. Social media like YouTube, Twitter, and Facebook allow competitors, employees, customers, and partners to be loud, fast, and public in ways that John Peter Zenger, the father of freedom of the press, never imagined. As the brochure for a seminar on social reputation management advertises, in an almost comically understated sentence, "It's no secret that consumers are talking about brands through social media and social networking."[13]

Great brand marketers know what it takes to build great brands, and there is no shortage of organizations, books, and training programs to help them elevate their efforts. However, for the risk-intelligent enterprise, investing in brand building is no longer enough. In a world filled with intentional and accidental brand saboteurs, companies need to aggressively play defense as well as offense. Brands are under constant attack, and brand stewards must systematically understand the risks that their brands face, the potential impacts, and the options for managing these risks. The only alternative is to let all that hard-won brand equity disappear faster than beer and chips at a Super Bowl party.

WHOSE JOB IS IT TO MANAGE BRAND RISK?

Few companies fully consider the potential for brand sabotage when it comes to hiring and training employees or setting policies for their employees to follow. Few companies have sufficient insight into the behavior and practices of their partners and suppliers to understand how much risk they actually face. Similarly, few companies have the capability to understand their customer base in its entirety, and conse-quently, most occasionally offend valuable customers who naturally assume that the companies know them better than they actually do.

Managing the risks associated with brand sabotage begins with the chief marketing officer but requires the vigilance and support of everyone across the enterprise. Even the board of directors has a role to play by determining that the right governance is in place to assess and contain risks to the brand.

WHAT THIS BOOK IS ABOUT

In the pages that follow, we'll share other stories of brand sabotage that should convince you that the threat is real and imminent, but also manageable. If you're reading this book, congratulations—you've already taken the first step in protecting your investment. Our goal is to convince you that there *is* a light at the end of the tunnel, and it's not just the headlamp of a train heading at you full speed.

We will provide you with the tools and frameworks to determine how susceptible your organization is to brand sabotage and what actions you can take to reduce its likelihood and impact. We will discuss roles and responsibilities within your organization for managing the risks of brand sabotage and we will identify how to make brand-risk intelligence a core competency.

You will also see that there are powerful lessons to be learned by looking at history. One of the more famous cases of brand sabotage took place almost twenty years ago when seven people died after taking pain-relief capsules that had been poisoned. The response of Johnson & Johnson—the parent company of McNeil Consumer Products Company, the manufacturer of the tainted capsules—is still the gold standard when it comes to responding decisively in the face of tragedy and still offers insights to those willing to listen. But we will also talk about more recent events, including the experience of US armed forces fighting insurgencies in Iraq and Afghanistan.

Brand Resilience starts with a discussion of why we think that brand risk is at an all-time high. We then move to a discussion of how the recent experiences of the top military field commanders can help inform the actions that you can take to protect your brand in today's high-speed and hyperconnected world. From there, we walk you through a seven-step program designed to make your organization battle-ready when it comes to managing brand risks. Finally, we conclude with a look at the challenges lurking around the next corner and what you can do to prepare yourself for them.

Building a great brand now requires building a resilient brand, and defense and recovery are the two keys to resilience. Perhaps the most apt guidance comes from the caption of a widely distributed ad showing Tiger Woods (prior to his Escalade escapade) standing in the rough. It reads, "It's what you do next that counts."[14]

PART ONE

WHY YOUR BRAND IS AT MORE RISK THAN YOU THINK IN A HIGH-SPEED WORLD

Chapter One

A BRAND NEW DAY

Valuable Brands, Fragile Brands

Close your eyes for a moment and consider the word *brand.*

Within milliseconds, images of the world's leading corporate brands, ranging from Nike to Apple to Disney, may flood your brain. Or, to be more *au courant*, Google, Facebook, Twitter, Wikipedia, Yelp, Foursquare, Urbanspoon, and YouTube.

The images inevitably consist of the iconic symbols, logos, and trademarks we encounter dozens of times a day on clothing, shopping bags, packages, sports arenas, office buildings, and homepages. Nike's swoosh, Apple's partially eaten apple, Google's font, Disney's Mickey Mouse, Geico's gecko, McDonald's golden arches, and Coca-Cola's script. If you're a baby boomer like me, you may think of Oscar Mayer's Wienermobile. If you're a millennial, maybe you'll think of the Red Bull MINI Cooper.

Think about it a little longer. We bet you can come up with brands associated with every aspect of life: sports, popular culture, politics, geographic regions, and even literature.

- **The Chicago Cubs**, our hometown team, is a winner when it comes to brand recognition, thanks in part to television station WGN and its national cable reach. Cubs-branded caps, hats, towels, pennants, and other assorted merchandise generate millions in annual sales.[1] If you have any doubts about the strength of the brand, try getting tickets to a home game at Wrigley Field on a Saturday afternoon in July.
- **The Olympics** has its distinctive five rings, theme song, torch, and thousands of athletes who proudly bear the title of Olympian. Every four years, television networks ante up a king's ransom to secure broadcast

rights ($2.2 billion for US rights to the 2010 Winter Olympics and 2012 Summer Olympics[2]), corporations shell out extraordinary sums to sponsor the games, and cities invest huge amounts of money to support their Olympic bids. The lucky bid winner then earns the right to spend boatloads more money to build the venues and facilities that will allow it to stage the Olympics and Paralympics for a stretch of approximately four weeks.

- **Paris Hilton** created incredible recognition first for herself and then for her Paris Hilton–branded products by parlaying a surname most known for its association with a global luxury hospitality chain. Her official website (www.parishilton.com) features footwear, fragrances, handbags, sunglasses, hair accessories, watches, sportswear, bedding, swimwear, and lingerie "collections" in addition to her blog, photos, videos, and other "news" items. Hilton, given as she is to tabloid coverage, personifies the idea of being famous for being famous as she graces the pages of *People* and *Us Weekly*. When Paris's brand wanes, any number of reality television stars, ranging from Kim Kardashian to Bethenny Frankel, are poised to replace her.[3]

- **Donald Trump** has his name emblazoned on the marquees of office buildings, hotels, and casinos. You can also tack on the advice books based on the Donald's business experience, a reality television show designed to test the mettle of would-be moguls, golf courses, a university, clothing, eyewear, leather goods, jewelry, furniture, lighting, home décor, mattresses, spring water, and vodka. Try to trump that.[4]

- **Barack Obama** was an electoral success due, in part, to the meticulous manner by which the Obama brand was developed, cultivated, and merchandised. Think of the photograph artfully converted into the now-famous campaign poster by artist Shepard Fairey (although apparently without first securing permission from the photograph's owner, the Associated Press), the simple but powerful theme of change (as in "Change We Can Believe In"), the patriotically colored O adorning bumper stickers and lawn signs, and the emotionally compelling personal narrative that informed not one but two bestselling books. In April 2009 Desirée Rogers, the former White House social secretary, asserted "we have the best brand on Earth: the Obama brand."[5] (Presidential adviser David Axelrod responded, "The president is a person, not a product. We shouldn't be referring to him as a brand."[6])

- We find **Sarah Palin**, the onetime mayor of an Anchorage suburb turned political dragon slayer, on the other side of the aisle. Palin and her running mate were self-styled "mavericks," with Palin willing to engage in a little self-parody by appearing on *Saturday Night Live* alongside her doppelgänger, Tina Fey, before taking up the mantle of political commentator. Ironically, they branded themselves with the name of a nineteenth-century Texas rancher, Samuel Maverick, who resolutely refused to brand his own cattle.[7] In 2009, Palin added the sobriquet "rogue."[8]

- Geographies have long been associated with brands, particularly when it comes to food. Think of the basics—cheese (Roquefort), wine (Burgundy), and meat (Prosciutto di Parma). But the lure of geographic links has spread beyond quaint agrarian regions of France and Italy. The December 14, issue of the *New York Times* (a clear geographic tie) carried an article on "**Brooklyn**: The Brand." Brooklyn-branded products mentioned in the article include pickles, salsa, beer, and chocolate. It also describes a new bar, The Brooklyneer, that features Brooklyn hot dogs, Brooklyn pickles, Brooklyn whiskey, Brooklyn ricotta, Brooklyn jam, and Brooklyn-brewed kombucha, despite being located in Manhattan. The bar's owners define a Brooklyneer as "someone who admires Brooklyn" and claim that they "merely wanted to share the food and drink they love with the rest of the city."[9]

- **Jane Austen**, the nineteenth-century author of romantic novels, is a brand. The opening paragraphs of her novel *Pride and Prejudice* appeared unattributed in the early ads for Barnes & Noble's ebook reader the Nook, as if daring the reader to identify the source. Legions of rabid Janeites eagerly consume new books, movies, and musicals that build upon her considerable legacy. *Pride and Prejudice and Zombies*, anyone?[10]

- Even terrorists have become brands. The January 31, 2010, edition of the *Wall Street Journal* carried an editorial titled "Carlos the Brand: The Jackal Has a Brand to Protect" that described an upcoming ruling by a court in Paris on a claim lodged by one Ilich Ramírez Sánchez, a.k.a. **Carlos the Jackal**. Carlos and his lawyer-cum-wife were "suing a French production company for the right to review and 'correct and edit' a made-for-TV film about him entitled 'Carlos.'" Carlos and his lawyer alleged that "the filmmakers...[were] out to 'demolish Carlos,'" whose aim in filing the suit was "to protect the intellectual property rights to his name and 'biographical image.'"[11]

- Barco Uniforms offers a line of *Grey's Anatomy* scrubs for nurses.[12] The article "Branding Operation" by *New York Times* columnist Rob Walker quotes a letter from a reader who writes, "How odd is it that a profession that asks people to trust its members to take life-or-death actions would advertise a brand based on a TV show on the job?"[13]

Was it always like this?

The word *brand*, based on an Old Norse word meaning "to burn," originally referred to the practice of herders burning marks onto the hides of their animals. The different marks on the livestock identified individual herders and, thus, their products. Over time, a brand became synonymous with the names and images that manufacturers developed to distinguish their products from those of their competitors. A variety of businesses claim to be the first to have registered a brand, including the British brewer Bass & Company, which used its distinctive red triangle on the barrels of ale that it shipped all over the world.[14]

It's a short hop, skip, and a jump from a red triangle to the Budweiser Tastebuds. We have moved beyond simple brand marks printed on products and shipping containers. Everywhere you look, you see a veritable sea of brands.

Consider food. In 1988, during a vacation in France dedicated to the consumption of copious amounts of fine food and wine, my wife and I were lucky enough to dine at a very special restaurant in Lyon, L'Auberge du Pont de Collonges. The restaurant's chef and owner was (and is) Paul Bocuse, one of the fathers of nouvelle cuisine and a recipient of the *Michelin Guide*'s coveted three stars.

My wife still talks about the food, ambience, and service more than twenty years later as her benchmark for fine dining. We were surprised, consequently, given this experience, to see the cabinets in the restaurant's entry hall filled with Paul Bocuse–branded merchandise available for sale to patrons. Hardly what we expected to see in this bastion of elevated taste.

That was then. Not long after our visit, Bocuse opened up a restaurant at Walt Disney's Epcot. Other Paul Bocuse restaurants have followed. Today, Paul Bocuse has a website that includes "l'Espace E-Boutique de Paul BOCUSE" and sponsors the Bocuse d'Or, a biennial culinary competition featuring teams from twenty-four countries. In retrospect, it seems that Bocuse was in fact an early innovator when it came to profiting from a chef's fame through branded books, television shows, prepared foods, and cookware. What seemed odd in the twentieth century is common practice in the twenty-first.

Chefs are not the only brand names when it comes to food. In Chicago, for example, grass-fed Tallgrass Beef (founded by brand-name journalist Bill Kurtis) is offered for home consumption as well as on the menus of the city's top restaurants. You can sip branded espresso at the local outlet of a global coffee chain, where you can also buy its branded blended drinks, branded coffee-related merchandise, and branded music using the store's branded stored-value card. Or you can buy the global coffee chain's branded ice cream or branded bottled coffee drinks at your branded superstore.

At Deloitte, the professional services firm where I have spent the past fourteen years of my career, we teach our new practitioners to think about what it will take to build their "personal brand" and counsel them that their professional success is directly related to these brand-building efforts. On more than one occasion, I have delivered a PowerPoint presentation in which I quote from Tom Peters's book *The Brand You 50*: "We are CEOs of our own companies: Me Inc. Our most important job is to be head marketer for the brand called You. Starting today you are a brand. The good news is that everyone has a chance to stand out. It's this simple: You are in charge of your brand."[15]

Not too long ago, I read an article about Bloggy Boot Camp, an event designed to help the participants (about 90 percent of them mothers) "take their blogs up a notch, whether in hopes of generating ad revenue and sponsorships, attracting attention to a cause or branching out into paid journalism or marketing." The title of the article? "Honey, Don't Bother Mommy. I'm Too Busy Building My Brand."[16] The article's title, if not the piece itself, was tongue-in-cheek, although I found a breathless endorsement of the article on Samson Media's blog, Playing in Traffic, which opened, "As you probably know by now, in today's business environment, it's ALL about your personal brand."[17]

A discussion on personal brands once led a colleague to refer me to the Interbrand website. Interbrand, a leading brand consultancy (as it says on their site, "started in 1974 when the world still thought of brands as just another word for logo"), offers a section on its website featuring its "Personal Brand Valuation" methodology.[18] I was mildly disappointed to discover that it's actually meant to help value celebrities and athletes for endorsement purposes, rather than for ordinary schlubs like me. But after the Tiger Woods incident, it's not surprising that advertisers and sponsors would be interested in tools for personal brand valuation.

You get the idea.

THE POWER OF UBIQUITOUS BRANDS

The explosive growth of brands should come as no surprise. While it's easy to poke fun at the self-promoters scrambling to build their personal brands, the fact remains that ubiquitous brands are incredibly powerful value-creation engines.

What do we mean by a "ubiquitous brand"? A ubiquitous brand is one where the brand's presence and reputation extends well beyond the products or services with which it was originally associated to the point where it generates substantial economic benefits for its owners above and beyond the margins generated by the sale of its core products or services.

In the 2010 study "BrandZ Top 100 Most Valuable Global Brands," by Millward Brown Optimor, the ten most valuable global brands (Google, IBM, Apple, Microsoft, Coca-Cola, McDonald's, Marlboro, China Mobile, General Electric, and Vodafone) collectively account for an eye-popping $693 billion of value.[19] The 2009 version of this same study notes that "in a year of global financial turmoil, when every key financial indicator plummeted, the value of the top 100 brands increased by 2 percent to $2 trillion."[20] Sounds like a much better performance than my investment portfolio during the same period. It also sounds like a great opportunity for a financial engineer to figure out how to create a class of securities based on brand value.

Ubiquitous brands attract customers like flowers attract bees. These customers often pay premium prices, despite the availability of less expensive and equally serviceable alternatives. The willingness of customers to wait years to plunk down $6,000 (or more, according to my wife, who knows about these things) to purchase a Birkin handbag from Hermès is just one example of the hold a ubiquitous brand can have on its customers. Other examples range from the Cheerios that you consume for breakfast in lieu of the generic oat cereals that sit alongside it on the grocery shelf, to the popular

BMW 3 Series that drivers continue to snap up despite the availability of much cheaper domestic alternatives.

Ubiquitous brands give their owners permission to enter new markets and launch new products and services in ways not available to owners of weaker brands. Take a look at how the market holds its breath whenever Apple drops the slightest hint of a new product launch. In the days surrounding the launch of Apple's iPad, the buzz was unbelievable. People may have criticized the price, the name, the features, and the functionality, but there was no lack of people talking, writing, blogging, and, tweeting—even though the product announcement preceded the actual availability by months. Apple has become an iconic brand, revered for its design aesthetic, distinctive advertising, and innovative products, and it was named the world's most admired company by *Fortune* in 2009.

Apple's success with its devices has also propelled the success of services and complementary products that adhere to Apple's design standards. In the company's reporting for the quarter that ended in December 2009, iPod sales grew 1 percent to $3.39 billion, while revenues from Apple-branded and third-party iPod accessories, iTunes-store sales, and other iPod services rose 15 percent to $1.16 billion.[21]

The proliferation of successful brand extensions and the growth of lucrative brand licensing exemplify the potential of strong brands to create value. The major sports leagues generate billions of dollars in incremental revenue each year from licensed merchandise such as video games, apparel, toys, and trading cards—more than $13 billion and growing. Westin's Heavenly Bed, designed to address travelers' concerns about the difficulty of enjoying a restful night while staying at a hotel, has been so successful that Westin now sells the bed through in-room catalogs, online, and at Nordstrom.[22]

WHAT ELSE CAN A UBIQUITOUS BRAND DO FOR YOUR COMPANY?

Ubiquitous brands are a magnet for talent, attracting employees as well as customers.

Like customers, employees relish being associated with a brand that radiates personality. What's good for the goose is apparently good for the gander. It should come as no surprise, then, that the lists of top brands and top employers correlate highly. Google, number one on the brand value list, ranks number four on *Fortune*'s 2010 list of "100 Best Companies to Work For."[23]

Customers flaunt their consumption of ubiquitous brands, and engaged employees can become the most conspicuous consumers of a ubiquitous brand's products and services. Visit an Apple store if you want to see highly satisfied employee advocates at work, serving highly loyal customers. According to Sanford C. Bernstein analysts, Apple reached $1 billion in annual retail sales faster than any retailer in history. Its stores generate more than $4,000 per square foot—a tidy sum, particularly when compared to $2,600 for Tiffany, no slouch in the branding department itself.[24]

Brand value, as calculated by Millward Brown Optimor and others, is real and significant and is clearly reflected in the stock prices of publicly traded companies. By their calculations, for example, 61 percent of American Express's market capitalization comes from its brand value. It's hard to believe that the most valuable assets of many companies don't show up on their balance sheets, thus avoiding the scrutiny that comes with financial regulation, reporting, and disclosure.

Because of the huge advantage conferred by employee advocates, measuring employee engagement and loyalty is now common practice. Organizations recognize that engaged and loyal employees are their best advertisements, while strong brands help to engage employees and keep them loyal.

IT TAKES HARD WORK TO DEVELOP UBIQUITOUS BRANDS

The critically acclaimed television show *Mad Men* is what used to be known as a water-cooler show. The day after the broadcast of a water-cooler show, workers in the office would gather around the water cooler (or perhaps the coffee machine) to discuss the show's latest plot developments and intrigues.

Mad Men is a show about the heyday of advertising, when any advertising agency that mattered was housed in a building located along New York's Madison Avenue. In *Mad Men*'s version of reality, its mostly male executives wear suits to work, drink cocktails at lunch, and have assistants to answer their phones and type their correspondence while they busy themselves creating brilliant television commercials and fabulous four-color magazine spreads featuring their clients' products. What a life.

Mad Men is mainly about creativity, with a little bit of account management thrown into the mix. The palette for this creativity is mass media—network television, newspapers, and national magazines—with the attendant millions of viewers and readers.

In the early 1960s, when *Mad Men* is set, virtually every household with a television watched network television—ABC, CBS, or NBC. There was no Fox, no CNN, no FX, no TBS, and certainly no AMC, *Mad Men's* home network.

CBS's *Gunsmoke,* a network television legend, symbolized the power and draw of network television in the early 1960s. *Gunsmoke's* 635 episodes ran from September 10, 1955, to March 31, 1975. It was the number-one-ranked show from 1957 to 1961.[25] Almost half of American households watched a typical broadcast, featuring James Arness as US Marshal Matt Dillon, Milburn Stone as Doc Adams, and Amanda Blake as saloonkeeper Kitty Russell. For years, viewers wondered about the true nature of the relationship between Marshal Dillon and Miss Kitty.

In the days portrayed by *Mad Men,* building a brand meant buying commercials on popular network television shows like *Gunsmoke.* Perhaps you'd also throw in some ads in a couple of major magazines and daily newspapers. With a decent media budget but without too much work, you could easily reach most American households.

Reaching the same portion of households is a lot harder and a lot more expensive today. Consumers are busy playing video games, surfing the web, updating their Facebook accounts, listening to their iPods, and following their friends on Twitter.[26] If they *are* actually watching a television show, it's probably on one of the dozens of cable channels available to them. Or on a DVR, a mobile phone, an on-demand video service, a portable MP3 player, an online video-sharing site, or any number of other technologies that allow them to see what they want when they want it. And they can happily do so without interruption by the commercials that were once the bedrock of brand building.

The decline of network television has been mirrored in virtually every advertising-supported medium that existed twenty years ago. *Reader's Digest*, which enjoyed peak US circulation of 17 million in the 1970s, had dropped to 8 million by 2009. Daily newspaper penetration dropped below 50 percent long ago, and almost every day brings new reports of newspapers going out of business. *Mad Men*, AMC's most popular show, regularly captures fewer than 2 million viewers for its regular broadcasts, although it garners additional viewers through the web and on-demand versions.

So, brand owners need creative new ways to do what used to be easy.

Building a brand today means much more than just spending money on mass media. The clusters of coworkers that gathered around the water coolers of the 1960s have been replaced by virtual communities that connect through social media—like the slyly named Watercooler, a startup in California that creates social games and sports-fan communities on Facebook and other top social networks. Its games and applications have been installed by more than 30 million users.[27]

Instead of a relatively straightforward mix of network television and other mass media, brand owners need to think about integrating more narrowly targeted elements like video programming, niche publications, event marketing, sponsorships, direct marketing, online marketing, social media, etc., ad infinitum.

Meanwhile, it's not getting any cheaper.

Take the Super Bowl, a barometer of advertising health, and one of the few broadcasts that has actually increased its absolute viewership since the '60s. The 2010 Super Bowl generated the highest viewership in broadcast history—as the *Hollywood Reporter* points out, the 2010 event "drew 106.5 million viewers...edging out 1983's *M*A*S*H* finale, which garnered 105.97 million viewers—although these figures also reflect the fact that the total "TV audience...[had] climbed from 218 million viewers to 292 million" between 1983 and 2010.[28] In 2011, Super Bowl viewership edged up again to 111 million viewers. (For the record, the stats are in table 1.1.)

Big opportunities come with big brands, but it's harder work than it used to be to realize the opportunity. The difficulty in delivering against these opportunities partly explains why chief marketing officers tend to have some of the shortest life spans in the executive suite. In figures compiled by Spencer Stuart's Greg Welch, the average CMO's shelf life

Table 1.1 Super Bowl: The barometer of advertising health

Super Bowl	Viewership	Cost for a thirty-second spot	Cost per thousand viewers
Super Bowl I (1967)	51 million	$42,500/CBS $37,500/NBC*	$.83/.73
Super Bowl XXI (1987)	87 million	$600,000	$6.90
Super Bowl XL (2006)	90 million	$2.5 million	$27.78
Super Bowl XLIV (2010)	107 million	$2.6 million	$24.29
Super Bowl XLV (2011)	111 million	$30 million	$27.03

*The only time the game was broadcast on two networks.

Sources: Bill Gorman, "Super Bowl TV Ratings," *TV By the Numbers*, January 18, 2009, http://tvbythenumbers.com/2009/01/18/historical-super-bowl-tv-ratings/11044; David Bauder, "Super Bowl 2010 Ratings," *The Huffington Post,* February 8, 2010, http://www.huffingtonpost.com/2010/02/08/super-bowl-2010-ratings-m_n_453503.html; "Super Bowl 2007," *Advertising Age, http://adage.com/Super BowlBuyers/superbowlhistory07.html;* Emily Fredrix, "Super Bowl Commercial Prices Fall for Second Time Ever," *The Huffington Post,* January 11, 2010, http://www.huffingtonpost.com/2010/01/11/super-bowl-commercial-pri_n_418245. html; "Sluggish Economy Pinches Super Bowl Ad Prices," MSNBC, http://www. msnbc.msn.com/id/34803473/; Richard Sandomir, "Super Bowl Dethrones M*A*S*H as Most-Watched Show in U.S. History," *The New York Times,* February 8, 2010, http://www.nytimes.com/2010/02/09/sports/football/09sandomir.html; Aaron Smith, "Is a $3 million, 30-second Super Bowl Ad Really Worth It?" CNNMoney.com, February 3, 2011, http://money.cnn.com/2011/02/03/news/companies/super_bowl_ads/index.htm.

is 75 percent shorter than that of the next-shortest-lived executive, the chief information officer, and 60 percent shorter than that of the other senior executives. CMO Mike Linton attributes this to the "marketer's dilemma," which requires CMOs "to hit the sweet spot that delivers today's results while building the brand for the long term."[29]

■ BRANDS ARE NOW ABOUT TRUST

Traditionally, brands have played a key role in communicating the quality of a product or service. As any good dictionary will tell you, quality means being free from defects, deficiencies, and significant variations. The International Organization for Standards (ISO) defines quality as "the totality of features and characteristics of a product or service that bears its ability to satisfy stated or implied needs."[30]

Successful brand owners develop measurable and verifiable quality standards and put processes in place to ensure that those standards are consistently and uniformly met. When you purchase a branded soap or visit a branded hotel or eat at a branded restaurant, you trust the brand to ensure that you enjoy a quality bar of soap, a quality hotel room, and a quality dining experience.

Quality also implies what *won't* happen as much as what will. A quality razor delivers a smooth shave, but also a safe one. A quality car comfortably transports its passengers from place to place without the need for unscheduled repairs. A quality meal is one that is enjoyable to eat, but also won't make you ill.

A friend from another country reported her initial experience in the United States shopping for cereal at a local grocery store. As she entered the cereal aisle, she was confronted with what seemed like miles of shelves, covered with an amazing array of sizes and varieties of transformed grains waiting for a bowl, spoon, and milk—far more choices than she had ever seen before. She froze. Her tension abated, however, when she recognized a cereal box containing "her brand" and she realized that the move to the United States didn't mean abandoning the familiar, and safe, choice.

There are plenty of ways to gauge the quality of a product or service. You can turn to Zagat or Yelp to help you find and select a restaurant. You can turn to J. D. Power to help you evaluate cars. If you want to buy a camera, a powerboat, a computer, a flat-panel television, a stove, a pair of running shoes, or a myriad of other products, you can easily find an Internet site, blog, or wiki that rates and describes it. In fact, we contend that you will quickly be overwhelmed by the incredible abundance of information about how to make the best possible selection among all of the options available to you.

Third party-evaluators have been with us for years. In 1936, Consumers Union, the parent company of *Consumer Reports,* was founded as "an expert, independent, nonprofit organization whose mission is to work for a fair, just, and safe marketplace for all consumers and to empower consumers to protect themselves."[31] But the current set of alternatives presents an astonishing breadth and depth of robust and easy-to-use information. Information that used to be expensive or time-consuming to obtain and difficult to digest is now cheap and easy, thanks to the thousands of webmavens that make the acquisition of this information their life's work.

In 2006, my colleague Alistair Davidson and I coauthored an article for *Strategy and Leadership* in which we described the growth of webmavens as key influencers on customer buying behavior. We also discussed the emergence of a new imperative for chief marketing officers focused on "maven management." While comments from webmavens can provide product managers with fresh intelligence on the failures and successes that customers are experiencing with their offerings, the bad news is that the negative feedback from just one or two influential webmavens can have dire results for a brand's reputation.[32]

Consumers are changing their habits as a result. Sixty-three percent of Americans (191 million), are actively using the Internet, and people now default to websites to help them understand and evaluate their options before making a major purchase. According to surveys completed by our colleagues at Deloitte, more than half of US consumers have purchased a product based on an online recommendation, and most consumers believe that it is relatively easy to obtain information about products that they are considering purchasing. The growth of mobile devices, along with the advent of fast mobile broadband networks, means that much of this information can be accessed and consumed even at the point of sale. Between 2007 and 2008, for example, the number of mobile Internet users increased from 12 percent to 18 percent of the US population.[33]

Perhaps because of this, quality levels are rising dramatically. The National Quality Research Center at the Ross School of Business, University of Michigan, administers the American Customer Satisfaction Index (ACSI).[34] ACSI measures satisfaction with the goods and services of hundreds of companies and public-sector organizations. A glance at ACSI's scores over the past ten years suggests that most have risen dramatically during this period. Manufacturing defects, service outages, and service delivery shortfalls have all decreased fairly significantly and fairly steadily. Your best option today is better than it ever was in the past, but so is the next best alternative.

All of this raises the question of why we even need brands anymore. What's their role in a world with great transparency of information and high overall quality levels?

Answer: We choose brands because we trust them.

We trust that they deliver quality, but we also trust everything that they stand for.

The brands that we choose use the right ingredients, purchased from the right suppliers, and produced by the right employees, in the right manner.

Freed from the burden of demonstrating quality, brands convey a much richer set of messages, which may include:

- I'm sustainable.
- I use fair labor practices.
- I don't pay bribes.
- I only use organic ingredients.
- I take care of my employees.
- I will safeguard your private information.
- I will configure my offerings based on your needs.

When we choose a brand today, it is as much about declaring who we are and what we value as it is about the product. We choose proudly and display those choices proudly. We have moved from mere consumption of a brand to a relationship with a brand. Our willingness to build these relationships with brands is what makes the most successful brands ubiquitous and therefore valuable.

Trust in a brand also means that we are willing to recommend a brand. This is the ultimate compliment that we can pay to a brand: making someone else aware of our trust and letting them know that it's okay for them to trust the brand as well. In fact, in their article "The Good, the Bad, and the Trustworthy," Paul Argenti, James Lytton-Hitchins, and Richard Verity (this really is his name, believe me) suggest that opportunities increasingly exist for companies to use "trustworthiness" as a source of competitive advantage.[35]

Various organizations have started to measure brand trust. Millward Brown, for example, identifies which brands are the most trusted and most recommended. In its report "Beyond Trust: Engaging Consumers in the Post-Recession World," Millward Brown introduces its proprietary metric, TrustR, "a new metric for understanding and strengthening the bond between consumers and brands." The top performer on the most recent study was Amazon.com. According to Millward Brown's CEO, Eileen Campbell, "the number one 'TrustR' brand in each of the 22 countries we researched was nearly seven times more likely to be purchased [than its competitors] and consumers were 10 times more likely to have formed a strong bond with these brands" versus other brands in general.[36]

Other firms offer tracking polls to measure brand trust and reputations daily, given how quickly opinions seem to shift. YouGov ("What the World Thinks") is an Internet-based market research organization launched in 2000 that relies on online panels to rapidly gather perceptions, opinions, and attitudes. YouGov's offering, BrandIndex, for example, "is a daily measure of public perception of 850 consumer brands across 34 sectors, measured on a 7-point profile: general impression, 'buzz,' quality, value, corporate reputation, customer satisfaction and whether respondents would recommend the brand to a friend."[37] It is based on interviews with nearly ten thousand adults per day, drawn from its panels of more than two million consumers across ten countries.

WHEN BRAND TRUST GOES BAD

The rise in importance of brand trust means that any breach of our faith in a brand can be fatal to the relationship. If "our brand" behaves in a manner that suggests our trust is misplaced, we terminate that relationship quickly and decisively. Unrepaired breaches are particularly harmful.

Competitors are also increasingly quick to jump on real and perceived breaches of trust. After one mobile phone company experienced problems with dropped calls in their latest phone and belatedly announced a fix involving "bumpers," a sort of protective case, a competitor unveiled full-page ads announcing "No Jacket Required," with the accompanying text "We believe a customer shouldn't have to dress up their phone for it to work properly." The target of the ad was instantly clear; there was no need to mention the competitor by name.[38]

Incredibly schizophrenic consumer behavior now appears to be the state of the world when it comes to brands. On one hand, we forge incredibly loyal bonds with brands. On the other, we abandon these brands when they prove unworthy. "Trust," as the 2010 *Edelman Trust Barometer* notes so eloquently, "is fragile."[39]

So, this is where we find ourselves: a world in which brands can be incredibly powerful, but more challenging and more expensive than ever to create and maintain, and less resilient.

Under these conditions, building a resilient brand—and defending it against both intended and unwitting acts of brand sabotage—needs to be your number one priority.

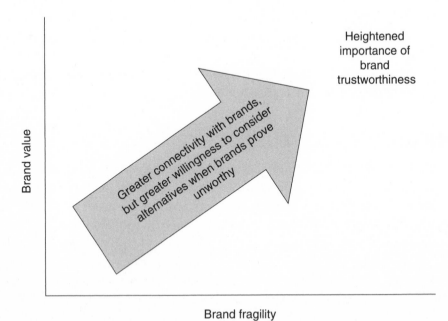

Figure 1.1 What happens when brand value and brand fragility grow simultaneously?

KEY TAKEAWAYS

WHAT WE KNOW...	...AND WHAT YOU CAN DO
■ Ubiquitous brands generate extraordinary value for their owners.	■ Put processes in place to assess brand value and measure changes in brand value over time, just like you would with any critical asset.
■ It takes hard work to develop ubiquitous brands.	■ Track spend on building and maintaining brand value.
■ Brands are now about trust.	■ Understand how your customers feel about your brand, in terms of trust.
■ Untreated breaches of trust can be fatal.	■ Establish the mechanisms for detecting and averting acts of brand sabotage; ensure that brand resilience is an organizational priority.

Chapter Two

MARKETING AS WARFARE

The New Insurgency

If there is one attitude more dangerous than to assume that a future war will be just like the last one, it is to imagine that it will be so utterly different that we can afford to ignore all the lessons of the last one.

—Sir John Slessor, Marshal of the Royal Air Force
and author of *Air Power and Armies*

The first, the supreme, the most far-reaching act of judgment that the statesman and commander have to make is to establish ... the kind of war on which they are embarking; neither mistaking it for, nor trying to turn it into, something that is alien to its nature. This is the first of all strategic questions and the most comprehensive.

—Karl von Clausewitz, *On War*

RALLYING THE TROOPS

Marketers relish tough military metaphors when it comes to describing their heroic efforts to win market share and beat the competition.

The link between the language of marketing and the language of warfare appears to date back only about thirty years. But the marketing-as-warfare metaphor has taken off in a way that only a few business concepts ever do.

Two of the military strategy books that have become required reading for many marketers as well as beacons for military leaders are *The Art of War* and *On War*.

The Art of War is a Chinese military treatise authored by Sun Tzu in the sixth century BC. Jesuit missionary Jean Joseph Marie Amiot translated the book into French in 1772, and British Royal Field Artillery officer Everard Ferguson Calthrop completed the first English translation in 1905 (although critics seem to prefer subsequent translations, including those by the novelist James Clavell and US Marine Corps Brigadier General Samuel Griffith). Mao Zedong, Vietnamese general Nguyen Giap, and Douglas MacArthur are said to have been devotees of the book.

On War (*Vom Kriege*) is a book on war and military strategy by Prussian general Karl von Clausewitz. It was published posthumously in 1832 by Clausewitz's wife and an unnamed collaborator, based on the unfinished manuscripts left by Clausewitz when he died. The book was first translated into English in the late nineteenth century and, like *The Art of War,* has been read by most modern military commanders. The Marine Corps manual *Warfighting* draws considerably upon Clausewitz's work, as well as *The Art of War.*

Both books focus on the strategies and tactics to render one's enemy impotent. Both books provide ample colorful quotes, like this one, by Sun Tzu: "Speed is the essence of war. Take advantage of the enemy's unpreparedness; travel by unexpected routes and strike him where he has taken no precautions." And there's this one, by Clausewitz: "In war, the will is directed at an animate object that reacts." With powerful language like this, it's not surprising that marketers' ears perk up. These guys have been dead for centuries and they can still sell it!

The seminal factor in establishing the link between military strategy and marketing was an article by Philip Kotler and Ravi Singh in the Winter 1981 issue of the *Journal of Business Strategy.*[1] Kotler, a well-known professor and pundit, is the author of one of the most widely known graduate-level marketing textbooks.

Kotler and Singh start their article with an oft-repeated quotation from advertising executive Albert W. Emery: "Marketing is merely a civilized form of warfare in which most battles are won with words, ideas, and disciplined thinking." Then they go on to reference prominent military strategists, including Clausewitz.

Kotler and Singh set the stage for others to further develop this metaphor, such as Bill Parks, Steven Pharr, and Bradley Lockeman, who in 1994 published an article in the Kelley School of Business's journal, *Business Horizons,* titled, "A Marketer's Guide to Clausewitz: Lessons for Winning Market Share."[2] Parks and his coauthors assert that "the metaphor of battle is useful in understanding the art of winning market share. Just as in war, the reality of market share battles is that the success of the victor depends on the failure of the loser."

Two of the strongest and most prolific proponents of the marketing-as-warfare metaphor are Al Ries and Jack Trout. Ries and Trout are well-known marketing strategists and prolific authors who worked together for more than twenty-five years. Starting with their book *Positioning: The Battle for Your Mind* in 1981, they went on to publish *Marketing Warfare* in 1986, *Bottom-Up Marketing* in 1989, and *22 Immutable Laws of Marketing* in 1993.

In *Marketing Warfare,* Ries and Trout proclaim, "We think the best book on marketing was written by a retired Prussian general, Karl von Clausewitz. Entitled *On War,* the 1832 book outlines the strategic principles behind all successful wars...In war, you win by outwitting, outflanking, and overpowering the enemy. The territory you take is only a reflection of your ability to do these things. Why should marketing be any different?"[3]

Ries and Trout discuss the principles of four types of warfare:

- Defensive warfare: "Defensive war is a game for a market leader only. There are three principles to follow, the most surprising of which is the strategy of attacking yourself and not the enemy."
- Offensive warfare: "Offensive warfare is a game for the No. 2 or No. 3 company in a field. The key principle is to find a weakness inherent in the leader's strength and attack at that point."
- Flanking warfare: "The most innovative form of marketing warfare is flanking. Over the years most of the biggest marketing successes have been flanking moves."
- Guerilla warfare: "Most of the players in a marketing war should be guerillas. Smaller companies can be highly successful as long as they don't try to emulate the giants in their field."

Ries and Trout also offer up case studies of four epic marketing wars: the cola war (Pepsi-Cola versus Coca-Cola), the beer war (national versus local brands), the burger war (McDonald's versus Burger King versus Wendy's), and the computer war (IBM versus everyone else).

Marketing Warfare was a great commercial success, and Ries and Trout went on to write a number of other best-selling books on marketing and branding, both together and with other collaborators. Several of their books have been updated and reissued, including a 2006 twentieth-anniversary edition of *Marketing Warfare*. We can only assume that their publisher's decision to issue the anniversary edition of the book signals that the marketing-as-warfare metaphor continues to resonate with marketers and business executives.

We didn't have to look far to find an example of the marketing-as-warfare metaphor in our own backyard. Two of our colleagues recently authored an article in our journal, *The Deloitte Review*, titled, "The Battle for Brands in a World of Private Labels."[4] The article focuses on the fast growth of private-label grocery products and how consumer product manufacturers can respond. Private labels now represent 20 percent of grocery store and 18 percent of supercenter sales. Between 2006 and 2009, private labels showed market share increases across 74 percent of products in the personal care, household goods, and food and beverage categories in the United States. Subheads in the article include "The Battle for Brand Loyalty" and "Are You Ready for Battle in a World of Private Label Goods?" and the opening illustration features a can of private-brand peaches jousting with a can of national-brand peaches, with can openers standing in for lances and shopping carts in lieu of horses.

In August 2010, a *Wall Street Journal* article described Procter & Gamble CEO Robert McDonald's leadership focus in vivid military terms. "As a US Army paratrooper, Robert McDonald trained to fight enemies in jungles, deserts and the Arctic. Now, going into his second year as chief executive of Procter & Gamble Co., the former military man is mounting a two-pronged attack on a very different battlefield—the global consumer-products industry. His missions: To win back ground lost as frugal shoppers have opted for cheaper alternatives to P&G's goods, and to conquer countries now dominated by rivals."[5]

THE MARKETING-AS-WARFARE METAPHOR WORKS BY CREATING A LASER-LIKE FOCUS ON DESTROYING THE ENEMY

The first principle of warfare, according to von Clausewitz, is to engage and **overwhelm the enemy**. He notes, "The invention of gunpowder and the constant improvement of firearms are enough in themselves to show that the advance of civilization has done nothing practical to alter or deflect the impulse to destroy the enemy, which is central to the very idea of war."

Once the enemy is identified, good war propagandists dehumanize and demonize the enemy in an effort to gain popular support for the war effort. Consider the recent example of George W. Bush's signature rhetorical legacy, the "Global War on Terror." Although the terminology may have been over the top, it was successful, in the short term, in channeling our collective post–9/11 rage by focusing on al Qaeda and Osama bin Laden. The term favored by Obama administration officials, "overseas contingency operations," is hardly the rallying cry evoked by the "Global War on Terror" when it comes to inspiring popular support.

While many companies are reluctant to name competitors outright in their external marketing communications, few shy away from doing so internally. As marketers, we need clear targets, even if they are expressed in euphemistic terms involving market share (remember the advice from the authors of "A Marketer's Guide to Clausewitz: Lessons for Winning Market Share": "The reality of market share battles is that the success of the victor depends on the failure of the loser"). By choosing a particular competitor to tackle, a company gives a face, not to mention a name and a personality, to the enemy. This makes it much easier to evoke strong emotions and gain the commitment of your constituents.

Second, military language conveys a sense of **decisiveness and purpose**. Clear objectives, a clear plan, clear tactics, and a clear means of measuring success.

The US Army's mission, for example, as described on its website, is unambiguous: "to fight and win our Nation's wars by providing prompt, sustained land dominance across the full range of military operations and spectrum of conflict in support of combatant commanders."[6] It's perfectly clear what the army is trying to achieve: "fight and win." It's no surprise that marketing executives find the sense of purpose and piercing clarity that military language creates compelling.

Third, the marketing-as-warfare metaphor implies that marketing as well as military operations can be organized around a series of tightly coordinated and well-executed **campaigns**, each with a well-defined strategic goal.

It's not entirely accidental that the word *campaign* has been repurposed from its military roots to describe other endeavors, including elections and marketing pushes. A good marketing campaign, like a good military campaign, involves carefully crafted objectives, supported by intense preparation, careful management, tightly coordinated execution, and post-execution evaluation and assessment. For marketers, campaign management software provides the technological infrastructure for coordinating these activities.[7]

Fourth, marketers as well as military leaders need to carefully plan and orchestrate their use of **weaponry**. Rather than air, land, and sea power, however, marketers rely on the "four P's" of marketing. Just as theater commanders in a war zone need to coordinate their use of land, air, and sea forces, any marketer worth his or her salt can wax eloquent when it comes to discussing the four sets of marketing weaponry: (1) product functionality, appearance, quality, packaging, and brand; (2) pricing, including discounting, allowances, and financing options; (3) place (i.e., distribution), including locations, channels, and direct sales; and (4) promotion, including advertising, public relations, and other marketing activities.[8]

IS MARKETING WARFARE STILL RELEVANT?

The fundamental premise of the marketing-as-warfare metaphor is that **marketing is a zero-sum game against known enemies**. Our gain is your loss. We measure success in market share. If our marketing efforts help us increase the size of the market, that's good, but if our marketing efforts increase market size *and* our market share, that's even better.

By 1996, the marketing-as-warfare metaphor had become so widespread that a revisionist article appeared in *Business Horizons* titled, "Marketing as Warfare: Reassessing a Dominant Metaphor."[9] The article, authored by Aric Rindfleisch, professor of marketing at University of Wisconsin's School of Business, questions the marketing-as-warfare metaphor's applicability in a world in which traditional competitors often find themselves collaborating rather than fighting head-to-head in a zero-sum game.

Rindfleisch argues that the assumptions underlying the marketing-as-warfare metaphor no longer apply—it's not just about "kill or be killed" when it comes to marketing. Collaboration, in the form of strategic alliances, joint research and product development, co-branding, and distribution agreements may actually allow both sides of a traditional rivalry to thrive. By equating marketing with warfare, marketers risk blinding themselves to the growth opportunities available through collaboration. Perception becomes reality.

The decade plus since Rindfleisch's article has vindicated him, providing ample evidence that the traditional rules and approaches

Table 2.1 Marketing-as-warfare: The old model

The four elements of the marketing-as-warfare metaphor	Old model of warfare: A zero-sum game against known enemies (i.e., competitors)
1. Focus on overwhelming a clearly identifiable opponent.	Your enemies and allies are easy to identify. You battle your enemies on a limited number of fronts, with steady support from your allies.
2. Start with a clear purpose and clear long-term objectives.	You have clear objectives, a clear plan, clear tactics, and a clear means of measuring success: gains in market share.
3. Organize operations around an integrated set of carefully planned and coordinated campaigns.	You can organize operations around a series of tightly coordinated and well-executed campaigns, each with a well-defined strategic goal, which is good since it often takes weeks or months to deploy your assets. Scale matters.
4. Carefully manage the mix of weapons that you select from a tried-and-true, battle-tested arsenal.	Weapons evolve along predictable paths and trajectories.

for defining markets and competitors need to be tossed out. After all, which of those rules could have predicted that phone manufacturers would be competing with camera manufacturers and sitcom addicts would get their fix through their computers?

Every day, we see more and more examples of companies working closely with their toughest competitors on multiple fronts. Our firm, one of the world's largest professional services providers, regularly teams with the world's largest technology companies. However, at the same time that we go to market with these companies, we also serve them as clients, use them as suppliers for technology products and services, and compete head-to-head with them.

So, the first problem with the marketing-as-warfare metaphor and model, highlighted by Rindfleisch and amply demonstrated by experience, is that we can't always afford to focus single-mindedly on engaging and overwhelming a clearly identifiable opponent under well-defined circumstances, governed by well-understood rules.

But that's only the beginning of the problem. Here are the realities that confront brand stewards today:

- **Sometimes, assaults to the brand come from unpredictable sources.** Exhibit one: Tiger Woods. Other examples of unpredictable sources (which we will discuss more in chapters 3 and 4) range from restaurant employees who (for fun) decide to create a video featuring unsavory food preparation practices, to disgruntled customers who become vociferous voices in every medium possible, to CEOs who clearly failed PR 101 training.
- **Sometimes, assaults to the brand are unintended consequences of other activities and decisions.** Virtually every decision that touches a customer can wind up unintentionally damaging the brand, be it pricing, promotions, packaging, design, naming, formulation, or choice of suppliers. A second-tier supplier who gains notoriety for unfair labor practices can potentially do more damage to your brand than a more deliberate frontal assault from a conventional competitor.
- **The frequency of brand assaults has increased.** As brands become more ubiquitous and their activities become more visible, they attract more critical attention than ever before. At the same time, it has become easier and cheaper to launch assaults and counter-assaults, if you look at the example of WikiLeaks's repeated disclosures of confidential government documents throughout 2010.

- **Speed kills.** The pace at which damage can be done to a brand is unbelievably quick. At times, waiting overnight to respond is way too long. As a result, a marketer's ability to systematically plan activities and campaigns has been compromised.
- **Scale doesn't matter (as much).** In a world in which small can appear big and big can appear small, larger doesn't necessarily mean better.
- **The "weapons" used in brand assaults are more diverse and less conventional.** Social media—Twitter, Facebook, YouTube, etc.—are the obvious new category of weapons, but in the right hands, almost anything can become a weapon.

The new model (summarized in table 2.2) is one in which the old rules of warfare no longer apply. The scariest part of this new world

Table 2.2 Marketing-as-warfare: The new model

The four elements of the marketing-as-warfare metaphor	The new model of warfare: Random assaults from unexpected and accidental sources
1. Focus on overwhelming a clearly identifiable opponent.	You're not sure exactly whom you're supposed to be fighting, much less why. Attacks can come from unexpected sources and in unexpected locations. Every aspect of your business, from the quality of the products that you produce to the people who represent you to the labor practices of the companies that supply you, could be an opening for an attack.
2. Start with a clear purpose and clear long-term objectives.	Some days, success consists primarily of living to fight another day and minimizing damage to your brand.
3. Organize operations around an integrated set of carefully planned and coordinated campaigns.	Speed often trumps scale. Your ability to react quickly and improvise partially offsets the inability to plan ahead.
4. Carefully manage the mix of weapons that you select from a tried-and-true, battle-tested arsenal.	New technologies have created a new class of brand threats. New weapons for attacking your brand are being developed and deployed daily in totally unpredictable ways and with much more destructive power.

is that not all of the individuals who do damage to your brand *mean* to do harm. Many are accidental or seemingly random acts. But intent matters less than impact.

So, although we will refer collectively to the activities that threaten your brand as **brand sabotage** and those who participate in these activities as **brand saboteurs**, we're going to take liberties with these definitions to include both intentional and unintentional acts. See table 2.3 for an example of brand sabotage in action.

Table 2.3 Applying marketing-as-warfare: An illustration

The four elements of the marketing-as-warfare metaphor	Brand sabotage in action
1. Focus on overwhelming a clearly identifiable opponent.	Your employees post a video on YouTube that is viewed more than a million times. Unfortunately, in this video, which they filmed in one of your facilities, your employees appear in their uniforms as they disparage your products. They think this is a joke.
2. Start with a clear purpose and clear long-term objectives.	You ignore the video and hope it will go away. It doesn't go away. Instead, it gets picked up by every new- and traditional-media outlet. Everyone wonders why you haven't responded.
3. Organize operations around an integrated set of carefully planned and coordinated campaigns.	You take the bull by the horns and respond with a Twitter feed and your own YouTube video in an effective effort to defuse the situation. You plan and execute these countermeasures in a matter of hours.
4. Carefully manage the mix of weapons that you select from a tried-and-true, battle-tested arsenal.	You wind up using some of the very same social media to gather customer feedback to help you reformulate your products, jumpstart growth, and gain significant market share.

◾ SHIFTS IN MILITARY STRATEGY SUGGEST A NEW METAPHOR FOR BRAND STEWARDS: MARKETING AS COUNTERINSURGENCY

Random assaults, anonymous enemies, threats of friendly fire: These all sound like the types of insurgencies that we read about daily in places like Iraq and Afghanistan. Well, today's marketing battlefront bears more and more resemblance to those military battlefronts. Perhaps we can learn something from today's military commanders.

Several years ago, the US military recognized that its approach to warfare needed to be updated. Its officers were trained to fight conventional wars and conventional battles but found instead they were fighting counterinsurgencies. As it had for our marketers, the world had shifted beneath their feet.

In this new world, military strategists fortunately found a new playbook to supplement their well-worn copies of *The Art of War* and *On War*. *The US Army/Marine Corps Counterinsurgency Field Manual FM 3-24* is the new playbook.[10] We believe that any brand steward can learn a lot from this book.

First, a little background. *The Counterinsurgency Field Manual* is a US Army field manual. Field manuals contain detailed information and instructions for soldiers serving in the field. There are more than five hundred field manuals in use, many of which are in the public domain.

The Counterinsurgency Field Manual was released in December 2006 and bore the imprimaturs of two then lieutenant generals, David Petraeus of the US Army and James Amos of the Marine Corps. Both have since been promoted to four-star rank and have been given significantly expanded roles and responsibilities. *The Counterinsurgency Field Manual* involved an unusual and unprecedented amount of participation from non-military contributors and unconventional thinkers, such as Lieutenant Colonel John A. Nagl, author of *Learning to Eat Soup with a Knife: Counterinsurgency Lessons from Malaya and Vietnam.*

The Counterinsurgency Field Manual is freely available online and available for purchase from the University of Chicago Press with additional material. For the University of Chicago Press edition,

Sarah Sewall, a former Pentagon official and Director of the Carr Center for Human Rights Policy at Harvard's Kennedy School of Government, contributes an introduction "that places the manual in critical and historical perspective, explaining the significance and potential impact of this revolutionary challenge to conventional U.S. military doctrine."[11]

As the University of Chicago Press's website explains, "When the U.S. military invaded Iraq, it lacked a common understanding of the problems inherent in counterinsurgency campaigns. It had neither studied them, nor developed doctrine and tactics to deal with them. *It is fair to say that in 2003, most Army officers knew more about the U.S. Civil War than they did about counterinsurgency.*" The *U.S. Army/Marine Corps Counterinsurgency Field Manual* was written to fill that void."[12]

Although *The Counterinsurgency Field Manual* is written expressly for a military reader (just as *The Art of War* and *On War* were written for military readers), its guidance has striking parallels with the guidance that is appropriate for brand stewards, given the new marketing realities.

Five big takeaways for brand stewards can be found in *The Counterinsurgency Field Manual*:

1. At first, you may not recognize that your brand is under attack: "One common feature of insurgencies is that the government that is being targeted generally takes a while to recognize that an insurgency is occurring. Insurgents take advantage of that time to build strength and gather support. Thus, counterinsurgents often have to 'come from behind' when fighting an insurgency."[13]

2. Your natural tendencies to respond in a conventional manner to attacks on your brand may be misguided. Sometimes, the more you protect your brand, the less secure your brand may be; the more force you use, the less effective it is; and doing nothing is the best response when it comes to protecting your brand: "Another common feature is that forces conducting COIN [counterinsurgency] operations usually begin poorly ... They falsely believe that armies trained to win large conventional wars are automatically prepared to win small, unconventional ones. In fact, some capabilities required for conventional success—for example, the ability to execute operational maneuvers and employ massive firepower—may be of limited utility or even counterproductive

in COIN operations. Nonetheless, conventional forces beginning COIN operations often try to use these capabilities to defeat insurgents; they almost always fail."[14]

3. When it comes to building a resilient brand, the winner is the one who learns more quickly: "In COIN, the side that learns faster and adapts more rapidly—the better learning organization—usually wins. Counterinsurgencies have been called learning competitions. Thus, this publication identifies 'Learn and Adapt' as a modern COIN imperative for U.S. forces."[15]

4. Some of the most effective weapons for counterinsurgents are not those aimed directly at brand saboteurs, and many important decisions are not made by CMOs: "Counterinsurgents often achieve the most meaningful success in garnering public support and legitimacy...with activities that do not involve killing insurgents...Lasting victory comes from a vibrant economy, political participation, and restored hope...Successful COIN operations require competence and judgment by Soldiers and Marines at all levels...Senior leaders set the proper direction and climate with thorough training and clear guidance; then they trust their subordinates to do the right thing."[16]

5. If a tactic works this week, it might not work next week; if it works in this market, it might not work in the next: "Competent insurgents are adaptive...Insurgents quickly adjust to effective COIN practices and rapidly disseminate information throughout the insurgency. Indeed, the more effective a COIN tactic is, the faster it may become out of date because insurgents have a greater need to counter it. Effective leaders at all levels avoid complacency and are at least as adaptive as their enemies. There is no 'silver bullet' set of COIN procedures. Constantly developing new practices is essential."[17]

The Counterinsurgency Field Manual contains an appendix titled "A Guide to Action." The suggested actions are organized around three pillars: Plan, Prepare, and Execute. We have taken the long list of suggested actions and boiled it down to seven steps for marketers and brand stewards anxious to adopt and practice the principles of effective counterinsurgency. (See table 2.4.)

The marketing equivalent of conventional warfare (i.e., the need to compete against identifiable competitors) probably won't completely disappear anytime soon. So don't throw away your copies of *The Art of War* and *On War*, and don't forget all

Table 2.4 Seven steps of effective brand counterinsurgency

Action pillar	Step	Explanation
Plan	1. Assess brand risks.	Begin to understand the potential threats faced by your brand, including their source and potential impact.
Prepare	2. Galvanize your brand troops.	Ensure that your employees and executives are actively engaged in detecting, preventing, and mitigating brand risks.
	3. Deploy your brand risk early warning systems.	Build your capabilities and systems to detect assaults on your brand early in the planning, preparation, and execution cycle.
Execute	4. Repel the attacks on your brand.	Actively respond to actual assaults in the appropriate timeframe and at the appropriate level.
	5. Learn and adapt your brand defenses.	Learn from each assault and adapt your behavior and tactics.
	6. Measure and track brand resilience.	Measure and track your performance in managing brand risk and building brand resilience.
	7. Generate popular support for your brand resilience campaign.	Broaden your internal and external bases of support, including your "volunteer army."

the lessons that Kotler, Singh, Ries, and Trout and the rest of the marketing-as-warfare advocates have taught you. When it comes to marketing and branding, beating the competition and gaining market share is still good. There is still plenty of need to invest energy in systematically understanding competitors, their strategies, their marketing plans, and their intentions.

But (and this is a big *but*) it's time to match offense with defense and begin to balance the conventional warfare mindset with the counterinsurgency mindset. Defense doesn't get a lot of attention until something bad happens, and then everyone wants to know why you didn't do something to prevent it. But then it's too late. Our goal is to equip you to do what you need to do before that is the case.

In the chapters that follow, we will dive deep into each of the seven steps listed in table 2.4. We'll start by trying to assess the true nature of the threats that your brand faces in a world filled with brand saboteurs and insurgents.

KEY TAKEAWAYS

WHAT WE KNOW...	...AND WHAT YOU CAN DO
■ Although "marketing as warfare" has been a compelling metaphor for marketers looking to "rally the troops," it may be running out of steam.	■ Carefully consider how much you rely on military language and metaphors to engage and focus your marketing resources.
■ "Marketing as counterinsurgency" may be a more appropriate metaphor, given today's marketing environment.	■ Adopt a counterinsurgency mindset in defending your brand, with an emphasis on learning faster and adapting more rapidly.
■ Effective counterinsurgency programs are built around the three pillars of planning, preparing, and execution.	■ Commit to a seven-step program that starts with assessing brand risks and includes galvanizing your troops, establishing your early warning systems, repelling attacks as they occur, adapting your defenses, tracking your success in defending your brand, and expanding your base of popular support.

THE STREISAND EFFECT AND THE PARADOXES OF COUNTERINSURGENCY

The Counterinsurgency Field Manual highlights a number of paradoxes one might encounter when conducting counterinsurgent operations, including the idea that sometimes doing nothing is the best reaction: "Often insurgents carry out a terrorist act or guerrilla raid with the primary purpose of enticing counterinsurgents to overreact, or at least to react in a way that insurgents can exploit."[18]

Companies can find themselves in a similar situation, when taking action against a threat may amplify the threat rather than squelch it. The emergence of numerous social networking and social media sites has made such situations increasingly delicate.

One of the more famous examples has given the phenomenon a name: the Streisand effect. Blogger Mike Masnick coined the term in 2005 to describe the paradox that trying to suppress something online will make it all the more visible.

Masnick was writing in reference to a 2003 incident in which the singer Barbra Streisand sued to remove a photograph of her residence that was part of a collection of twelve thousand photographs documenting the California coastline. Prior to Streisand's attempt to remove the photograph, the website had generated roughly four hundred hits. After news of her $10 million lawsuit to remove the photograph was made public, more than 420,000 visitors viewed the site.[19] Oh, and by the way, Streisand lost her case and had to pay $177,000 in legal fees. The photo remains on the site to this day.[20]

Celebrities are not the only ones to suffer consequences from the misapplication of force in response to a brand threat. Nestlé's response to a Greenpeace video critical of the company's supply chain practices propelled the Greenpeace campaign into the worldwide spotlight, generating 1.5 million views for a video that prior to Nestlé's intervention had generated fewer than a thousand hits.[21]

In September 2009, the popular technology and culture blog Boing Boing posted a critique of a Ralph Lauren ad that showed an impossibly thin model. The blog intended to call attention to the frequent overzealous post-processing to make already thin models appear even skinnier.[22] The initial post generated 158 user comments, 364 Facebook shares, 135 tweets and 0 Diggs. Ralph Lauren issued a takedown notice on the grounds of copyright infringement. The blog responded to the takedown notice with a second post that generated 620 user comments, 1574 Facebook shares, 1843 tweets, and 2,779 Diggs and was picked up by the Huffington Post, ABC News, and hundreds of smaller websites as well.[23]

These examples mirror a common occurrence in counter-insurgent operations: the commission of a relatively minor attack in the hope that a disproportionate response will result, generating significant ill will and hostility toward the military. In the face of such threats, *The Counterinsurgency Field Manual* advises, "If an assessment of the effects of a course of action determines that more negative than positive effects may result, an alternative should be considered—potentially including not acting."[24]

PART TWO

SEVEN STEPS FOR MANAGING BRAND RISK AND RECOVERY

Chapter Three

STEP ONE, PART ONE

Assess Brand Risks—The Enemy Within

Without good intelligence, counterinsurgents are like blind boxers wasting energy flailing at unseen opponents and perhaps causing unintended harm. With good intelligence, counterinsurgents are like surgeons cutting out cancerous tissue while keeping other vital organs intact.

—The Counterinsurgency Field Manual

BRAND RISK IS AN UNAVOIDABLE CONSEQUENCE OF DOING BUSINESS

We use the term **brand risk** to describe anything that directly threatens brand value. Brand risk threatens brand value by rupturing the trust that a customer has in the brand. Brand risks may include:

- disgruntled employees blogging about how poorly they feel you treat them,
- third-party websites posting scathing reviews of your new products,
- your executive team behaving boorishly,
- a less than well-thought-out change in product packaging or formulation that generates significant negative customer feedback,
- repeated deep discounting policies that make customers question whether they should ever pay full price for your products,
- unethical competitors anonymously spreading disinformation about your brand on a blog, and
- unhappy customers posting music videos about poor service on YouTube.

Get the picture?

Brand risk can happen anywhere and anytime unless you put a program in place to recognize and prevent it.

In chapter 1, we looked at how ubiquitous brands generate extraordinary value for their owners. In fact, for many organizations, the financial value of the brand exceeds any single asset class that appears on the balance sheet and is a significant multiple of revenue and cash flow. We also discussed why brands are more about trust than they are about signaling quality. As a result, any breach in the trust that customers have placed in a brand can be fatal to brand value. While quality problems are one source of brand risk, many brand risks result from problems that have little direct relationship to quality (think Tiger Woods crashing into the fire hydrant).

Brand risk is contextual. The more valuable the brand, the higher the risk. Owners of the most valuable brands need to safeguard them and worry about brand risk much more than owners of less valuable brands.

We distinguish brand risk, by the way, from other types of risks, such as financial risks or legal risks. To the degree that we talk about these, we will discuss how poorly handled financial or legal risks create brand risks (and vice versa).

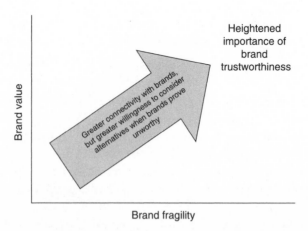

Figure 3.1 The "brand paradox": Explosive growth in brand value coupled with tremendous fragility

In our experience, today most organizations spend considerable time and resources building their brands, but very few organizations systematically identify and assess the risks that their brands face.

That's not to say that organizations do *nothing* relative to managing brand risk. However, the brand protection programs that we see tend to be either narrowly focused (e.g., managing brand licensing efforts), confined to the marketing department, or primarily *reactive* (e.g., containing the fallout associated with a major industrial accident).

Why?

The obvious answer is that it's no one's job. Check your CMO's job description to see whether it contains the term *brand risk*. The closest it probably comes is *reputation management*, and chances are it doesn't even include that. If it does appear, it will likely be down toward the bottom of the list of responsibilities, and we all know that items on the bottom of the list rarely get attended to.

Ironically, if you have a chief risk officer, our guess is that brand risk is not high on the list of his or her priorities, either.

Your COO? Unlikely.

Your CEO? Probably not.

Your board? Ditto.

It's not completely surprising that no one has this role specifically enumerated in his or her job description. In chapter 1, we discussed the relatively recent phenomenon of explosive growth in brand value coupled with tremendous fragility, leading to the heightened importance of brand trustworthiness. Think of this as the "brand paradox" that companies now need to manage.

You may be tempted to say, "Well, our CMO should take this on" when it comes to the issue of brand risk management. After all, the CMO is supposedly responsible for all things branding. That's fair, but the CMO won't be able to do the job without a lot of help. Brand risks do not begin and end in the marketing department—not by a long shot. In fact, brand risks can be the consequence of:

- engineering—the release of a new product with performance problems,
- finance—a significant tightening of its credit policies,

- IT—the inadvertent disclosure of confidential customer information,
- legal—the failure to protect trademarks from infringement,
- manufacturing—the use of non-sustainable ingredients in key products,
- marketing—the decision to update the packaging of a flagship consumer product,
- pricing—the *de facto* price increases that come through surcharges and extra fees,
- procurement—the use of offshore manufacturers with problematic labor practices, and
- the board—affiliations with other organizations that may be perceived as conflicts.

Or any other corporate department—you name it.

There can also be second-order brand risks that stem from poorly handled "situations" (e.g., delays in making a decision to recall a poorly designed product). Damage control is where reputation management activities are often focused. Unfortunately, this is akin to trying to extinguish a fire in a building that was built with no acknowledgment of fire codes and building standards.

The point is that almost anything that a company does, any decision it makes or stand it takes, can wind up coming back to haunt the company and diminish the brand that it has spent so much time, energy, and money building.

Brand risk is an unavoidable consequence of doing business. As several of our colleagues say in an article on risk management, "A diet of pure risk aversion likely will lead to extinction."[1]

Not convinced? Think about automotive or airline safety for a moment. The best way to avoid a car accident is never to drive, and the best way to avoid being killed in a plane crash is never to board a plane. Unfortunately, these are not options for many of us, just as avoiding all brand risks is not an option for most organizations.

That's why the National Safety Council introduced the notion of defensive driving, in 1964, and why the National Transportation Safety Board (NTSB) was launched in 1967 to "identify and promote lessons learned from accident investigations to help make transportation safer."[2] (We'll talk more about the pivotal role of the NTSB in reducing the risks associated with air transportation in chapter 8.)

Like automotive and air safety, the opportunity for effective brand risk management begins long before the accident occurs.

◼◼ LIKE COUNTERINSURGENCY, MANAGING BRAND RISKS STARTS WITH GOOD INTELLIGENCE

Effective brand risk management requires purposefully building your capabilities to:

1. understand and assess brand risks,
2. select the acceptable brand risks,
3. develop the appropriate brand risk mitigation strategies, and
4. minimize the likelihood of the unacceptable brand risks.

This is where **brand risk intelligence** comes into play. Just as *The Counterinsurgency Field Manual* describes counterinsurgency as an "intelligence-driven endeavor," effective brand risk management starts with good intelligence about the risks that your brand faces.

Your job as a newly appointed leader of marketing counterinsurgency efforts, consequently, will include a substantial amount of intelligence work—identifying potential points of attack and narrowing them down to the most serious ones—before you will be ready to take the actions necessary to combat threats to your brand. These efforts require constant vigilance since, as we pointed out in chapter 2, "insurgents are adaptive…[and] quickly adjust to successful COIN practices," and even a successful strategy may quickly "become out of date because insurgents have a greater need to counter it."[3] So, intelligence gathering in a world of counterinsurgency is a never-ending activity.

One of the primary reasons why risk-intelligence efforts fail is that they begin with false assumptions about what may or may not happen. As a result, such efforts don't come up with solutions for addressing possible, but highly unlikely, worst-case scenarios. Building strong brand risk intelligence requires a willingness to imagine the unimaginable and think the unthinkable and plan accordingly. Nassim Nicholas Taleb's bestseller *The Black Swan: The Impact of the Highly Improbable* discusses how we try to predict the likelihood of catastrophic events based on the past and on the assumption that the past will repeat itself.[4] As *Wired* editor and *Long Tail* author Chris Anderson writes in his review of Taleb's book, "Nassim argues that most of the really big events in our world are rare and unpredictable, and thus trying to extract generalizable stories to explain them may be emotionally satisfying, but it's practically useless. September 11 is one such example, and stock market crashes are another. Or, as he puts it, 'History does not crawl, it jumps.' Our assumptions grow out of the bell-curve predictability of what he calls 'Mediocristan,' while our world is really shaped by the wild power law swings of 'Extremistan.' "[5]

THE FIRST JOB OF BRAND RISK INTELLIGENCE IS TO IDENTIFY POTENTIAL BRAND INSURGENTS (AND SOURCES OF BRAND RISK)

There are three elements to consider as part of your initial brand risk intelligence gathering.

- **Who?** Is the saboteur an employee or a competitor? A partner or a supplier? A customer or a self-styled maven?
- **What?** What are the specific brand risks that occurred? Did the act of sabotage cause significant damage in and of itself or was it part of a pattern of attacks that collectively damaged your brand? What is the potential threat if left unaddressed?
- **Why?** Did the saboteur intend to do damage, or was he or she actually trying to help? Or was he or she responding to be viewed as a provocation that demanded (in his or her eyes) a reply?

The chief difference between conventional warfare and insurgencies is that insurgents are generally not members of organized military or paramilitary forces. Insurgents don't sign up through conventional recruiting processes, don't undergo conventional training, don't use conventional weapons, and don't have conventional hierarchies.

An insurgent may literally be an army of one or part of a very loosely organized coalition with a constantly shifting membership. Insurgents' motives may also be more elusive than those of conventional forces. Some insurgents act with the noblest of intentions (e.g., righting a wrong, making the public aware of a problem) and some with the most mundane (e.g., being bored and trying to have some fun). Some insurgents display strong discipline, shared values, commonality of purpose, strict communications protocols, and predictable behaviors, but many may fall short on these dimensions when compared to conventional and long-established military forces.

But just because insurgents don't wear uniforms like the usual suspects, that doesn't mean that they don't do real damage. They're just harder to find. So don't underestimate the time and effort required to identify the *who* when it comes to brand risk management. You will need to consider a range of candidates, including:

- employees
- senior executives
- value-chain partners
- customers
- third parties
- competitors

Let's start with what's closest to home: your employees.

DON'T ASSUME THAT YOUR EMPLOYEES HAVE RECEIVED, MUCH LESS READ, THE MANUAL

Sabotage describes activities aimed at weakening or damaging an entity through subversion, obstruction, or destruction of property. The word is derived from the French word *sabot*, a type of wooden shoe worn in various European countries. The popular explanation is that fifteenth-century Dutch workers threw their *sabots* into the gears of textile machinery because they feared that the machinery would render them obsolete (i.e., the workers, not the shoes).[6]

While this popular explanation has a romantic allure, the etymology is suspect, and the term probably evolved from meaning "to execute badly" to its current usage in the late nineteenth or early twentieth century, when organized labor began to systematically use sabotage as a tool to secure worker rights.

The etymology of *sabotage* notwithstanding, the image of *sabot*-wielding employees deliberately taking actions that damage an organization and its brand evokes (or should evoke) fear and concern. Employees who are out to settle scores with their employers can do significant damage to a brand, specifically through disclosure of trade secrets (e.g., recipes, manufacturing processes) as well as customer lists and marketing plans.

Don't delude yourself, however, into thinking that the only threat comes from angry employees. There are also countless examples of unintentional but equally damaging employee-initiated brand sabotage. You need to worry about both the witting and the unwitting acts of brand sabotage.

When we hire employees, we assume that employees will do what they can to avoid undermining brand value. That's why, when they do undermine it, it's particularly distressing and surprising. When the actions of employees—the people you pay to help you succeed in the market—create brand risks, you naturally feel betrayed. To paraphrase Shakespeare's King Lear, how sharper than a serpent's tooth it is to have a thankless employee!

When it comes to employees and brand sabotage, what can go wrong?

Lots!

When Employees Snap

Let's meet our first group of category of insurgents: employees who decide to turn rogue.

The decision to turn rogue may be prompted by a variety of motives, ranging from a sense of being mistreated, to a belief that the company endangers the greater good, to pure greed. Rogue employees may also be motivated by the desire to get even, the need to feel important, or the wish to embarrass a particular executive.

Often, the resulting actions take the form of leaks of valuable or embarrassing information. The leaked information may not even be true, but that probably doesn't matter until it's too late.

The late journalist Daniel Schorr once described leaks as "accidental seepage—a lost document, a chauffeur's unwary anecdote, loose lips in the Pentagon." But according to Schorr, the notion of a leak has migrated away from a passive and unintentional event. "Today, when information 'is leaked,' it is a witting (if sometimes witless) action."[7]

One of the most famous leaks was the case of the Pentagon Papers in the summer of 1971. Daniel Ellsberg, an employee of a major defense contractor and former Pentagon staffer, leaked a

Department of Defense study on United States and Vietnam relations to Neil Sheehan, a reporter at the *New York Times*. The *Times* started publishing the material in June of 1971; publication was temporarily derailed due to a court order, then resumed in the form of excerpts over a multi-day period. In the meantime, Ellsberg shared this material with a number of other national newspapers. These papers went ahead and published the document while the *Times* was tied up in court.

Ellsberg, a veteran analyst with years of experience, made a deliberate decision to share these materials because he felt that Americans needed to know exactly what the US government was up to in Vietnam. Ellsberg felt that the disclosure of these materials would facilitate that awareness and that leaking the materials was a moral act.

Ellsberg's leak wound up being the cause of a second leak, with even more dire consequences than the first.

As a result of Ellsberg's leak, President Richard Nixon decided to dispatch a squad of "plumbers" to the office of Ellsberg's psychiatrist. Nixon's hope was to uncover information that would be personally damaging to Ellsberg and allow the government to discredit him. "Convinced that we were responding to a national security crisis…" the "plumbers" broke into the psychiatrist's office in Beverly Hills on September 3, 1971, to photograph Ellsberg's files, but found nothing.[8] More than thirty-five years later, Egil Krogh, Nixon's deputy assistant, wrote, "The premise of our action was the strongly held view within certain precincts of the White House that the president and those functioning on his behalf could carry out illegal acts with impunity if they were convinced that the nation's security demanded it."[9]

Emboldened by this view, "plumbers" were dispatched to the offices of the Democratic National Committee's offices in Washington's Watergate Complex almost ten months later. Frank Wills, a security guard, noticed tape covering several door latches and called the police. The "plumbers" were caught in the act before they were able to leave DNC's offices.

The break-in provided the opportunity for another leaker, FBI associate director Mark Felt (a.k.a. Deep Throat), to disclose details of the bungled burglary to the *Washington Post*. The backlash associated with the Watergate break-in and the disclosure of Nixon's involvement eventually led to the first and only resignation of a sitting US president.

In addition to causing Nixon to resign, the Watergate break-in added a suffix to our language, "-gate", used to describe a situation where someone unsuccessfully attempts to cover up an embarrassing situation. When Apple held a press conference regarding reception problems with its iPhone 4, Apple leader Steve Jobs, in an effort to defuse the situation, described it as "not antenna-gate."[10] Nevertheless, Apple did offer free "bumpers" (a protective rubber case to reduce antenna interference) to customers with reception problems, and the executive in charge of mobile devices left the company shortly after the incident.[11]

In June 2010, US Army private Bradley Manning was arrested for leaking tens of thousands of classified army documents to the website WikiLeaks. WikiLeaks was founded in December 2006 and its website went live early the following year. On its website, WikiLeaks describes itself "a multi-jurisdictional public service" and states its commitment to the concept of "principled leaking" as a way for "whistleblowers, journalists and activists who have sensitive materials to communicate to the public."[12]

By many accounts, it appears that Manning's leak, like Ellsberg's, was deliberate. But, as Ben Zimmer writes in the *New York Times*, we've gone from tiny pin-prick leaks to a dam breach. The "release of the Afghan war logs...stretched the semantics of *leak* to a bursting point."[13]

Almost forty years separates the two events, but the second event has provoked extensive discussions about how the two compare with one another. Ellsberg, for example, in an interview in the aftermath of the WikiLeaks disclosure, described "the parallels [as] very strong," as he actively justified Manning's leaks on moral grounds.[14]

Since the initial leak of the Afghan war papers, thousands of additional US government documents have been released by WikiLeaks. In the process, WikiLeaks has garnered unprecedented levels of notoriety, while government officials mentioned in the leaked documents have spent countless hours trying to repair the damage done by the disclosure of very confidential, and somewhat embarrassing, diplomatic communications.

What's instructive for our purposes are the stark differences between the two events. The Internet has changed everything—the velocity and momentum of leaked information, the ease of global dissemination, and the democracy of access.

In 1971, the concept of social media was not even a glimmer in someone's eye. In 1971, we didn't have YouTube, we didn't have Twitter, and we certainly didn't have WikiLeaks. In 1971, one couldn't upload gigabytes of documents and instantaneously make these documents available to anyone in the world with a web browser. By contrast, in 1971, a leaker needed access to a willing reporter from a major outlet to get the exposure available to anyone today through the Internet.

WikiLeaks and its functional equivalents have not just targeted governmental organizations. Commercial organizations have been targeted, as well—just visit WikiLeaks's home page if you have any questions.

Rogue employees are not a new phenomenon. It's just that going rogue has become much, much easier, and your brand is a lot less secure as a result. As L. Gordon Crovitz writes in the *Wall Street Journal*, "Modern technology makes everyone a publisher, including leakers. This means it's impossible to protect secrets....WikiLeaks...is a reminder that we must now learn to live with technology tools that we cannot control."[15]

Let's inch away from the case of employees who have gone rogue to the case of an employee who may temporarily go AWOL.

Ever have the experience of catching an employee on a bad hair day? As frequent travelers, we regularly encounter taxi drivers, flight attendants, hotel personnel, and restaurant employees who temporarily forget that, as paying customers, we're entitled to more than a modicum of civility, regardless of the personal setbacks that they may have experienced that day. While we have never had the experience of being cursed out on a public address system, we've had our share of rude, unpleasant, obnoxious, and insulting treatment at the hands of so-called "service providers."

Consider this example. Steven Slater, a flight attendant with a highly regarded airline loses patience with his passengers, curses out an uncooperative passenger over the plane's loudspeaker, grabs two beers, pulls the emergency exit chute, announces, "That's it, I'm done," and slides down the chute in an act of dramatic deplaning.

According to CBS News show *48 Hours,* this scenario followed the activities of an uncooperative "passenger [who] jumped up before the seatbelt sign was turned off to grab her luggage after the plane landed at Kennedy International Airport. She reportedly ignored... [the flight attendant] when he told her to sit down, and when... [the flight attendant] approached the passenger to tell her again to sit down he got hit in the head with her falling bag. When he asked her to apologize she responded with a foul refusal."[16]

Miss the story? Just Google "flight attendant meltdown."

It's not hard to imagine the final straw that causes a front-line employee to reach the tipping point and respond in kind to a disruptive, rude, and unruly customer.

Still, we expect that service personnel will behave better than that. It's their job, we think. They get paid to suffer indignities and they should know better than to act unprofessionally, no matter what the provocation.

Unfortunately, saying so doesn't make it so. Service personnel are under more stress than ever. At JFK Airport, there is a health clinic with programs in place to address worker meltdowns. The director of clinical services reports, "There are more people reacting to anger triggers now than ever before, in every part of the airline industry."[17]

And it's not just airline personnel. We are seeing more and more examples of customer service representatives, cashiers, hotel lobby clerks, waiters, bank clerks, and sales associates reacting to "anger triggers."

And when this happens with your employees, you have to assume that the activity will be captured in words, if not pictures, and quickly posted to name-your-favorite-social-media-outlet for everyone to see. In real time. Everywhere. Unfortunately, for you, in today's instant-replay world, you can no longer assume that events best forgotten will be. With the Internet, social media, and search engines, brand-damaging incidents are memorialized forever, just one or two clicks away.

When it comes to brand reputation, social media have let the proverbial genie out of the bottle, and there is no way that you're going to get it back in.

Ignorance Is Not Bliss

Let's move along the brand sabotage spectrum from the employees who willfully align themselves with the insurgents and those who temporarily go AWOL to the ones who just don't understand that whatever they do might matter. Consider these examples. Two employees, one chain-restaurant kitchen, one video camera. The employees are bored. They videotape themselves, in their uniforms, preparing food under staged unsanitary conditions. They post the video to YouTube. They think it's a joke. Millions of people watch the video. And, not surprisingly, millions stop eating at the restaurant chain.

A female employee just out of college drops an email to colleagues at a leading professional services firm asking them to vote for the best-looking male colleague. While this contest is not something that would be totally out of character in a college setting, it's far less appropriate in today's workplace. In a matter of days, the email has found its way to virtually every major professional and financial services firm in the world. The forwarded email includes a variety of salacious comments.

The fact of the matter is that many employees don't see anything wrong with this. They don't understand that this behavior is as damaging as if they deliberately sought to hurt the brand. They just don't get it.

Like the costumed characters in a theme park, they need to realize that they're no longer just employees but cast members who are always on stage. Social media make the entire world a potential stage.

When Loyalty Becomes Rigidity

Finally, along the brand sabotage spectrum, we have employees determined to do the right thing, no matter what.

Mindless adherence to policies and procedures, regardless of circumstances, is also a recipe for disaster. An employee who never deviates from what's required could wind up doing more harm than good. We've all seen employees forced into situations in which following policy and procedure causes unintended injuries to some of a company's most loyal and valuable customers.

As a customer, how many times have you found yourself saying, "But you don't understand, I'm a really valuable customer. You don't want to treat me this way"? Mr. or Ms. By-the-Book Employee is not always the best brand advocate in a world where missteps are noticed and publicized.

The solution is not to abandon all rules and all policies and all procedures, but to teach employees and their managers when to put aside the playbook and "call an audible."[18] Adaptability can be a key differentiator. As *The Counterinsurgency Field Manual* says "the side that learns faster and adapts more rapidly—the better learning organization—usually wins. Counterinsurgencies have been called learning competitions."[19]

WHEN IT COMES TO BRAND RISKS, SENIOR EXECUTIVES SHOULD, BUT DON'T ALWAYS, KNOW BETTER

The Counterinsurgency Field Manual states, we expect "senior leaders [to] set the proper direction and climate with thorough training and clear guidance; then they trust their subordinates to do the right thing."[20]

Similarly, we expect senior executives to adhere to a higher set of standards than the average employee just as military officers are expected to adhere to a higher set of standards than, and set examples for, enlisted personnel. Article 133 of the Uniform Code of Military Justice makes these expectations crystal clear: "Any commissioned officer...who is convicted of conduct unbecoming an officer and a gentleman shall be punished as a court-martial may direct."[21]

Lately, it seems like we need an Article 133 for senior executives when it comes to brand sabotage. Unless their behavior consistently sets the appropriate example, it's awfully hard to expect that subordinates will have the necessary training and guidance to do the right thing.

Recently, we have been inundated with articles about senior executives forced out of office due to "conduct unbecoming," such as:

- inappropriate relationships with subordinates,
- inappropriate interactions and relationships with vendors,
- inappropriate and insensitive comments to the press (or inappropriate and insensitive comments when they thought that the press wasn't listening),
- inappropriate financial transactions,
- inappropriate use of corporate assets and facilities,
- excessive compensation for questionable performance,
- excessive and costly post-retirement perks, and
- insensitive, arrogant, or off-key behavior (e.g., traveling by private jet to Washington, DC to request a publicly funded bailout).

Most of the time, however, being forced out of office does not equate to being fired for cause—although very occasionally, it does mean that someone leaves office without the humongous termination payment stipulated in his or her contract.

John Hofmeister, who served as president of Shell Oil Company from 2005 to 2008, is the author of *Why We Hate the Oil Companies* (written and published before the most recent oil spill in the Gulf of Mexico). He describes visiting fifty cities from mid-2006 to early 2008 as Shell's president to meet with business leaders, community leaders, government representatives, the general public, and Shell's wholesalers and retailers. In the process of traversing the country, he discovers how corporate leaders create their own reputation for arrogance, leading to the stunted relationship between the industry and the public.

Hofmeister identifies three issues when it comes to the problem that some executives have in communicating and the problems that this creates for them. While his remarks and point of reference focus on the oil industry, they could apply to a number of other industries that have seen the erosion of customer trust.

- Messages that strain your credibility with customers and lack authenticity: "Are the messages that are sent out what we really believe? Or are we merely saying things that we hope will give us a temporary advantage?"[22]

- The tendency of wealthy company executives to live in their own bubbles, at something of a remove from the world: *"Bunker mentality describes many oil company responses to public outcries."*[23]
- The lack of transparency: "Oil companies have generally resisted the candor and forthcoming style of communications that other industries call best practice."[24]

As far as senior executives are concerned, you can just assume that every single act that violates real and imagined standards will be captured, posted, and disseminated quicker than you can say "Eliot Spitzer" and "Client #9."

In chapter 5, we'll return to the specific question of what organizations can do to mitigate brand risks associated with employees and senior executives, including policies, procedures, processes, access, and training. For now, let us agree that aligning the behavior of employees and executives with the brand and reducing resulting brand risk offers fertile territory to explore.

BRAND RISKS OFTEN BEGIN WITH OPERATIONAL DECISIONS

In addition to the specific "brand busting" behaviors that need to be changed, we also need to consider the policies, processes, and procedures that potentially create brand risks.

Imagine if every significant corporate decision required a brand risk review. Would your brand be more secure, or would this just add more cost and time and reduce your nimbleness in a world where agility is essential to success?

What are the areas where a brand risk review process might be most relevant?

- brand licensing
- new product introductions, including brand extensions
- outsourcing and selecting suppliers and partners
- product pricing
- use of confidential customer information

Brand Licensing

As brands have become more valuable, brand owners have discovered the opportunity to significantly increase revenues and profits through licensing deals with third parties.

In July 2009, a colleague and I suggested brand licensing as a tactic for financial relief and brand revitalization in an article in *Advertising Age*.

"Brand licensing stems from a simple concept: The owner of the brand provides selected brand-exploitation rights to a third party in exchange for compensation, typically a percentage of the gross or net sales generated through the use of the brand by the licensee. With the right brand definition and investment, brand licensing can generate significant additional returns on the initial investment."[25]

In the article, we provide examples of the success that leading brands have had with licensing activities, ranging from Westin's "Heavenly Bed" deal with Nordstrom[26] to Godiva Chocolatier's arrangements with Diageo for a chocolate liqueur[27] to stadium-naming rights for the major professional sports leagues. But we also caution would-be franchisors to worry about the potential risks associated with brand licensing: "Licensors need to manage risks such as brand dilution (from poor quality control), brand confusion (from mismatched products) and other brand-erosion risks resulting from unchecked licensee relationships. The lure of 'easy money' can lead marketing executives to make undisciplined choices over time. But by treating brand licensing as a strategic decision, CMOs can position themselves to achieve high returns for their most important assets."[28]

New Product Introductions

Recently, a company with one of the world's premier consumer brands tested a cheaper, similar-named version of one of its core premium products, but eventually decided to end the test prior to full product launch. Apparently they felt that an attempt to capture a segment of customers with a "value" play was not worth the introduction of a potential rival to its core premium brand.

When Apple introduced its iPad, the media and blogosphere were atwitter with comments about the name and its suggestion of a feminine hygiene product. The *New York Times* headline read "What's in a Name? For Apple, iPad Said More than Intended,"[29] while the *Wall Street Journal's* headline was "Apple Tablet Draws Jeers, Legal Rumblings over iPad Name."[30]

Every new product introduction offers an opportunity to extend the brand by reaching new customers and increasing the value that is provided to existing customers. But each new product introduction potentially provides fuel to critics and competitors.

Outsourcing and Selecting Suppliers and Partners

In 2009, the Nobel Prize Committee awarded the Nobel Memorial Prize in Economics to Oliver Williamson. Williamson's field of study is transaction-cost economics. Transaction-cost economics explains why it makes sense for firms to perform some activities internally and others externally. Transaction-cost economics also explains why some outsourcing is done through spot markets, while other outsourcing is done through ongoing relationships. Williamson's work builds on the work of Ronald Coase, another Nobel laureate, who introduced the concept of transaction costs in his seminal article, "The Theory of the Firm." If you want to understand the intellectual underpinnings for the modern outsourcing, offshoring, reshoring, and onshoring phenomena, you would be well served to read Coase.

One of the potential by-products of fragmenting activities across multiple players is fragmented accountability for end-to-end quality. While contracts serve as a good-faith attempt to deal with this fragmented accountability, no single contract can cover every possible contingency and risk.

One risk that tends not to be well covered by contracts with value-chain partners is brand risk. Typically, contracts deal with one obvious source of brand risk: potential misuse of intellectual property, ranging from logos to brand names. If your contracts don't deal with these risks in excruciating detail, it's time for a new lawyer and new contracts. As you cross borders, the risk associated with these factors increases exponentially.

But other brand risks abound when it comes to value-chain partners. Looking backward across the supply chain, risks to the brand generally tend to fall into the following categories:

- **Environmental impact/sustainability**: The supplier uses ingredients or engages in practices that are environmentally unsafe. In the winter of 2010, Nestlé found itself the subject of attacks via YouTube, its own Facebook page, and Twitter. The attacks claimed that Nestlé contributed to the destruction of Indonesia's rain forest through its purchase of palm oil from an Indonesian company that allegedly cleared rain forest to establish palm plantations. One report on the attacks described a mock Kit Kat commercial showing "an office worker opening [a Kit Kat] wrapper and snacking on [a] bloody orangutan finger."[31]
- **Labor practices**: The supplier engages in unsafe or irresponsible labor practices. Recent examples here have included hiring of underage workers, unsafe labor conditions, substandard wages, unsafe living conditions in company housing, poor hygiene at facilities, and inadequate medical treatment for workplace accidents. These concerns began years ago as apparel manufacturers outsourced operations to Asia; they have now become commonplace across multiple categories. For suppliers that operate exclusively in the United States, the comparable issue is immigration and the use of undocumented workers.
- **Product safety**: The supplier uses inferior or contaminated ingredients. This problem has increased tremendously in recent years across categories, particularly in the case of food products. "Nearly one in six Americans is stricken by food poisoning each year and more than 3,000 die," according to two studies released in late 2010 by the US Centers for Disease Control and Prevention.[32] Recent examples of contaminated food categories include peanuts, eggs, beef, and pet food. We'll discuss food safety in more depth in chapter 7. A notable example outside of food was the use of lead paint by a supplier to a manufacturer of highly regarded children's toys.
- **Reputation**: The supplier is affiliated with other organizations, including governments, with significant reputation problems, creating a "guilt by association" risk to the brand.

Distribution partners can generate very similar brand risks, as well as additional ones. Because distribution partners often are the company's face to the customer, any brand-destroying behavior on the part of the distribution partner is particularly visible. The processes in which these behaviors are most likely to occur include:

- advertising;
- merchandising, including product display;
- information disseminated about products at the point of sale;
- ordering;
- pricing and discounting;
- returns (a.k.a. reverse logistics);
- warranties and repairs.

The question to ask yourself is whether sufficient safeguards are in place to ensure that distribution partners are aligned with your expectations for the brand.

Product Pricing

Pricing practices can create brand risk in two ways.

First, hidden charges, surcharges, extra charges, penalties, and the like add up quickly. High prices, in the form of extra charges, can create considerable risks for a brand by giving the impression that the brand is trying to take advantage of customers. The poster child for extra charges lately is the airline industry, where fees are assessed for checked baggage, rebooking, "preferred seating," and onboard snacks. At least one airline has made much of its free bag policy, with advertising trumpeting this policy.

Second, excessive promotions and discounts can damage a brand as well, when the discounts signal to customers that regular prices are too high. "Excessive promotions train the consumer to wait for deals and can shift the focus from product attributes to prices."[33] Recent research indicates that the ability of manufacturers to charge premium prices for branded products has eroded considerably.

Use of Confidential Customer Information

The final area where we are seeing more and more examples of decisions that might benefit from brand risk reviews is in the use of confidential customer information. There are two areas in particular where customer sensitivity to use of confidential information seems particularly prickly: information acquired through web-browsing activities, and location-based information.

Most organizations publish their privacy policies. Often, this information is sent to us, and most of us read these policies with the same diligence and attentiveness that we apply to insurance policies and warranty information. Until we discover otherwise, we assume that the company with whom we have the relationship will safeguard our confidential information (e.g., earnings, social security number, financial holdings).

The confidentiality of behavioral information falls into a fuzzier areas, particularly when it involves leveraging the digital footprints that we all leave when we browse the web. We all should be familiar with the concept of "cookies," small text files that are exchanged when we visit a website. Cookies are the tools that allow us to customize a website's appearance and automatically populate our usernames when we return to a website to sign in.

The latest advances in digital marketing involve "personalized remarketing" or "personalized retargeting," in which ads seem to stalk a consumer from website to website. The technique was explored by dedicated start-ups (e.g., Criteo), then Google tested it in 2009 and made it available to all advertisers on its AdWords network in March 2010.

Criteo's website explains the concept to advertisers:

> Personalized retargeting allows you to effectively re-engage with your potential customers after they leave your website using targeted advertising banners. While browsing your website, Criteo tags your potential customers with an anonymous cookie [meaning that no personally identifiable information is stored] and tracks the product they have shown interest in. When potential customers leave your website and visit other pages on the Internet, Criteo finds your lost prospects and retargets them with unique personalized banner ads featuring product-level recommendations based on their browsing history on your website. Each Criteo banner is created per viewer in real-time optimizing the placement, creative, and products displayed to achieve the highest click-through-rate (CTR).[34]

Location-based information falls into a similar vein. Many technologies, including most mobile phones, facilitate the identification of the location of the user. Knowing a customer's location could provide advertisers with a great opportunity to create highly targeted offers that kick in at the geographically appropriate times. Shopkick, for example, offers coupons and bonuses every time a subscriber walks into the location of a retail partner.[35]

Creepy, or effective? Or both?

Paul H. Rubin, a professor of economics and law at Emory University, argues that most consumers have misconceptions about privacy on the web. Rubin's view is that most information gathered on the web is used anonymously and that consumers are rarely harmed by this practice because it is anonymous. Rubin also argues that greater availability of information helps markets work better and that "the cost of privacy is less efficient markets."[36]

Whether or not you subscribe to Rubin's arguments about how customers benefit collectively and individually from greater information, customer fears about use of confidential information are unlikely to go away. A December 2010 survey conducted by *USA Today* and Gallup Inc. "suggests most US Internet users are aware they are being tracked online by advertisers and are troubled by the practice."[37] Meanwhile, the Federal Trade Commission has indicated its support for giving consumers a "Do Not Track" option to protect consumer privacy.[38]

A SPECIAL NOTE REGARDING TRANSFORMATIONAL EVENTS

While a variety of operating decisions can generate potential brand risks, particular attention needs to be paid to what we describe as "transformational events." A transformational event is one that could fundamentally reshape the internal and external perceptions of a brand and, in doing so, unexpectedly damage brand value.

Obvious examples of transformational events are mergers, acquisitions, and spin-offs or divestitures. Any change of ownership carries the risk that the brand will change and that the new owner will not maintain the same relationships with customers as the old owners. Similarly, major restructurings raise customer fears that vital elements of the brand experience will be eliminated (e.g., because of cheaper ingredients or lower service levels). As with mergers and acquisitions, restructuring efforts require treading carefully to manage the potential for brand risk.

We have now finished looking at the brand risks that can emanate from within the extended borders of your organization—your employees, your executive leadership team, and your value-chain partners, ranging from suppliers to distributors. For enemies within, motivations are not always clear. In many of the cases we discussed, we have accidental insurgents—individuals whose actions create brand risks but whose intentions were never to do so.

In chapter 5, we'll come back to the question of what steps you can take to reduce the likelihood that such brand threats will ever arise. Much can be accomplished in this regard, we will argue, by making the accidental insurgents deliberate participants in your brand risk management program.

When we talk about the topic of brand sabotage with executives, however, our experience is that they tend to immediately think of the potential brand risks that can emanate from beyond their borders—dissatisfied customers, cantankerous critics, and unruly competitors—mostly because these kinds of brand attacks are more purposeful, and therefore scarier.

In the next chapter, we'll take a more careful look at these threats—the ones you were probably most afraid of in the first place.

KEY TAKEAWAYS

WHAT WE KNOW...

- Brand risk is an unavoidable consequence of doing business.
- Like counterinsurgency, managing brand risks starts with good intelligence.

- The first job of brand risk intelligence is to identify potential brand insurgents.
- Don't assume that your employees have received, much less read, the manual.
- When it comes to brand risks, senior executives should, but don't always, know better.

- Brand risks often begin with operational decisions:
  - ❑ Brand licensing
  - ❑ Introducing new products or extending the brand
  - ❑ Outsourcing and selecting suppliers and partners
  - ❑ Product pricing
  - ❑ Using confidential customer information

...AND WHAT YOU CAN DO

- Embed your brand risk management efforts into your ongoing operations.
- Ensure that your brand risk intelligence activities consider worst-case scenarios as well as the most likely scenarios.
- Never assume that brand insurgents will identify themselves.
- Enroll your employees in your brand risk management efforts.
- Recognize that senior executives must be included in your employee enrollment efforts.
- Consider what might change if every significant corporate decision required a brand risk review.

WHAT IS RISK INTELLIGENCE?

Our colleagues Frederick Funston, Stephen Wagner, and Henry Ristuccia write in their article "Risk Intelligent Decision-Making: Ten Skills for Surviving and Thriving in Uncertainty":

> A diet of pure risk aversion likely will lead to extinction... *Risk intelligence* is both the capability to produce and then effectively act upon such intelligence in order to achieve the desired results. Some level of failure is essential for innovation and experimentation. The enterprise needs to determine acceptable versus unacceptable differences between actual and expected performance. Otherwise, intolerance of any level of failure will lead to risk aversion and competitive disadvantage....
>
> In this broad context, success often requires the embedding of risk intelligent capabilities throughout all levels of the organization—from directors to executive leadership to business units and all employees.[39]

Funston, Wagner, and Ristuccia argue that risk intelligence efforts typically fail when an organization exhibits one or more of the following behaviors:

- relies on false assumptions,
- fails to exercise vigilance,
- ignores velocity and momentum,
- is unable to make the key connections and manage complexity,
- is unable to imagine failure,
- relies on unverified sources of information,
- maintains inadequate margins of safety,
- focuses exclusively on the short term,
- is unwilling to take enough of the "right" risks,
- lacks operational discipline.

Chapter Four

STEP ONE, PART TWO

Assess Brand Risks—Beyond Your Borders

Few insurgencies fit neatly into any rigid classification. In fact, counterinsurgent commanders may face a confusing and shifting coalition of many kinds of opponents, some of whom may be at odds with one another.
　　　　　　　　　　　　—The Counterinsurgency Field Manual

It's time to turn our focus from the enemies within to the enemies that live beyond your borders.

Although there are notable exceptions, much of the internally generated brand sabotage that we've just discussed is accidental—employees, executives, and value chain partners can and do inadvertently damage the brand that provides them with a livelihood. Often, carelessness is the culprit, not malicious intent. By contrast, when we look beyond the extended borders of the enterprise, we find a whole raft of intentional brand insurgents, whose motivations range from responding to real or perceived breaches of trust to inflicting serious and lasting brand damage. As with real insurgents, these external brand saboteurs sometimes converge in unpredictable ways.

When we consider external sources of sabotage, four obvious categories spring to mind:

- Customers
- Reviewers
- Gadflies and ideologues
- Competitors

Let's take each of these, in turn, beginning with your customers.

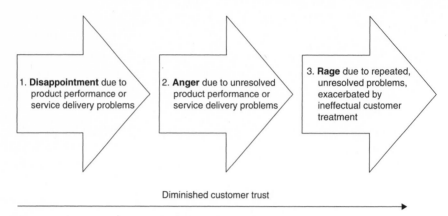

Figure 4.1 The three steps to losing a customer's trust

THINK OF YOUR CUSTOMER'S ACT OF BRAND SABOTAGE AS A *CRI DE COEUR*, MOTIVATED BY THE PERCEPTION THAT YOU HAVE LET THEM DOWN

"Trust is what creates customer loyalty, trust is what reduces transaction costs, and trust is what speeds up buying decisions."
—Ed Moran and Francois Gossieaux,
The Hyper-Social Organization[1]

Why would your customers try to sabotage your brand? After all, haven't your customers already made the choice to have a relationship with your brand? Haven't they extended their trust to you? How in the world could undermining your brand possibly help them?

It's really very simple: You've let them down. They no longer trust you to do the right thing.

It's rare that this loss of trust happens all at once. Losing a customer's trust is a three-stage process that begins with disappointment, moves to anger, and then, if not addressed, ends in rage. See figure 4.1.

Stage One: Disappointment

Stage one of losing a customer's trust is when you disappoint the customer. The disappointment can come from something big or something small, or it might just be the proverbial straw that breaks the camel's back. Most of us are disappointed with our suppliers now and then. Occasional disappointment over the course of a long relationship is inevitable. In a personal relationship, it can range from forgotten birthdays and anniversaries to communication miscues. Trust me, it happens. Ask my wife.

Disappointments happen in a supplier-customer relationship, too. Possibilities include:

- contaminated products,
- defective products,
- excessive wait times for customer service,
- hard-to-follow instructions,
- hard-to-understand pricing structures,
- inaccurate bills,
- late shipments,
- missing parts,
- product shortages,
- restrictive return policies,
- service delivery mishaps and outages, and
- unexpected warranty limitations.

In some cases, the problem might be that you screwed up. You didn't perform, you didn't deliver, or you didn't satisfy the expectations that you created with the customer. In the cases where you screwed up, it's your job to make it right before the situation moves from disappointment to anger. To do this, you need the mechanisms in place to identify what happened, whether you were truly at fault, and how you will fix the problem. Every world-class organization should have well-defined service recovery processes in place to handle exactly these situations.

In other cases, you may not exactly have done anything wrong. The customer misunderstood; a third party didn't perform; the weather intervened and caused a service disruption.[2] From the customer's perspective, something went wrong. It may not be your fault, but you'll be blamed.

Sometimes, it's best to shut up and fix the problem without worrying about who is at fault. Ten years ago, I worked with a major casual apparel direct merchant known for its outstanding service and generous merchandise return policies. In my initial tour of their headquarters, they showed me a pile of returned items that were actually the products of their chief competitor. Much to their chagrin, these misdirected returns, although infrequent, happened with some regularity. With a smile, they explained that they used to return the misdirected merchandise to the customers with instructions to send it the correct merchant. They eventually realized that it was just as easy to forward the returned merchandise directly to the competing merchant—who had come to a similar conclusion regarding their customers' returns of my client's merchandise—in the apparel industry's version of a prisoner-of-war exchange, rather than shift the burden back to the customer, even though the customer had made the mistake.

In still other cases, the disappointment is the outcome of a decision that you made. You added a fuel surcharge, you changed your return policies, or you decided to divert a shipment to a more important customer. In these cases, the disappointment is the result of a calculated risk that you took. The key here is that ideally you identified the risk in advance, appropriately assessed it, and moved forward, cognizant of the potential consequences.

On a recent fall weekend, I turned on my TV to watch the final match of the U.S. Open tennis tournament. Blank screen.

Time to call customer service.

I Googled the customer service number for my cable company. Then I realized that I had no Internet signal—because my Internet service is from the same provider that I use for cable. When I opened my browser, I received a message telling me that I needed to set up a new account. What was going on?

I popped my mobile wireless card into my computer and tried again. Different provider, different result. I was in business.

I called my cable company, ready to go through the usual rigmarole that comes with restoring my service, which generally involves turning devices off and unplugging them. Much to my surprise, the message that greeted me also informed me that I had been cut off due to non-payment of my bills.

What?

I went on hold.

Meanwhile, I opened up my electronic banking account and discovered that I had neither received nor paid a cable bill in three months.

While on hold, the cable company's interactive voice response system informed me that I could pay the bill by phone. Okay. I paid off the balance, including a fee for restoration of service, watched the TV and Internet signal spring back to life, and waited to speak to a customer service rep.

I waited almost ten minutes. My head was about to explode. When I was finally connected with someone, I explained to the representative that I wanted to be reimbursed for the restoration of service fee. I told him I had not been getting my electronic bill and that up to that point I'd had an impeccable record of on-time bill payment. He was polite. He was even apologetic. He removed the charge. I hung up. I had my cable back, I had my Internet back, I got my service fee waived, and my head had not exploded. Mission accomplished.

So, I was inconvenienced, disappointed, and annoyed, but given the result, this was hardly worth tweeting about, blogging about, or posting a video about on YouTube.

For many companies, the initial customer disappointment becomes an opportunity to shine. It's an opportunity for them to demonstrate their commitment to customer service and show that they care. It's an opportunity for them to undertake heroic acts and noble gestures. It's an opportunity to do the right thing.

If you ever read a book or attended a lecture about great customer service or "wowing" the customer, you have likely heard the story about the customer who returned a set of tires to Nordstrom. In the story, Nordstrom refunds the customer's money, even though Nordstrom is an apparel store that has never carried or sold tires. The story is generally used to illustrate the point that companies with great customer service "do the right thing," even when they don't have to.

Is the story true or not? Why would any customer ever mistake a high-end clothier for an automotive retailer? Why would any retailer ever refund money to a customer who was returning merchandise that had clearly not been purchased there? Snopes.com offers an interesting analysis of the possible truth behind the story (i.e., that the Nordstrom location where the incident supposedly took place had once been a tire store)[3] and even points out that Bernie Marcus, one of the founders of Home Depot, tells a similar story in his business memoir, *Built from Scratch*.[4]

Regardless of its accuracy, the Nordstrom legend is consistent with the experience of many companies. In general, speedy and effective responses to customer disappointments usually work in the company's favor. One of our utility clients has found that its most satisfied and engaged customers are actually the ones who have experienced a single power outage that was quickly resolved. Satisfaction and engagement, however, rapidly decline with the second or third outage, regardless how quick the response.

At our firm, we've actually organized our core client-service training around the concept of "moments that matter," with the goal of helping our professionals develop the appropriate responses to strengthen our client relationships. Handled well, a "moment that matters" results in a satisfied client and becomes a turning point in a potentially problematic relationship. Handled poorly, a "moment that matters" hastens a customer down the road from disappointment to anger.

Stage Two: Anger

Failing to address customer disappointment advances you to stage two, anger. You don't restore service. You don't refund the customer's money. You don't fix the bill. You don't recall the products. You don't replace the missing part. You don't return the customer's calls. You don't express remorse, and you certainly don't apologize.

Now the customer is not only disappointed—the customer is angry.

Some angry customers suffer in silence. Others desert you. Still others escalate their dissatisfaction in the form of either repeated requests, or complaints to third parties like the Better Business Bureau, regulatory agencies such as the Consumer Product Safety Commission, ombudsmen, or a consumer advocate in the media, like David Segal, who writes "The Haggler," a customer service column that appears in the Sunday edition of the *New York Times*.[5]

During stage two, the most active angry customers may go public. But often it takes just a little more to incite others to action.

Stage Three: Rage

Here's what it takes to move some customers from anger to rage: You

A. ignore them
B. blame them
C. belittle them, or
D. all of the above

Ever see the 1987 movie *Fatal Attraction*? (If you missed the movie, you can catch the relevant clip on YouTube.[6]) Michael Douglas plays a married lawyer who has a weekend fling with an editor (Glenn Close) who becomes obsessed with him. She stalks him, calls him at home, and even murders his daughter's pet rabbit. When he confronts her, she tells him that she will not be ignored. It really gets ugly after that. That's what rage looks like.

Ever reach out to a supplier who tells you that you wouldn't have a problem if you had followed procedures properly? Ever had a supplier who made you feel like an idiot? Remember how you felt? That's rage.

Responding ineffectively to a customer's anger can quickly move him from stage two to stage three. You have now irrevocably breached the customer's trust. The customer is officially enraged and is ready to get even. Be prepared to suffer the consequences: the loss of business from the individual customer, the public broadcasting of your sins, and efforts to enlist others in the cause.

Here's what is interesting about rage: Because of social media, individual rage can quickly become viral rage. Social media allow an enraged individual to rapidly share his or her rage publicly and find like-minded individuals. In minutes, the entire world can hear about what you did and can participate in a virally driven collective condemnation that can be downright scary.[7]

Consider the case of Procter & Gamble (P&G) and diaper rash.[8]

Diapers are a big part of P&G's business. Pampers generates $9 billion in annual revenues, more than 10 percent of P&G's total revenues.[9] Once customers select a brand of diapers, they tend to be very loyal.

Pampers keep babies dry because they contain an absorbent gel, which is poured into a bulky pulp material that's used in the diaper. In March 2010, P&G changed its manufacturing process. Instead of pouring the gel into the pulp material, P&G started printing it directly onto the diapers. The result was a 20 percent thinner diaper, which sounds like a good thing.[10]

Some customers, however, were not pleased. They believed that the newly reengineered diapers were causing their babies to break out into a diaper rash. They complained. P&G, a company that takes customer service very seriously, responded with a combination of direct customer outreach and postings to various web pages and social-media sites.

Apparently, some of these customers were not satisfied with P&G's response. Faster than you can say "talcum powder," a Facebook campaign was launched, complaints were lodged with the US Consumer Product Safety Commission (CPSC) and Health Canada, and a lawsuit was filed.[11]

P&G was convinced that its reengineered diaper was not the cause of the diaper rash and that they were the target of a campaign aimed at discrediting them They made the decision to fight back and fight back aggressively. Their response included an outreach campaign to "mommy bloggers" and proactive PR. This response wound up putting P&G, as the *Wall Street Journal* reported, "in the uncomfortable position of having to publicly blame or discredit its own customers."[12]

In fact, P&G turned out to be right.

In September 2010 P&G was absolved, with the US Consumer Product Safety Commission (CPSC) and Health Canada both concluding that there was no "link between the diapers and the [nearly 4,700] health complaints received." The CPSC press release also drily noted that "most babies exhibit diaper rash at least once in their lifetime."[13]

The diaper-rash episode is not the only example of unhappy customers publicly venting and generating viral rage.[14]

Table 4.1   Customer rage goes viral: An illustration

Incident #1: Airline damages checked luggage

The precipitating event	A musician checks his expensive musical instrument on an airline flight. Upon retrieving his checked instrument, he discovers that the instrument is damaged. The airline turns down his claims for compensation because he fails to report the damage in the prescribed time window.
The reaction	Said musician writes a trilogy of songs chronicling his tale of woe. The first installment is posted to YouTube and generates more than 9 million hits within a year. The song garners the #1 position on iTunes Music Store the week following its release, and *Time* magazine names the song to its list of the "Top Viral Videos of 2009." Musician subsequently gains notoriety as a speaker on customer service. Airline contributes the equivalent of the cost of the instrument to a not-for-profit organization.

Airlines seem to be a particularly easy target for unhappy customers.[15] See table 4.1 for one recent incident.

A journalist acknowledged the success of the above songwriter's campaign as "a sign of how the new social media have endowed consumers with unprecedented power in our constant struggle to hold corporations accountable and win civilized treatment for ourselves," but suggests that there are nuances to consider.

The airline could not have anticipated that it was picking a fight with someone who had a lot of viral-marketing strengths. The songwriter's efforts wouldn't have gone anywhere if he weren't incredibly persistent, nor would his song have become a hit if he didn't have an excellent country-pop voice...an affable personality that enabled him to declare image war on a publicly-traded company without seeming to harbour one ounce of bitterness, and a gift for writing a catchy chorus...So while the strategy was remarkably successful, it's not available to those of us who aren't moderately expert singer-songwriters...the chance [the airline] took by saying 'Tough luck' is one they can still probably take thousands of times over without hazard. And at the same time, the power of social media is available to the airline, too, and offers them some protection that corporations didn't have...30 years ago.[16]

The publicity generated by this incident reflects what happens when customer complaints go viral. These incidents are still the exception, not the norm. As brand stewards, we need to understand when we're dealing with the lone disgruntled customer and when we're dealing with a tsunami of dissatisfied customers who have found an individual to give voice to their frustration and sense of betrayal.

Sometimes, this stuff just gets goofy. Frito-Lay markets SunChips as a healthy product made with whole grains and low in saturated fat and cholesterol. And its website describes how it uses solar energy to cook its products. Frito-Lay started using compostable packaging, designed to break down in about fourteen weeks, for SunChips. But apparently, the compostable packaging is noticeably louder than the standard packaging.[17] The loudness of the packaging inspired a Facebook group called SORRY BUT I CAN'T HEAR YOU OVER THIS SUN CHIPS BAG, with more than 43,000 followers at last count. Frito-Lay has taken this in stride with comments on its website about the "different sound qualities" of its new bag and shelf signs that read, "Yes, the bag is loud. That's what change sounds like."[18]

Less than two months after the *Wall Street Journal* published a front-page article documenting this fracas ("Snack Attack: Chip Eaters Make Noise About a Crunchy Bag"), it published another article, "Sun Chips Bag to Lose its Crunch," which reported that "Frito-Lay...says it is pulling most of the biodegradable packaging it uses for its Sun Chips snacks, following an outcry from consumers who complained the new bags were too noisy."[19] Within a week, there was a new set of Facebook groups grousing about the demise of the bags.[20]

Your job is to understand when and where this rage is likely to occur and determine how you want to respond to and manage it. At the end of this chapter, we'll talk about the assessment component, and we'll outline potential responses in chapter 7.

VOLUNTEER REVIEWERS REQUIRE MORE AND MORE OF YOUR ATTENTION

An educated consumer is our best customer.

—Syms Corporation

Sy Syms (née Seymour Merinsky) built a fortune by "giving Educated Consumers® real bargains on real designer clothes." His stores offer a broad range of styles and sizes at affordable prices and, if you grew up in New York City, as I did, it was hard to avoid his ubiquitous ads, many of which starred Mr. Syms himself.[21]

Today, it's not just Syms's customers who are educated consumers. Customers have ready access to more information about products than they have ever had before. While they still learn about your brand from what you have told them, through your advertising and other marketing communications, much of what they know about your brand also comes from information you don't generate and can't control.

The research that we have conducted about buying patterns suggests that looking at online reviews and ratings prior to purchase is a critical step for most customers today. Access to online reviews and ratings through mobile devices has accelerated usage.

Most mature brand management organizations have long had people and processes in place to deal with the professional reviewers and analysts. While professional reviewers and analysts do make mistakes, they generally adhere to strict editorial standards and rigorous fact-checking processes that decrease the likelihood of unsubstantiated and erroneous assertions about your offerings. However, more and more online reviews are now generated by web users, so constraints are virtually nonexistent and just about anything goes.

Many of the reviews can be found on the websites of vendors that have decided, as Amazon did, to "tap into the passion that consumers [have] for products and shopping." Although many websites allow reviewers a great deal of latitude, they generally reserve the right to restrict or remove reviews. Amazon's website, for example, publishes very specific guidelines for reviews and other user-generated content, including reserving the right "to restrict or remove any and all uses or Content that we determine in our sole discretion is harmful to our systems, network, reputation, or good-will, to other Amazon.com customers, or to any third party" and "remove reviews that include any of the following: objectionable material...promotional content...inappropriate content...[and] off-topic information."[22]

Just assume that whatever you are offering, there are websites out there that permit your would-be customers to read what current and former customers have to say.[23] In addition, there are websites focused exclusively on user-generated reviews, ranging from Epinions ("You can read and write reviews on millions of products and services"[24])to Pissed Consumer ("Tell the World. Be Heard"[25]) to Viewpoints ("Let's review") to Yelp ("Real people. Real reviews"[26]).

Angie's List, which was started by Angie Hicks in Columbus, Ohio, in 1995 to review contractors, now includes reviews of doctors and other local service providers and serves more than a million customers. As its website states, "Angieslist.com puts reliable information and resources at the fingertips of its members, so they can access it anytime they need help—whether it's for a major home renovation, an emergency car repair, finding a new dentist or even a clown for their kid's birthday party."[27]

Given the increasing number and influence of volunteer reviewers, you need to focus energy on managing them as part of your counterinsurgency efforts.

BE PARTICULARLY WARY OF IDEOLOGY-INSPIRED BRAND INSURGENTS

Ideas are a motivating factor in insurgent activities. Insurgencies can gather recruits and amass popular support through ideological appeal...The most powerful ideologies tap latent, emotional concerns of the populace...Ideology provides a prism, including a vocabulary and analytical categories through which followers perceive their situation.

—The Counterinsurgency Field Manual

Gadflies and other ideology-inspired brand insurgents did not start with social media.

In April 1906, President Theodore Roosevelt delivered a stirring speech in conjunction with the laying of the corner stone of the Cannon House Office Building in Washington, D.C. The speech introduced "the man with the muck-rake," a character from the seventeenth-century classic *The Pilgrim's Progress*, to describe what was required to expose economic, political, and social evils. In the speech, Roosevelt commended the activities of would-be muckrakers:

> There are, in the body politic, economic and social, many and grave evils, and there is urgent necessity for the sternest war upon them. There should be relentless exposure of and attack upon every evil man whether politician or business man, every evil practice, whether in politics, in business, or in social life. I hail as a benefactor every writer or speaker, every man who, on the platform, or in book, magazine, or newspaper, with merciless severity makes such attack, provided always that he in his turn remembers that the attack is of use only if it is absolutely truthful.[28]

Roosevelt's speech occurred in the Progressive Era, a period of American history when calls for reform were important parts of the political landscape and investigative journalists and authors were particularly influential. The breakup of John D. Rockefeller's Standard Oil is generally attributed, in part, to Ida Tarbell's 1904 book *The History of the Standard Oil Company* (first serialized in *McClure's Magazine*), while Upton Sinclair's 1906 work *The Jungle* garners much of the credit for the Pure Food and Drug Act, passed in 1906.

Muckrakers did not die with the Progressive Era.

In 1965, Ralph Nader, best known nowadays as an occasional presidential candidate, wrote a book about automotive safety titled *Unsafe at Any Speed*. Although Nader looked broadly at automotive safety issues, the book is remembered mainly for its accusations of handling and stability problems with General Motors' rear-mounted-engine vehicle the Corvair. Although tests subsequently completed by the National Highway Traffic Safety Administration concluded that the Corvair compared favorably to other contemporary vehicles in handling and safety, it was too late to prevent Corvair sales from going into a tailspin. GM stopped production of the vehicle in 1969.[29]

GM came under new fire from filmmaker Michael Moore in 1989 with *Roger & Me*, a film focused on Moore's attempts to confront GM CEO Roger Smith about the impact of downsizing on Flint, Michigan.

Other books and films have targeted different industries, including:

- fast food: *Super Size Me* and *Fast Food Nation*,
- chemical manufacturing: *A Civil Action*,
- private security: *Blackwater: The Rise of the World's Most Powerful Mercenary Army*, and
- banking: *Wall Street*.[30]

Ideologues and gadflies tend to be concerned with a common set of issues, such as:

- environmental impact,
- excessive greed,
- health,
- labor conditions,
- product safety, and
- undue corporate influence on government officials and regulators.

Sometimes, ideology becomes intertwined with more mercenary objectives, particularly in today's highly litigious society. In September 2010, newspapers carried the obituary of Edward Swartz, "The Nader of the Nursery." Swartz was a product liability attorney and founder of World Against Toys Causing Harm (WATCH), a not-for-profit organization designed to "educate the public to the dangers lurking in many toys and children's products." Swartz authored two exposés, *Toys that Don't Care* and *Toys that Kill*, and, through WATCH, began issuing an annual list of the "10 Worst Toys" in 1973. Swartz continued to pursue product liability cases, winning his largest toy case victory in 1991 with an award of $3.1 million in a choking case.[31]

Goldman Sachs included brand risk as part of its discussion of risks in its annual report for the first time in 2009, after the plethora of negative attention associated with the financial crisis. In addition to the other risk factors, the report discusses how adverse publicity could have "a negative impact on our reputation and on the morale and performance of our employees, which could adversely affect our businesses and results of operations."[32] In September 2010, Goldman began to run its first national advertising campaign since it went public in 1999. David Wells, a spokesman for Goldman, said about the campaign that "we need to provide to a broader audience a better understanding of who we are and what we need to do. This is meant to help do that."[33]

The difference between the enraged customer and the contemporary muckraker lies in their motivation—one is enraged by how he or she was treated as an individual, while the other is enraged by the company's principles and practices, broadly speaking. These differences in motivation, however, won't prevent coalitions from forming.

■■■ COMPETITORS ARE INCREASINGLY QUICK TO CAPITALIZE WHEN YOU STUMBLE

In the 1960s, Dick Tuck, a Democratic political operative, gained notoriety for his effectiveness in derailing Richard Nixon's campaign for governor of California. Tuck's specialty was political mischief, and he is particularly remembered for a rally in Los Angeles's Chinatown, where he put Chinese language signs that questioned a loan Howard Hughes made to Nixon's brother in the place of more benign signs reading "Welcome."

Tuck's "Chinatown Caper" is emblematic of a species of political dirty tricks, ranging from digging up and, now with the help of social media, publicizing unfortunate but true comments a candidate made early in his or her career, to the questionable use of Photoshopped images and creative editing to suggest activities and events that never, in fact, occurred. As Mark Leibovich writes, in a *New York Times* article about Tuck and other "merry pranksters," "The Internet makes it easier to commit wrongdoing and harder to conceal it."[34]

Compared to political competitors, business competitors generally play fair. There are exceptions, such as when the CEO of one retailer anonymously blogged negative comments about a competitor (which also happened to be an acquisition target). However, concerns about regulators and litigation, combined with a general feeling that what goes around comes around, are usually pretty effective in keeping competitors in line.

Nevertheless, one of the things that we noticed during the last recession is that companies have become less timid about opportunistically capitalizing on competitive missteps and using social media to take on competitors head-to-head. In the most recent economic downturn, this competitive sniping tended to take the form of ads with very targeted messaging aimed at competitive weaknesses, sometimes accompanied by special offers encouraging a competitor's customers to try the alternative. For example, Dunkin' Donuts focused on positioning itself as a more economical alternative to higher-priced specialty coffee retailers with its "Breakfast, NOT Brokefast" campaign, while the United States Postal Service got in on the act with its "A simpler way to ship" campaign for its priority mail shipping services.[35]

It's a fine line between what's fair game and what's off limits when it comes to competitive acts of brand sabotage. When human lives and public safety are involved, it's probably safe to assume that competitors will be loath to undermine you, lest they be accused of poor taste and timing. In less weighty situations, don't be surprised if your competitors are more inclined toward acts of mischief when it comes to poaching your customers.

NEVER UNDERESTIMATE THE IMAGINATION OF POTENTIAL SABOTEURS

External brand saboteurs can be incredibly imaginative when it comes to the weapons that they improvise to damage your brand. You need to be equally imaginative in identifying the possibilities and the likelihood of their appearance.

Take the example of the 9/11 attack, where al Qaeda terrorists used commercial aircraft as their weapons of choice. *The 9/11 Commission Report* notes that the federal government should have considered this possibility.[36] "[S]ince al Qaeda and other groups had already used suicide vehicles, namely truck bombs, the leap to the use of other vehicles such as boats (the *Cole* attack) or planes is not far-fetched."[37] Unfortunately, the *Report* concludes, "[i]magination is not a gift usually associated with bureaucracies."[38]

By contrast, here is a case of trying to think ahead. After the 2010 oil spill in the Gulf of Mexico, BP recognized the power of web-based searching and purchased a number of search terms associated with the words *"oil," "spill,"* and *"BP."* If you search these words on Google or Bing, the first hit is a sponsored link to BP's website, specifically, to a page labeled "Gulf of Mexico Response," which describes everything that BP is doing "to make this right." Bravo to BP for its new-media savvy.

If you add the word *lawsuit* or *damages* to your search, the same sponsored link appears. But appearing alongside it is a sponsored link for a law firm that asks if you've been affected by the gulf oil spill.[39] To borrow a phrase from another industrial company, this is "imagination at work."

SUCCESSFUL BRAND COUNTERINSURGENCY BEGINS BY ASSESSING THE POTENTIAL THREATS FACED BY YOUR BRAND, INCLUDING SOURCE AND POTENTIAL IMPACT

One common feature of insurgencies is that the government that is being targeted generally takes a while to recognize that an insurgency is occurring. Insurgents take advantage of that time to build strength and gather support. Thus, counterinsurgents often have to 'come from behind' when fighting an insurgency.

—The Counterinsurgency Field Manual

In this chapter and the preceding one, we have spent time looking at the potential sources of brand sabotage. In chapter 3, we looked at the "enemies within," specifically employees, executives, and value chain partners. In this chapter, we looked beyond the borders of your enterprise at customers, individuals, and organizations that review products and services; at gadflies and ideologues (a.k.a. muckrakers); and at competitors. In providing you with examples of how brand sabotage can occur, we've tried to convey several critical points worth recapping:

- Brand risk is a natural consequence of operating decisions that you make. The goal is not to avoid brand risk but to be aware of it and incorporate brand risk proactively into your key decisions.
- Brand risk can come from both internal and external sources.
- Brand risk existed long before social media ever appeared; social media, however, can play a role similar to that of an accelerant in a fire by speeding the spread and intensifying the impact.

- Managing brand risk requires vigilance in the short term, with a perspective on the long term.
- Brand risk management efforts can fail if you underestimate the imagination of potential saboteurs and are unwilling to imagine the unimaginable.

Here are the key questions that you should be asking about your company as you assess internal and external threats:

- Are we actively identifying and evaluating the risks to our brand as part of our strategic and operational decision making?
- Do we regularly and systematically look at the many potential sources of brand risks to identify and assess potential brand-damaging activities that have occurred and those that might occur?
- Are we educating our employees about the concept of brand value and risk and helping them to assess the impact of their activities and decision making on our brand? Do we have policies in place to prevent them from intentionally or unintentionally undermining our brand? Have we trained them in what to do when they observe acts of brand sabotage?
- Have we built the capabilities to monitor and track potential brand risks, including understanding what is going on with competitors and, more broadly, across the industry?
- Do we have plans in place to respond to acts of brand sabotage?
- Are we deliberately and purposefully harvesting insights when attacks on our brand do occur?
- Are we actively measuring brand value and do we understand how it is affected by brand-damaging events?
- Have we created a broad group of collaborators capable of helping us defeat brand insurgents?

KEY TAKEAWAYS

WHAT WE KNOW...	...AND WHAT YOU CAN DO
■ Think of your customer's act of brand sabotage as a *cri de coeur* motivated by the perception that you have let them down.	■ Monitor your performance relative to customer expectations. Track where individual customers are in the disappointment-anger-rage cycle and identify appropriate mitigation plans.
■ Volunteer reviewers require more and more of your attention.	■ Create the capability to proactively engage with and manage volunteer reviewers.
■ Be particularly wary of ideology-inspired brand insurgents.	■ Avoid knee-jerk reactions. Your natural tendencies to respond in a conventional manner to attacks on your brand may be misguided. Sometimes, the following is true: ❑ The more you protect your brand, the less secure your brand may be; ❑ The more force you use, the less effective it is; and ❑ Doing nothing may be the best response when it comes to protecting your brand.
■ Competitors are increasingly quick to capitalize when you stumble.	■ Assume that competitors will join the attack.
■ Never underestimate the imagination of potential saboteurs.	■ Become a learning organization. When it comes to building a resilient brand, the winner is the one who learns most quickly.

Chapter Five

STEP TWO

Galvanize Your Brand Troops

Effective COIN operations require competence and judgment by Soldiers and Marines at all levels ... Senior leaders set the proper direction and climate with thorough training and clear guidance; then they trust their subordinates to do the right thing.

—The Counterinsurgency Field Manual

Effective performance often requires the embedding of risk intelligent capabilities throughout all levels of the organization—from directors to executive leadership to business units and all employees.

—Funston, et al., "Risk Intelligent Decision-Making: Ten Essential Skills for Surviving and Thriving in Uncertainty"[1]

Whether we're talking about real troops fighting real insurgents or your brand troops fighting brand insurgents, an effective counterinsurgency program requires leaders to fully engage the hearts and minds of those they lead. Preventing brand sabotage begins with building awareness of the threat and its consequences, and teaching employees to assume personal responsibility for preempting, detecting, and reducing the possibility of its occurrence.

This is a place where real leadership is required on the part of a company's executive team—to define the mission, to set the climate and culture, and to train and guide individual employees. The three critical ingredients for effectively engaging your brand troops are:

- a clear mission,
- a purposeful outreach program, and
- a strategy for employee ownership of the mission.

Let's take a slight detour from our counterinsurgency model and look at a powerful example of how another organization developed broad support to help it deal with a major threat. It's the experience of the United States Forest Service in fighting the threat of wildfires.[2]

Let's start with a brief history. The Forest Service was established in 1905 as an agency of the US Department of Agriculture and was charged with the management of the approximately 193 million acres of public lands in national forests and grasslands. For perspective's sake, 193 million acres is equivalent to the size of Texas.

Fighting wildfires is a key responsibility of the Forest Service. The facts and figures contained in their 2007 report paint a stark picture of the challenge of eliminating wildfires. According to the Forest Service's "Large Wildfire Cost Review," 2007 wildfires burned an astonishing total of 9.32 million acres at a federal cost of nearly $1.8 billion. This total included twenty-seven individual fires costing more than $10 million each, with total suppression costs approaching $547 million, and total burned territory of approximately 3 million acres. During 2007, there were 12,261 wildfires caused by lightning, but almost six times as many were caused by human error.[3]

Those are the facts. If you want a more descriptive perspective on wildfires, we recommend reading two books.

Young Men and Fire, by Norman MacLean (who also wrote *A River Runs Through It*), is a riveting account of a wildfire fighting tragedy that took place in 1949 in Mann Gulch, a remote area of Montana. In addition to documenting the devastating fire that took the lives of twelve firefighters and a forest ranger, MacLean describes many of the changes in modern firefighting techniques that emerged from a close analysis of the fire.[4]

Timothy Egan's more recent book *The Big Burn* covers an earlier but equally devastating fire in the Bitterroot Mountains on the Idaho-Montana border and provides context for the creation of the Forest Service and its subsequent focus on fighting wildfires.[5]

Shortly before the 1949 Mann Gulch tragedy described so vividly by MacLean, the Forest Service launched a campaign to reduce the threat of wildfires through public awareness and active engagement. Walt Disney allowed the Forest Service to use the animated character Bambi in its initial public service announcement ads, but only on a temporary basis. The search for a permanent mascot culminated in the selection of another animal, Smokey Bear (more commonly, but incorrectly, referred to as Smokey the Bear as a result of a popular song and a Little Golden Book that used the unofficial "the").

The initial Smokey Bear campaign used the slogan "Smokey Says—Care Will Prevent 9 out of 10 Forest Fires." The slogan quickly morphed into "Remember...Only YOU Can Prevent Forest Fires" and more recently shifted to "Only YOU Can Prevent Wildfires" to include grassland fires as well as forest fires.

The premise behind the initial Smokey campaign was that many wildfires are the result of carelessness, and by alerting the general populace to this reality, the threat could be reduced. Examples of fire-causing human error include unsafe and unattended campfires, improper disposal of cigarettes and other smoking materials, unsafe burning of debris, poorly maintained outdoor equipment such as lawnmowers, fireworks, and children playing with matches and lighters.

The Smokey campaign continues to run today, and after more than sixty years it is the longest running public service campaign in the United States. According to the Ad Council, more than 95 percent of US adults and 77 percent of US children recognize Smokey Bear and his message. In his book *The Art of Cause Marketing: How to Use Advertising to Change Personal Behavior and Public Policy*, Richard Earle describes Smokey as one of the most "ownable, memorable and empathetic icon[s]" ever used to represent a cause campaign.[6]

What worked about Smokey?

- A clear mission that connects the target audience emotionally to the cause: "Only You Can Prevent Wildfires"
- A deliberate outreach to the masses: a campaign supported by commercials, songs, books, and eventually a website
- A specific strategy for getting the average American to take ownership of the mission: educational materials, a "Get Your Smokey On Pledge," an interactive website, and a newsletter, for example

Oh, and let's not forget the appeal of the cute mascot himself, Smokey (although today, we might be more inclined to create an avatar).

With these guidelines, let's see how we can apply the lessons from Smokey Bear to our fight for brand resilience.

THE FIRST STEP IN GALVANIZING YOUR TROOPS IS TO DEFINE A CLEAR MISSION THAT LINKS YOUR TROOPS TO THE CAUSE OF BRAND RESILIENCE

Most of us view mission statements as overly broad, fluffy, and meaningless, written in haste at some offsite retreat because we needed something to say when someone asked us about our mission statement. This is not always true, but regardless of how much time, energy, and brainpower went into their development, most corporate mission statements provide little in the way of practical, day-to-day guidance.

By contrast, like Smokey Bear, real soldiers talk about their mission with a degree of clarity that most of us civilians will never fully comprehend. *The Counterinsurgency Field Manual* defines "mission" in the context of counterinsurgency:

- **Clarity to permit decentralized execution:** *"Mission command* is the conduct of military operations through decentralized execution based upon mission orders for effective mission accomplishment. Successful mission command results from subordinate leaders at all echelons exercising disciplined initiative within the commander's intent to accomplish missions."
- **Mutual trust and mutual understanding that subordinates will do the right thing:** "It requires an environment of trust and mutual understanding...Under mission command, commanders provide subordinates with a mission, their commander's intent, a concept of operations, and resources adequate to accomplish the mission. Higher commanders empower subordinates to make decisions within the commander's intent. They leave details of execution to their subordinates and expect them to use initiative and judgment to accomplish the mission."

So, if the mission for our employees is to protect the brand and mitigate reputational risk, and a successful mission requires clarity to permit decentralized execution and mutual trust and understanding that subordinates will do the right thing, how are we doing?

The answer for most organizations is probably "Not very well." We haven't provided the clarity to permit decentralized execution, and we certainly haven't created the mutual trust and understanding that allows subordinates to do the right thing.

If you need support for these comments, we offer up our own organization's research—specifically, the "Ethics & Workplace" surveys that my firm, Deloitte, launched in 2007 under the sponsorship of our chairman, Sharon Allen. Sharon is fervently committed to the topic of building winning workplaces, which led her to commission what has become a series of annual surveys.[7] These surveys are typically done with the assistance of a third party research firm and respondents include both randomly selected employed adults and executives from Fortune 1000 companies.

Our two most recent surveys provide sobering news on the issues of clarity and trust. First, the 2009 survey, which looked at reputational risk in the workplace, found that "74% of employed Americans surveyed believe it is easy to damage a brand's reputation via sites such as Facebook, Twitter, and YouTube." That's an unusually high percentage by any account, and one that might normally suggest that enterprises and employees are well aligned to respond to this threat.

However, given this consensus, what we found was astonishing:

- Corporate boards are not focused on reputational risk related to social media. Only 15 percent of executives surveyed say that reputational risk and social media are boardroom issues, although 58 percent agreed that they should be.
- Few companies have specific programs in place to deal with reputational risk related to social media.
- Employees don't seem to know what programs are in place, don't seem to care, and don't seem ready to change their behavior.
  - Almost one-quarter of employees surveyed don't know if their company has a policy regarding use of social media.
  - Almost half of survey respondents say that a company policy would not change how they behave online.
  - More than half of employees surveyed contend that social media pages are none of an employer's business.
  - Nearly one-third of employee respondents say they never consider what the boss would think before posting materials online.

- More than one-quarter of employees surveyed don't consider the ethical consequences of posting comments, photos, or videos online.
- More than one-third of survey respondents don't consider their boss, their colleagues, or their clients when posting comments, photos, or videos online.

These results are disturbing, to say the least.[8]

Now, let's take a look at the 2010 survey, which focused on the issue of trust in the workplace. The 2010 survey asked employees about their relationships with employers and discovered the following:

- One-third of employed Americans surveyed plan to look for a new job when the economy gets better.
- "Of this group of respondents, 48 percent cite a loss of trust in their employer and 46 percent say that a lack of transparent communication from their company's leadership . . . [as] their reasons for looking for new employment at the end of the recession."
- More than a third of employees surveyed indicate that their trust in the most senior leadership of their enterprises—i.e., their company's board—has decreased.

The executives surveyed are even more pessimistic. Their respective figures for lack of trust and transparent communications are 65 percent and 48 percent.

We can't pretend that we have the recipe to restore employee-employer trust in today's economic environment. This is a big problem and one that should be a priority for every global executive. As Sharon Allen remarked about the implications of our 2010 survey, executives need to focus on establishing and reinforcing a values-based culture if they expect to positively shape the behavior of employees over time, regain trust, and drive business performance.

Nevertheless, we can offer up three specific recommendations for how to address this issue in the context of the brand resilience problem that we are trying to solve.

Recommendation #1

Embed brand intelligence throughout your organization.

Executives should communicate to employees the importance of building and preserving brand value.

This means helping employees to answer the following questions:

- Why is brand value so important to enterprise success?
- What drives enterprise brand value?

As part of this, executives should be very clear about the types of activities that destroy brand value and the potentially devastating impact of these activities on brand value and, ultimately, enterprise value.

Let's go back to Smokey for a moment. The pure facts and figures about wildfires certainly captured our attention—more than 9 million acres of forest and grassland destroyed in a single year, and six times more wildfires resulting from human carelessness as from lightning and natural causes. We're convinced that sharing the equivalent brand facts with your employees will capture their attention.

How would you answer the following questions?

- How many of your employees know your brand value?
- How many of your employees know how this brand value has changed over time?
- How many of your employees know how the value of your brand compares with that of your competitors?
- How many of your employees have heard the full range of brand sabotage stories that have taken place in the last two to three years?

Recommendation #2

Persuade employees that they are the first and most important line of defense when it comes to protecting brand value.

We believe that trust starts by asking others to do the right thing and giving them the opportunity to do so. When it comes to brand resilience, executives need to help employees see that they are on the front lines in detecting and reducing acts of brand sabotage, and to ask them to step up to that role.

Even though I grew up in New York City, one of my favorite activities in my middle-school years was camping, thanks to the Boy Scouts. As a Boy Scout, Smokey's messages about campfire safety were drilled into me: Never leave fires unattended; sift through the ashes to make sure that the ashes are cool to the touch before you vacate your campsite. Today, Boy Scouts have gone one step further and encouraged scouts to carefully consider stoves as an alternative to campfires to reduce both environmental impact and the risk of wildfires. Smokey's slogan—*only YOU can prevent wildfires*—was, and continues to be, unambiguous.

Have you sent the same unambiguous message—*only YOU can prevent brand sabotage*—to your employees? Have they heard it and do they care?

Mission clarity (protect the brand), coupled with an invitation to participate in this mission, are the foundation for employee engagement when it comes to brand resilience.

ENGAGING YOUR TROOPS REQUIRES A PURPOSEFUL AND SUSTAINED BRAND RESILIENCE OUTREACH PROGRAM

If you go back to our 2009 Ethics & Workplace Survey, you may note that a significant portion of employees were not aware whether their employer even had a policy regarding social media. This is certainly one indicator of the need for a purposeful and sustained brand resilience outreach program.

A common complaint that we frequently hear from our clients' employees (as well as our own!) is that communications programs tend to be programs du jour. Employees recognize that they can often ignore a particular program with the knowledge that the program will soon disappear and be replaced by the next program that has captured the CEO's fancy.

A key reason for the effectiveness of Smokey Bear is the campaign's durability. Smokey himself has been refreshed and updated, but the same core message has been in place for more than sixty years. Long before the Internet was invented, long before the wars in Iraq and Afghanistan that provided the insurgency metaphor we use in this book, and long before many of the iconic brands of today were born or launched, Smokey was in place and on the job. The campaign has also been a multimedia campaign, with television and print advertising, posters and site-based advertising, a school visitation and public appearances program, licensed merchandise, and even a child's storybook and song.

So, what might a brand resilience outreach program look like?

A brand resilience outreach program must be tied to the life-cycle of your employees. Ideally, the awareness of brand value begins during the recruitment cycle, with questions designed to test the alignment between the company's brand and the prospective employee's values. Tony Hsieh, CEO of Zappos.com and author of *Delivering Happiness: A Path to Profits, Passion, and Purpose,* describes his recruitment process in an interview with Bigthink.com.

> We actually last year had over 25,000 people apply to work at Zappos and we only hired 250 of them, so about 1%. I think I heard the stat that it's actually harder to get into Zappos than into Harvard. So I'd say our recruiting team does a good job of screening on the front end. And, yes, it is true, they are not perfect and there are times when people do make it through the process, but then everyone that's hired goes through a four-week training program, the same training program that our Call Center Reps go through, and it's pretty hard to fake something for four weeks. And so we also use the training program as...almost like an extended interview.[9]

Additional brand resilience outreach efforts should be coordinated with employee on-boarding and promotions.

Second, brand resilience outreach becomes particularly important whenever a company undergoes a significant change, whether it's a merger, divestiture, major new product launch, enterprise cost reduction, or new market entry. Each of these events can present an opportunity for employees to question what the brand stands for and an opportunity for you to remind them of the same messaging about brand value that you previously communicated.

A BRAND RESILIENCE OUTREACH PROGRAM SHOULD BE ROOTED IN CLEAR PRINCIPLES AND VALUES

Most organizations have dealt with the mechanical aspects of branding through the development of visual identity standards. Although you may never have seen it (or quickly forgot it after you did see it), a copy of these visual identity standards is most likely posted on your company intranet. Often, an organization's visual identity standards are described as "brand standards," but they're usually concerned only with "look and feel." If you need examples, just Google "brand standards" and you'll find dozens of examples of corporate brand standards manuals. While these are important, they are *not* the standards we're talking about.

Johnson & Johnson regularly shows up on lists of top companies to work for and most admired companies. Around the same time the Forest Service launched its Smokey campaign, Johnson & Johnson launched "Our Credo."[10] *Credo* is Latin for "I believe" and describes a statement of principles and beliefs. If you read "Our Credo," it's perfectly clear what Johnson & Johnson stands for.

The operative words in "Our Credo" are "We are responsible," and many observers attribute Johnson & Johnson's responsiveness during various corporate crises to the internal importance of "Our Credo" and Johnson & Johnson's strong adherence to its principles.

Following the principle of a strong internal message, many companies have started to publish guidelines specifically focused on social media. IBM was one of the first companies to introduce a policy on social computing, and it has made its policy statement publicly available online.[11] The policy was originally developed in 2005, with a focus on blogging, and was updated in 2008 and 2010. IBM notes that they review the guidelines "periodically so that they may evolve to reflect emerging technologies and online social tools."

Though the statement is almost 2,700 words long, preventing us from reprinting it here, we recommend that you add it to your list of required reading. The policy statement starts by recognizing that online collaboration allows "IBM and IBMers to share with the world the exciting things we're learning and doing," and "advocate[s] IBMers' responsible involvement today in this rapidly growing environment of relationship, learning and collaboration."

It also provides very specific guidelines, ranging from not disclosing proprietary and enterprise performance information to respecting copyright laws, as well as useful coaching tips, such as "Don't pick fights, be the first to correct your own mistakes," and "Try to add value. Provide worthwhile information and perspective."

There are other highly effective models available, too. In an online article published at Ragan.com, Dallas Lawrence identifies six "great examples of employee social media policies", all of which are publicly available (see table 5.1).[12]

Table 5.1 Six social media policy examples for employees

Company	Social media policy focus
Kodak	Kodak makes its social media policy available in the form of an online brochure aimed at sharing "tips." Its ten rules start with living the Kodak values and include "Keep your cool" and "Heed security warnings and pop-ups."[a]
Yahoo	Yahoo's personal-blog policy includes "Legal Parameters" as well as "Best Practice Guidelines."[b]
Coca-Cola	As Dallas Lawrence notes, Coca-Cola "takes a break from all things digital to reinforce its traditional company values and brand identity. The soft-drink conglomerate recognizes that consistency is crucial when building and maintaining brand equity. In order to create a strong, cohesive image, the same message should be broadcast across all channels." Coca-Cola also requires that "all associates who wish to officially represent the Company online must complete the Social Media Certification Program prior to beginning or continuing these activities."[c]
Kaiser Permanente	According to Lawrence, Kaiser's policy on blogging stands out because of its emphasis on building community.[d]
Bread for the World	Lawrence points out Bread for the World's emphasis on the mission-driven nature of its communications, including social media.[e]
General Motors	GM wins Lawrence's approval with its focus on "educating its employees about the importance of transparency."[f]

[a] *Social Media Tips*, Eastman Kodak Company, 2009, http://www.kodak.com/US/images/en/corp/aboutKodak/onlineToday/Kodak_SocialMediaTips_Aug14.pdf.

[b] "Yahoo! Personal Blog Guidelines: 1.0," Yahoo!, http://jeremy.zawodny.com/yahoo/yahoo-blog-guidelines.pdf.

[c] "The Coca-Cola Company: Online Social Media Principles," The Coca-Cola Company, http://www.viralblog.com/wp-content/uploads/2010/01/TCCC-Online-Social-Media-Principles-12–2009.pdf.

[d] "Kaiser Permanente Social Media Policy," Kaiser Permanente, April 30, 2009, http://xnet.kp.org/newscenter/media/downloads/socialmediapolicy_091609.pdf.

[e] "Bread for the World's Social Media Policy," Bread for the World website, October 27, 2009, http://www.socialmedia.biz/social-media-policies/bread-for-the-worlds-social-media-policy/.

[f] "General Motors Social Media Policy," General Motors, http://www.conference-board.org/htmlEmail/pdf_files/Social-Media.pdf.

At a minimum, an effective social media policy:

- acknowledges the potential value of social media to the company and the individuals involved;
- highlights the relevant legal issues, including the protection of intellectual property rights;
- identifies core principles, particularly as they relate to privacy and transparency;
- spells out expectations for individual involvement, including behavioral expectations, and ties these back to overall expectations regarding employee conduct; and
- asks employees to take on a positive role in protecting the brand. For example, Coca-Cola's policy asks employees to "Be a 'scout' for compliments and criticism" and to notify the company of both positive and negative comments they find online.

Here are some questions to keep in mind when it comes to reaching out to employees:

- Are we engaging with our employees regarding the issue of brand value at the most critical points in their lifecycle with us, starting with recruiting?
- Are we prepared to stick with this for the long term rather than replacing it with another program du jour?
- Have we put clear policies and guidelines in place for our employees regarding the use of our brand?
- Have we put clear policies and guidelines in place for our employees relative to the use of our brand and social media?

FOR YOUR BRAND RESILIENCE EFFORTS TO BE EFFECTIVE, YOUR BRAND TROOPS NEED TO OWN THE MISSION

Under mission command, [local commanders] control...the resources needed to produce timely intelligence, conduct effective tactical operations, and manage operations...Mission command encourages the initiative of subordinates and facilitates the learning that must occur at every level. It is a major characteristic of a COIN force that it can adapt and react at least as quickly as the insurgents.

—The Counterinsurgency Field Manual

Social media provide a powerful platform for collaboration. Collaboration, as the IBM social computing policy notes, is all about individual and institutional learning, enabling us to tap into the experiences and insights of a broad group of individuals.

Now, imagine if all of your employees shared their insights and learning about brand sabotage with each other, and collaborated on actively seeking out opportunities to eliminate the potential for such incidents.

Recommendation #3

Employee ownership of the brand resilience mission requires three elements:

- The ability to recognize brand threats and potential threats
- The willingness to share knowledge of these threats
- The ability to communicate these threats to other employees so that they can adapt their behaviors appropriately

The first element, the ability to recognize brand threats and potential threats, starts with employee education. We talked previously about the need for reaching out to employees at each point of their lifecycle, from recruiting through on-boarding and promotions. While it's important to communicate the guidelines and principles embodied in the types of policies that we just covered, simply communicating these guidelines and principles will not suffice.

Rather, the focus of your brand resilience education efforts should equip your employees with the ability to recognize brand threats and potential threats—a sort of brand sabotage litmus test. Developing this ability requires a focus on situational awareness.

Situational awareness, as described by counterterrorism experts Fred Burton and Scott Stewart, "is the process of recognizing a threat at an early stage and taking measures to avoid it. Being observant of one's surroundings and identifying potential threats and dangerous situations is more of an attitude or mindset than it is a hard skill...[that] can be adopted and employed by anyone." For

Burton and Stewart, the "important element of this mindset is first coming to the realization that a threat exists...This is why apathy, denial and complacency are so deadly."[13] *The Counterinsurgency Field Manual* provides similar counsel: "Before commanders deploy their units, they make every effort to mentally prepare their Soldiers or Marines for the anticipated challenges, with a particular focus on situational awareness."[14]

The second element of ownership is a willingness to share knowledge of threats. Coca-Cola's social media policy politely asks employees to serve as scouts for compliments and criticism: "Even if you are not an official online spokesperson for the Company, you are one of our most vital assets for monitoring the social media landscape. If you come across positive or negative remarks about the Company or its brands online that you believe are important, consider sharing them."[15]

We are also seeing examples of organizations that are strongly committed to building and maintaining great brands invite employees to identify ways in which the organizations are not living in accordance with their brands. These invitations are meant to be interpreted broadly across all aspects of the organizations' operations and provide a way to capitalize on the experience of line employees in trying to "deliver the brand."

The third element of ownership is communicating with other employees about collective learning so that each individual employee can benefit from the experiences of others. This is where we must venture beyond the roadmap that we developed based on lessons learned from Smokey Bear. Ironically, the very same social media that accelerate brand sabotage can also facilitate and accelerate the sharing of "tribal knowledge" among employees. Imagine, for example, if you had a blog where every employee report of brand sabotage was posted and other employees could comment on these postings, including suggestions of how to change or avoid them—a much more efficient and interactive online version of the old suggestion box.

With any program like this, an important component is to publicly thank and recognize the contributors. One important lesson learned from social media is that contributors value recognition immensely, and the ability to build their reputations is often more appreciated than any other type of recognition that employees achieve.

The opportunity for employees to participate in strategically important activities, such as brand resilience efforts, can have spill-over effects on employee performance and commitment. According to our colleagues Cathy Benko and Molly Anderson,

> as employees participate...they become better versed in organizational strategy, operations, and happenings, and therefore contribute more and perform better than those who do not participate in this way...Greater collaboration and transparency inside a firm...can result in a greater sense of community and pride in the organization, creating a cadre of brand ambassadors...Getting collaboration right...expands the pool of potential team members and taps in to a range of insights.[16]

Here are some questions to ask yourself to facilitate employees owning your brand resilience mission:

- Have you taught your employees how to recognize what activities could potentially sabotage your brand?
- Are your employees willing to share what they learn about acts of brand sabotage, and have you provided them with the platform for doing so?
- Have you allowed employees to benefit from what their colleagues have observed and reported?
- Have you captured this collective learning and incorporated them into your brand resilience programs?

KEY TAKEAWAYS

WHAT WE KNOW...

- The three critical ingredients for effectively engaging your brand troops are a clear mission, a purposeful outreach program, and a strategy for employee ownership of the mission.

- The first step in galvanizing your troops is to define a clear mission that links your troops to the cause of brand resilience.

- Engaging your troops requires a purposeful and sustained brand resilience outreach program.

- For your brand resilience efforts to be effective, your brand troops must own the mission,

...AND WHAT YOU CAN DO

- Consider what programs you can create that will have the impact and enduring value of Smokey Bear.

- Commit to sharing information with your employees about brand value, including drivers of brand value, competitive brand value, and the potential impact of acts of brand sabotage.

- Assess whether you are committed to engaging your employees in the brand resiliency war for the long term. Develop a clear strategy for engaging with your employees regarding the issue of brand value at all critical points in their lifecycle. Create clear policies and guidelines for your employees about the use of the brand that address, but are not limited to, social media.

- Focus your educational efforts on giving your employees the situational awareness capabilities to recognize brand sabotage. Provide them with the platform and motivation to share what they learn. Capture these lessons and share them broadly to identify additional safeguards and tactics that you should build into your brand resilience programs.

MANAGING THE REPUTATIONAL AND BRAND RISK ASSOCIATED WITH SOCIAL MEDIA

An interview with John Callahan, national director of knowledge management, Deloitte Services LP

What are the objectives of the new training program?

The course focuses on the issue of the personal behavior of our partners, principals, directors, and employees. The course first explains social media for the uninitiated (a.k.a the "Gen O"—as in *old*). Then, through a series of real-world scenarios, it highlights how existing Deloitte policy and our values should shape personal behavior when using social media—and that's social media both inside our firewall and outside in the public domain. Ultimately, the course focuses on protecting the employee, the firms, our clients, and our brand from undue risk.

Why did you decide to require all employees to participate?

We realized, as do most organizations now, that in this social media environment, there is no way to review and pre-approve all employee blog, wiki, or discussion board comments prior to posting. That, in fact, would go against the very nature of social media.

But publishing something before it goes through layers of review and approval is a very difficult concept for our organization. The oldest and deepest part of our business DNA is based in the audit business, where "check and double-check" before issuing an opinion has been the name of the game for over a century. When you combine those DNA-level instincts with the litigious nature of our profession, and the fact that we're a partnership without incorporation protections, and that parts of our business are heavily regulated (with regulators watching closely!)—well, you can then understand why the distributed authorship and instant publishing of social media cause a lot of concerns among our senior leaders. In fact, that's what led to

➡

the decision that the course will be mandatory—for everyone from our CEO to our newest recruit.

What made Deloitte decide to develop this training?

An internal audit report of the Deloitte U.S. Firms pointed out weaknesses in our governance over implementation of social media tools. I was responsible for authoring the formal management response to the internal audit review, and then for implementing the proposed corrective actions. The course was one of those proposed actions.

Did Deloitte take any different approaches from what it normally does when it developed this new training?

To be honest, it has not been an easy or quick journey.

We started with a broad review of our existing policy set, and then developed a detailed whitepaper that defined for policy-makers in Deloitte what our position would be vis-à-vis use of these tools. The whitepaper was written by representatives of our talent department, knowledge management, office of general council, risk management, and others from both the United States and the Deloitte Touche Tohmatsu global network of member firms. Through many, many iterations, that document took six months to complete (see above re: "check and double-check"), but this was new ground we were covering. Up until that time, we didn't have an agreed-upon position.

We then turned the whitepaper into a learning storyboard script. Given the nuances of this whole topic, our proposed wording was very precise. A third-party vendor then turned the script into an interactive course, but the alpha version came across as if one were sitting in a law school course. So we pared back a lot of the legalese, cut the course from one and a half hours to just sixty minutes, and focused on the scenarios.

We started this journey in January 2009—so it took almost two years to get the course out the door.

What types of examples do you cite in the course?

Unintended breach of client confidentiality in personal comments made on Facebook; inadequate protection of proprietary Deloitte information when participating in an online public discussion forum; very importantly, distinguishing between the "authoritative content" that the firms have published (methods, tools, approaches, etc.) versus "user generated content"—a critical regulatory issue; being clear when one is speaking on behalf of oneself versus speaking on behalf of Deloitte; not posting inappropriate, potentially offensive material on personal sites if then choosing to "friend" coworkers or clients; respect for intellectual property rights and copyright.

Given the subject, how does the design and delivery of the course differ from other courses and training?

One key focus is that our individual responsibility is not only for our own actions, but also to help "tend the garden"—meaning we all should be on the lookout for others' online contributions that might violate Deloitte policies or values, and then take appropriate steps to remedy the situation (which we define in the course). Essentially, in this new environment, we should be looking out for one another, for the firms, our clients, and the brand. We hope the message comes through in the way the scenarios are structured.

How much of the course focuses on guidelines and principles as opposed to examples, and how much focuses on developing situational awareness?

Setting aside the upfront "Social Media 101" introduction, there are ten scenarios in all, each one requiring probably four minutes to complete. We created a "half time" after the first five scenarios specifically to talk about general guidelines for folks to keep in mind. The guidelines are mostly common sense but nevertheless are important to say.

What reactions do you expect from practitioners?

It's a required course, so I've been warned that, by default, everyone will dislike it. And that I'll receive many emails saying exactly that in a variety of colorful ways.

We do expect pushback. The Gen Xers will say, "I've been using these tools since I was in a highchair. Why are you teaching me about them?!?" The Gen Oers (as in *old*) will say, "I'm never going to use these tools. Why are you teaching me this?!?"

The answer to the Gen Xers is that they now have to use the tools under a professional code of conduct and a set of policies that govern behavior both in and out of the office.

The answer to the Gen Oers is that they will frequently now be supervising teams who are using these tools, so they are ultimately responsible.

Regardless, my inbox will still overflow.

What comes next?

The course itself will become part of all new hires' first ninety days' requirements after they come aboard. It will be updated periodically to reflect technology changes, as needed.

Chapter Six

STEP THREE

Deploy Your Brand Risk Early Warning Systems

Establishing a reliable source network is an effective collection method. Military source operations provide the COIN equivalent of the reconnaissance and surveillance conducted by scouts in conventional operations...[and] serve as "eyes and ears" on the street and provide an early warning system for tracking insurgent activity...

Insurgents have their own reconnaissance and surveillance networks. Because they usually blend well with the populace, insurgents can execute reconnaissance without easily being identified. They also have an early warning system composed of citizens who inform them of counterinsurgent movements. Identifying the techniques and weaknesses of enemy reconnaissance and surveillance enables commanders to detect signs of insurgent preparations and to surprise insurgents by neutralizing their early warning systems.

—The Counterinsurgency Field Manual

By now, we hope that your counterinsurgency instincts have started to kick into full gear.

You took the first step by undertaking a pretty rigorous and dispassionate assessment of the potential threats. You looked at your employees, your executive team, your supply chain and distribution partners, and—we hope—yourself. You took a close look at your customers and competitors, while trying to stay mindful of the reviewers, critics, gadflies, and ideologues that have been around forever and are in full flower lately thanks to the web. As a result, you should have a much better sense of the potential sources of attack, the modes of attack, the intentions behind the attack, and where you may be the most vulnerable, and have started to build your defenses.

You took the second step with an intensive effort to engage your employee population. You realized that you need to get them to take ownership of the brand resilience mission. You educated and sensitized them, asked them to keep their eyes peeled for criticisms and compliments, and gave them the infrastructure to report back what they see and hear. They're mobilized, galvanized, and fully enlisted in your efforts.

However, you still need to build additional reconnaissance and surveillance capabilities to complement the efforts of your employees and allow you early visibility into insurgent activities. Think of these additional capabilities as your brand risk early warning system. The goal of this chapter is to identify what steps you can take to build these capabilities and stay one step ahead of the insurgents.

PREDICTING BRAND SABOTAGE IS HARD

Chapter 2 discussed three aspects of insurgency that make the development of early warning capabilities particularly challenging:

1. **At first, you may not recognize that your brand is under attack**. As it says in *The Counterinsurgency Field Manual*, "the government that is being targeted generally takes a while to recognize that an insurgency is occurring. Insurgents take advantage of that time to build strength and gather support. Thus, counterinsurgents often have to 'come from behind' when fighting an insurgency."[1]
2. **Insurgents never stop inventing new ways to sabotage your brand**. Studying past insurgent activities and erecting defenses against the types of attacks that occurred yesterday still leaves you vulnerable to the newest improvised forms of brand sabotage. Typically, when you devise effective counterinsurgency measures, the insurgents come up with new approaches for attacking your brand. "Indeed, the more effective a COIN tactic is, the faster it may become out of date because insurgents have a greater need to counter it."[2]
3. **This stuff happens fast**. In fact, make that really, really fast—and it spreads like wildfire.

So, learn to live with the fact that you're not going to prevent every possible incident of brand sabotage from occurring and just be content if you can stop some before they overwhelm you. That's the focus of this chapter. In chapter 7, we will discuss how to deal with the attacks that make it past your early warning systems.

As you will see, your early warning system can involve a mix of volunteer contributors who actively report individual incidents (an "everyone-as-an-informant" approach to sourcing intelligence about possible acts of brand sabotage), and active "listening" and monitoring of Internet chatter, particularly on social media sites. Your approach can range from leveraging some of the capabilities that are already embedded within social media platforms, to building your own feedback generator, to relying on the plethora of third-party solutions focused on reputation management.

IN THE FIGHT AGAINST BRAND SABOTAGE, EVERYONE CAN BE PART OF YOUR EARLY WARNING SYSTEM

In June 2006, *Wired* magazine published an article by Jeff Howe about what he calls "the new pool of cheap labor: everyday people using their spare cycles to create content, solve problems, even do corporate R & D." Howe's article is credited with introducing a new term to describe this phenomenon: crowdsourcing.[3]

Howe subsequently authored the book *Crowdsourcing: Why the Power of the Crowd Is Driving the Future of Business* and launched the website Crowdsourcing.com.[4] What's Howe's definition of crowdsourcing? "Crowdsourcing is the act of taking a job traditionally performed by a designated agent (usually an employee) and outsourcing it to an undefined, generally large group of people in the form of an open call."[5]

Wikipedia, which was launched in 2001, five years before Howe's article, is probably the most familiar example of crowdsourcing. In the pages that follow, we explore two examples of crowdsourcing that focus more on crisis detection and tracking. The first relies on an existing social media platform, Twitter, while the second uses a bespoke platform. The common thread between them is the reliance on crowds to help gather information that in turn allows for the pinpointing of natural disasters and manmade crises. This crowdsourcing can complement the approaches that we already discussed in chapter 5 for engaging your employees in your efforts to detect brand sabotage.

The US Geological Survey Twitter Earthquake Detection (TED) Project[6]

People like to tweet after earthquakes. After an earthquake, they often rapidly report that an earthquake has occurred and describe what they've experienced.

—USGS Seismologist Paul Earle[7]

Earthquakes are impossible to prevent, hard to predict, and devastating in their effects.

In the United States, our front line of defense against earthquakes is the United States Geological Survey (USGS). The USGS is "a science organization that provides impartial information on the health of our ecosystems and environment, the natural hazards that threaten us, the natural resources we rely on, the impacts of climate and land-use change, and the core science systems that help us provide timely, relevant, and useable information."[8] Among the key services provided by USGS are earthquake detection, monitoring, and notification. According to the USGS, "Earthquakes are one of the most costly natural hazards faced by the Nation, posing a significant risk to 75 million Americans in thirty-nine States."[9]

As of 2010, the USGS has a new weapon in its arsenal for earthquake detection, monitoring, and notification. It's Twitter, the microblogging service where Justin Bieber has more than 7.5 million followers (Twitter.com/justinbieber). In our humble opinion, using Twitter for earthquake detection seems like a much more noble application.

Robert Scoble was the first to figure out the link between Twitter and earthquakes. Scoble, a frenetic blogger, social media junkie, and former Microsoft technical evangelist, writes at Scobleizer.com. Back in 2007, he began noticing that he could find news about earthquakes more quickly through Twitter than any other media, including the ultra-reliable and ultra-timely website maintained by the USGS.

In May 2008, Scoble picked up a tweet about a devastating earthquake in China—one that ultimately caused more than 68,000 deaths, injured more than 374,000 people, and left almost 5 million people homeless. He began aggregating and redistributing tweets about the earthquake, and his redistributed tweets found their way to many established news outlets, including the BBC and the *New York Times*, which subsequently reported the story.

Scoble's excitement about being able to report the event is palpable.

> I reported the major quake to my followers on Twitter before the USGS website had a report up and about an hour before CNN or major press started talking about it... How did I do that? Well, I was watching Twitter on Google Talk. Several people in China reported to me they felt the quake WHILE IT WAS GOING ON!!... It's amazing the kind of news you can learn by being on Twitter and the connections you can make among people across the world.[10]

In a post to the BBC News blog dot.life, posted shortly after the story surfaced, Rory Cellan-Jones wrote, "Let's see, as this story unfolds, whether this is the moment when Twitter comes of age as a platform which can bring faster coverage of a major news event than traditional media, while allowing participants and onlookers to share their experiences."[11]

The concept was not lost on the USGS. Using funding from the American Recovery and Reinvestment Act, the USGS is "developing a system that gathers real-time, earthquake-related messages from the social networking site Twitter and applies place, time, and key word filtering to gather geo-located accounts of shaking. This approach provides rapid first-impression narratives and, potentially, photos from people at the hazard's location. The potential for earthquake detection in populated but sparsely seismically-instrumented regions is also being investigated."[12]

According to an article about TED by Timothy Hurst on the website Ecopolitology.com, "TED uses an application programming interface that aggregates tweets based on keywords like 'earthquake' and 'tremor' to pull tweets about a particular earthquake into a database. Then the USGS generates an e-mail report containing the magnitude, location, depth below the surface, number of tweets about the earthquake broken down by their location, and text of the first 40 or 50 tweets."[13]

TED is not perfect. As USGS scientist Michelle Guy indicates, "Another kink that we have in the system is out-of-context tweets. So for example, there's often tweeting about enjoying Dairy Queen's Earthquake brownie desserts or maybe even a good game of Quake. Once we are aware of these kinds of trends, then we can try to filter out tweets that might, for example, have both the words 'earthquake' and 'brownie' in them."[14]

Right now, TED (at Twitter.com/usgsted) has a relatively small number of followers, at less than 7,000—compared to Scoble's 164,000-plus followers (Twitter.com/scobleizer)—so it would be hard to declare it an unqualified success. But the important thing is, it's an example of how crowdsourcing might work in an environment where every second counts—as it will in the event of brand sabotage.[15]

Ushahidi.com[16]

Ushahidi.com came into being in the aftermath of Kenya's disputed election in early 2008 as a collaborative effort by a volunteer group of "citizen journalists" over a long weekend after a Kenyan lawyer named Ory Okolloh posted the idea on a blog. (*Ushahidi* means "testimony" in Swahili.) The initial version of Ushahidi consisted of a website that allowed ordinary Kenyans to report incidents of violence via mobile phone or web. The outputs included an "incident map."

From Kenya, Ushahidi spread to South Africa, where it was used to help map incidents of xenophobic violence. Then, Humanity International, "a philanthropic organization committed to building peace and advancing human freedom"[17] provided seed funding to develop a more robust, open-source application "that any person or organization can use to set up their own way to collect and visualize information. The core platform will allow for plug-ins and extensions so that it can be customized for different locales and needs."[18]

According to the description on its website, "Ushahidi builds tools for democratizing information, increasing transparency and lowering the barriers for individuals to share their stories...The Ushahidi Platform allows anyone to gather distributed data via SMS, email or web and visualize it on a map or timeline. Our goal is to create the simplest way of aggregating information from the public for use in crisis response."[19]

The list of Ushahidi applications now includes the Sudan Vote Monitor, the Chile Crisis Map, the Haiti Crisis Map, Snowmageddon: The Cleanup, Atlanta Crime Maps, Vote Report India, and Swineflu .Ushahidi.com.

A *New York Times* article, "Africa's Gift to Silicon Valley: How to Track a Crisis," authored by Anand Giridharadas, describes the irony of innovative thinking and entrepreneurship coming from an impoverished region. Giridharadas brands Ushahidi's philosophy as "everyone-as-informant mapping" and envisions using this approach as a counterinsurgency tool in the war on terror. "Imagine if any Pakistani could send an anonymous text message to the authorities suggesting where to look. Each location could be plotted on a map. The dots would be scattered widely, perhaps, with promising leads indistinguishable from rubbish. But on a given day, a surge of dots might point to the same village, in what could not be coincidence. Troops could be ordered in."[20]

Imagine that.

IT'S AMAZING WHAT YOU CAN LEARN BY JUST LISTENING

If you liked the television show *24*, you'll like this.

In June 2010, Gatorade, the PepsiCo-owned sports drink maker, went public with their "Gatorade Mission Control Center" inside its Chicago headquarters, "a room that sits in the middle of the marketing department and could best be thought of as a war room for monitoring the brand in real-time across social media."[21]

In a move that demonstrated Gatorade's digital-age savvy, social media cognoscenti Adam Ostrow, editor in chief at Mashable.com, was invited to visit the site. Ostrow describes himself as "responsible for the editorial management and direction of one of the most widely read blogs in the world, covering the latest technologies, trends, and individuals that are driving the current evolution of the Web."[22]

According to Ostrow's report, the room includes a number of extra-large monitors that help display both dashboards and data visualizations of social media mentions that are relevant to Gatorade, its competitors, its athletes, and related topics. The goal of the project, according to Carla Hassan, Gatorade's senior marketing director of consumer and shopper engagement, is to "take the largest sports brand in the world and turn it into the largest participatory brand in the world."[23]

As Ostrow points out, you don't need to go to Chicago to see the Gatorade Mission Control Center in action. Just go to YouTube and search for it. As you'll see in the video, Gatorade's focus is broad: "Whenever people are talking, clicking, typing about our brand, Mission Control is there to listen." The video cites a list of objectives: "monitor online discussions, proactive social media outreach, track brand attributes, monitor sports landscape, track media performance, track sports trends and buzz... Through these conversations, we gather the insights that influence our communications, that influence our product, our brand, setting the stage for digital leadership."[24]

YOU DON'T NEED TO BUILD YOUR OWN COMMAND CENTER TO LISTEN TO WHAT PEOPLE ARE SAYING ABOUT YOU

It all started with clipping bureaus.

What's a clipping bureau? If you had read the May 30, 1932, issue of *Time* magazine, you would have come across an account of the Original Henry Romeike Press Clipping Bureau that included this sentence: "As everyone knows, the function of a clipping bureau is to supply customers with clippings from newspapers everywhere mentioning either their names, manufactured products or any designated subject." The article goes on to tell the story of how Romeike invented the concept in Paris in the late nineteenth century before moving to London and then to New York.[25]

Here is the description of the Henry Romeike clipping crew, in full swing in its Manhattan loft in 1932: "About 60 young women sit at benches, expertly scanning the 1,900 dailies and 5,000 weeklies... Pasted on a wall before each girl's eyes is a typewritten list of clients and subjects most difficult to remember. The bulk of the 7,000 names and words for which she must watch is carried in her head."[26]

When I finished graduate school in 1980 and started working at Time Incorporated, clipping bureaus were still commonplace. We subscribed to a number of clipping services that scanned a wide variety of media to identify articles of particular relevance and saved us the trouble of reading each and every newspaper, magazine, and periodical ourselves. We would regularly get a package of clippings and broadcast summaries, usually attached to a buck slip indicating the names of the next recipient to whom the package should be routed.

At some point, we went from bureaus that physically cut and clipped articles to media monitoring services and "listening services, which monitor in real time hundreds of thousands of news sources, blogs and websites what people are saying about specific products or topics."[27]

The purveyors of these solutions range from Dow Jones & Co., which publishes the *Wall Street Journal*, and Nielsen, the privately held media-research firm, to smaller suppliers that focus more on reputation management.

Let's take a quick look at what's available to give you a better sense of what you can and cannot expect from one of these "listening solutions." Each of these purports to replace either clipping bureau services or relatively expensive customized market research.

Dow Jones, for example, offers Dow Jones Insight, which describes itself as a "media analysis service" that processes "more than 1.5 million articles in 23 languages from press release wires, newspapers, magazines, radio and TV transcripts, Web sites, blogs and message boards" on a daily basis.[28]

Its pitch is that "from these articles, we extract thousands of concepts—people, companies, brands, issues, events, messages, positive and negative words or phrases—and match them to the interests of our clients...We present the results in charts and graphs that make trends, warning signals and opportunities instantly obvious. We can also immediately alert communications professionals to surprises—concepts just beginning to be associated with their organization."[29] When it talks about the value it provides to its customers, its description includes:

- evaluation of spokesperson, brand and message performance;
- competitive benchmarking;
- pinpointing of journalists and bloggers writing about your brand;
- trend analysis.

Dow Jones offerings allow you to understand your favorability (which they call "sentiment analysis"), threats to your reputation, past media coverage and the extent to which issues tend to linger in the press, the impact of your media efforts, and your progress in relation to goals.

Nielsen, whose market-research offerings range from the Claritas database to radio and television ratings, offers Nielsen BuzzMetrics ("Millions of Consumers Are Talking—Are You Listening?"). According to its website, "Nielsen BuzzMetrics' services and solutions uncover and integrate data-driven insights culled from nearly 100 million blogs, social networks, groups, boards and other CGM [consumer-generated media] platforms."[30]

Not surprisingly for a leading market-research company, Nielsen emphasizes the care and methodological rigor that it takes to harvest data from a broad range of sources, cleanse it, ensure its relevance, and analyze it. Nielsen also offers complementary capabilities to conduct surveys through an online-recruited but demographically and behaviorally weighted panel.

According to Nielsen, BuzzMetric's services provide the tools to understand what customers are saying about you, which can help you with brand management, new product development, and campaign tracking and measurement.

In June 2010, BuzzMetric became part of NM Incite, a newly announced joint venture between Nielsen and McKinsey & Company. NM Incite combines Nielsen's monitoring capabilities with McKinsey's consulting capabilities "to realize the promise of social media intelligence."[31] Its solutions include tracking brand threats, with the goal of helping "identify—in near real-time—threats and opportunities and understand the full scope of what lies ahead to avoid and diffuse or capitalize on it."[32]

But Dow Jones, Nielsen, and McKinsey are far from the only game in town when it comes to understanding the buzz that your brand is generating.

ListenLogic, LLC, founded in 2007 and formerly known as Apptastics, LLC, purports to "translate the millions of online consumer conversations taking place each day into high-value strategic insights that inform and empower brands.... [Its] proprietary technologies and rigorous research methodologies deliver...consumer insights and market intelligence that helps Global 1000 companies drive innovation and build competitive advantage."[33]

ListenLogic's offerings consist of a suite of "Involved Consumer" business intelligence products. These include insights into a consumer's ethnicity, interests, and demographics to understand their attitudes, needs, and product motivations (icProfile); the activities, products, and affinities correlated with the consumption of a product (icTopic); the trigger events and behaviors along a consumer's purchase path (icTrigger); longitudinal tracking and trends for competitive benchmarking and awareness (icTrend); and relevant conversations that consumers participate in online (icVerbatim).[34]

Specifically, in the social media area, ListenLogic offers a social media analytics technology, RESONATE, "to efficiently monitor social media, measure consumer opinion and, engage consumers...[by mining] all forms of public data on blogs, social networks, forums, news, and other CGM [consumer generated media]."[35] These capabilities power a series of complementary services to "proactively identify and assess online threats as they occur in near real-time."[36] These services include a "Social ThreatDesk...manned by dedicated analysts who identify and escalate both known and unknown threats to key stakeholders across your enterprise,...[notify] stakeholders daily, and...[measure] the impact of any threats throughout their duration. The Social ThreatDesk...is available globally in multiple foreign languages."[37]

ListenLogic's website lists a number of clients, including interactive agencies, large pharmaceutical brands, food and foodservices companies, large financial services institutions, national retailers, eCommerce brands, entertainment companies, and membership organizations.[38]

Another up-and-comer when it comes to understanding the buzz that your brand is generating is ReputationDefender.[39]

ReputationDefender was founded in 2006 by Michael Fertik, a Harvard-trained entrepreneur, lawyer, and author, and its investors include the leading venture capital companies Kleiner Perkins Caufield & Byers, Bessemer, Floodgate, and Jafco. Serving consumers and businesses, ReputationDefender offers a variety of subscription services that go beyond just monitoring what is being said about your brand on the web. ReputationDefender also allows you to remove inaccurate, inappropriate, hurtful, and slanderous information, and to influence the search results associated with your personal or corporate brand.

We had a chance to speak briefly with Fertik on the phone, and he repeatedly emphasized ReputationDefender's focus on going beyond monitoring to "prophylactically" remove potentially damaging material that ReputationDefender discovers. It's a colorful way of putting it, but it does offer something clipping services never could!

NOT EVERYTHING YOU LEARN FROM LISTENING MATTERS—AND NOTHING YOU LEARN FROM LISTENING MATTERS IF YOU DON'T HAVE A PROCESS FOR TAKING ACTION

Whether you build, buy, rent, or cobble it together, you need some kind of early warning system to be an effective counterinsurgent. As you select the right approach for your brand, here are a couple of factors to consider:

- **Disambiguation challenges**
  The 1932 *Time* article on Romeike's clipping service illustrates the disambiguation challenge perfectly:

  The marking girls, who earn about $20 a week, are a liability until they have about two years' experience. Even then they are not infallible. A client named Levy was sent dozens of clippings about a tax levy. The Country Gentleman received various references to country gentlemen. An olive growers' association got clippings about the death of Film Actress Olive Thomas. A man who wanted all items on batteries had to weed through stories about arrests for assault and battery. Matters improved after the girls were paid a straight wage instead of piece work.[40]

Disambiguation challenges will be with us for a while. Remember the USGS's Twitter Earthquake Detection project turning up out-of-context tweets about Dairy Queen's Oreo Brownie Earthquake. Once you recognize the potential ambiguity, you can filter it out. But until then, you, like poor Mr. Levy who received clippings about a tax levy, may have to live with less precision than is desirable.

There are at least two factors that can/will likely exacerbate disambiguation challenges in the near term. As you include more and more non-English source material in your monitoring base, precision will become challenging, particularly when you deal with colloquial expressions. Similarly, as you include more and more non-textual source material (e.g., video) in your monitoring base, it may be harder to pinpoint relevant results.

- **Weighting: understanding what's noise and what's not**
How do you understand which tweets matter and which ones don't?

Klout offers a service that may be helpful. Klout is a privately held company based in San Francisco whose goal is to "accurately measure influence and provide context around who a person influences and the specific topics they are most influential on." The result is a Klout Score that "measures overall influence through 25 variables broken into three categories; True Reach, Amplification Score and Network Score."[41]

Klout offers an application programming interface that allows other software applications to integrate Klout Score into their offerings. Klout customers include social media dashboard provider Hootsuite; Twitter business-intelligence monitor Tap11; and web-based social media engagement, management, and reporting solution CoTweet.

Over- or underestimating the influence of a source can be as dangerous as missing it altogether.

- **Data visualization**
A number of the early warning systems (e.g., Ushahidi, Gatorade's Mission Control Center) employ data visualization techniques to display results.

In the case of Ushahidi, the visualization technique is relatively straightforward. Ushahidi uses Google mapping to display the geographic location of incidents. Areas with particularly high incident rates pretty quickly become evident.

The problem with data visualization is that in the wrong hands it quickly becomes confusing rather than illuminating. If you want a primer on what works and what doesn't work when it comes to data visualization, pick up any of Edward Tufte's trilogy of self-published books *The Visual Display of Quantitative Information* (1983), *Envisioning Information* (1990), and *Visual Explanations* (1997).[42]

■ **Moving from early warning to action**
Our focus in this chapter has been on building early warning capabilities. This means some form of intelligence gathering to detect potential incidents of brand sabotage. Through early detection, the appropriate actions can be determined and executed.

In our description of approaches, we discussed both building your army of volunteer informants (we'll discuss how this can be accomplished in chapter 10) and using listening solutions to gain a sense of what's being said and what it means.

The key to an effective early warning system is to put the pieces together and have a clear line of sight to an action plan. One of the major criticisms of the American intelligence efforts associated with the 9/11 attacks was not insufficient intelligence but the failure to understand the implications of the intelligence that had been gathered and use it as the basis for action.

So, if you do put together an early warning system, you'll also need to be crystal clear regarding the processes for reviewing the information that you gather and assigning responsibility for acting on the intelligence that you accumulate.

KEY TAKEAWAYS

WHAT WE KNOW...

- Predicting brand sabotage is hard.
  - At first, you may not recognize that your brand is under attack.
  - Insurgents never stop inventing new ways to sabotage your brand.
  - This stuff happens fast.
- In the fight against brand sabotage, everyone can be part of your early warning system.
- It's amazing what you can learn by just listening.

- You don't need to build your own command center to listen to what people are saying about you.
- Not everything you learn from listening matters—and nothing you learn from listening matters if you don't have a process for taking action.

...AND WHAT YOU CAN DO

- Learn to live with the fact that you're not going to prevent every possible incident of brand sabotage from occurring. Focus on building early warning capabilities that allow you to reduce the time you spend in a purely defensive mode.
- Consider opportunities for crowdsourcing information about potential sources of brand sabotage.
- Ensure that you have the listening capabilities to monitor chatter related to your brand across multiple media sources.
- Take a close look at the off-the-shelf listening solutions available.

- It's not enough to monitor chatter. You need processes in place to filter out what's irrelevant, communicate what is relevant in a compelling manner, and assign responsibility for responding.

Chapter Seven

STEP FOUR

Repel the Attacks on Your Brand

Any use of force can generate a series of reactions. There may be times when an overwhelming effort is necessary to destroy or intimidate an opponent and reassure the populace. Extremist insurgent combatants often have to be killed. In any case, however, counterinsurgents should calculate carefully the type and amount of force to be applied and who wields it for any operation. An operation that kills five insurgents is coun-terproductive if collateral damage leads to the recruitment of fifty more insurgents.

—The Counterinsurgency Field Manual

Remember when you were a little kid and your mother taught you the proverb "Sticks and stones may break my bones, but words will never hurt me"? We do, but when it comes to brand value, names can and will often hurt you. Names, rumors, innuendos, malicious gossip, slanderous stories, and the like can all hurt the value of your brand, and that's exactly what we mean by brand sabotage. Larry Weber's book *Sticks & Stones: How Digital Business Reputations Are Created Over Time and Lost in a Click* provides numerous examples of how quickly and how far reputations can sink—that is, if you're not convinced by the ones we've already shared![1]

This chapter is about repelling the attacks on your brand that make it past your early warning systems and defenses. We will talk about what you can do and when you should do it. We will also discuss the ins and outs of offering apologies and making amends. In chapter 8, we will undertake a variation of what is known in the military as an "after action report"—a summary that takes a retrospective look at an event, with the goal of harvesting insights that change future behavior.

▌ THINK OF A BRAND ATTACK AS AN EVENT, WITH THE OPPORTUNITY FOR PRE- AND POST-EVENT ACTIONS

In developing this book, we have worked with three graduate business school students, Amit Gupta, Yueyuan "Tim" Li, and Gopal Subramaniam, along with their teacher, Kapil Jain, to build a normative model for brand resilience. They've found it challenging. As Kapil told us, "You've given us a very tough problem to solve!"

The discussions with Amit, Tim, and Gopal helped our thinking in two fundamental ways. First, they suggested focusing on the event-driven aspect of brand sabotage and introduced the term "brand shock" to describe the result. Second, they urged us to think about the timeline associated with brand shocks and how organizations respond to them.

Let's start with the idea of "brand shocks."

A shock is a violent, sudden, unexpected, or traumatic act or event. Think of the shock generated by an ungrounded electrical wire or the aftershocks that follow an earthquake. Shock can also mean the state of distress, disbelief, horror, surprise, or disappointment that follows the initial jolt or violent event. Remember "Shock and Awe," the doctrine that shaped the United States' 2003 Operation Iraqi Freedom campaign? First introduced in *Shock & Awe: Achieving Rapid Dominance,* a 1996 National Defense University publication authored by Harlan Ullman and James Wade Jr., the doctrine calls for rapidly overwhelming an enemy and destroying its will to resist or mount a defense.[2] "Shock and Awe" operates on both meanings of the word *shock*.

In chapters 3 and 4, we identified the sources and types of brand shocks you need to concern yourself with. Just to refresh your memory, we covered both the internal and external threats that you need to consider (see table 7.1).

So, think of each and every one of these threats as a type of brand shock. Each brand shock can be characterized along a number of dimensions (see figure 7.1).

Table 7.1 Internal and external threats to brands

The enemy within...	...and beyond your borders

■ employees
  ❑ leaks of valuable and/or embarrassing information
  ❑ egregious customer mistreatment
  ❑ unprofessional or brand-inconsistent behavior
  ❑ excessively rigid interpretation of policies and rules
■ senior executives
  ❑ conduct unbecoming (inappropriate relationships with subordinates or third parties, inappropriate or insensitive remarks, inappropriate or illegal financial transactions, inappropriate use of corporate assets, blatantly excessive compensation and perks, tone-deaf behavior)
■ unforeseen consequences of operational decisions
  ❑ brand licensing
  ❑ handling and use of confidential customer information
  ❑ introducing new products or extending the brand
  ❑ outsourcing and selecting suppliers and partners
    ■ environment and sustainability issues
    ■ labor practices
    ■ product safety
    ■ affiliations
■ product pricing and discounts
	■ customer rage
	  ❑ return/exchange policies
	  ❑ perceived mistreatment or poor service
	  ❑ product quality and safety issues
	■ reviewers
	  ❑ product and service quality and safety concerns
	  ❑ product and service functionality concerns
	  ❑ product and service pricing concerns
	■ gadflies and ideologues
	  ❑ environmental concerns
	  ❑ excessive greed
	  ❑ health concerns
	  ❑ labor conditions
	  ❑ product safety
	  ❑ undue influence on government officials and regulators
	■ competitors
	  ❑ price or value attacks
	  ❑ product or service quality attacks

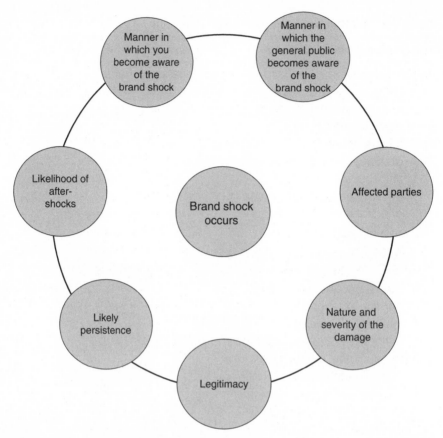

Figure 7.1 Brand shock

Please note that the actual event, the manner in which you become aware of the brand shock, and the manner in which others become aware of the brand shock could be one and the same.

Let's take an example, outlined in table 7.2.

The two characteristics that stand out when you consider how to respond to such an event are the likely persistence of a brand shock and the likelihood of aftershocks. Persistence appears to be a function of both (1) the uniqueness of the brand shock (e.g., a clever and well-executed musical video about damaged luggage); and (2) the resonance (i.e., the extent to which others will find the reports of the brand shock to be compelling, usually because they can personally relate to the incident).

Table 7.2 Brand shock: An example

The anatomy of a brand shock	
The actual event	■ Airline damages a passenger's luggage (as in the case we discussed in chapter 4).
Manner in which you become aware of the brand shock	■ Passenger complains (multiple times).
Manner in which others become aware of the brand shock	■ Passenger creates a clever music video parody and posts it to YouTube. Video is picked up and amplified by numerous websites and media.
Affected parties	■ Limited to passenger whose luggage was damaged by the airline.
Nature and severity of the damage	■ Low
Legitimacy	■ Bona fide complaint, although initial proposed remediation fell within stated guidelines.
Likely persistence	■ High due to: ❑ Creativity of the video, ❑ Broad resonance (average consumer can relate to the problem).
Likelihood of aftershocks	■ High: Brand shock may stimulate other consumers to articulate similar concerns.

A brand aftershock is an artifact of the initial brand shock that usually results from others identifying closely with the complaint. Imagine if every airline passenger who has ever had their luggage lost creates a music video after viewing the initial one, or at least re-tweets the link. A brand aftershock could also be a function of how an organization responds to an initial brand shock (e.g., an oil spill occurs in the Gulf of Mexico, then the CEO's immediate comments don't appear to reflect the degree of compassion that victims and observers desire). Sometimes, as we discussed in chapter 2, the cure can be worse than the wound that you're trying to treat.

Certainly, social media increase the likely persistence of brand aftershocks by accelerating and simplifying the distribution of information. However, it seems that every book that we pick up lately about social media is a polemic about how social media fundamentally change the world. We agree, but only to a point, so we were delighted to read Malcolm Gladwell's essay "Small Change: Why the revolution will not be tweeted" in the October 4, 2010, issue of the *New Yorker*.[3] If you accept the arguments that Gladwell presents in the essay, you agree that we are attributing a far more meaningful impact to social media than they deserve when it comes to enlisting people in a cause, whether it's a charitable movement or an attack on a brand.

Gladwell's thesis is that there is a big difference between the "strong tie" phenomenon that characterizes high-risk social activism—like the 1960 sit-ins at the Woolworth's in downtown Greensboro, North Carolina—and the kind of social activism associated with social media (e.g., the Save Darfur Coalition on Facebook). "The platforms of social media are built around weak ties... The Internet lets us exploit the power of these kinds of distant connections with marvelous efficiency... But weak ties seldom lead to high-risk activism."[4]

Gladwell goes on to argue that while social media do increase participation, they achieve this precisely by lessening the motivation that participation requires. This high participation, Gladwell asserts, masks the weak ties between participants and causes observers to overestimate the eventual impact of this "activism." As a result, more often than not a well-coordinated and tightly executed response to a brand shock by a company committed to maintaining its image can trump the weak ties of brand shock executed through a social media.

"If Martin Luther King, Jr., had tried to do a wiki-boycott in Montgomery," Gladwell writes, "he would have been steamrolled by the white power structure... The things that King needed in Birmingham—discipline and strategy—were things that online social media cannot provide."[5]

Amit, Tim, and Gopal suggested constructing a "brand shock time continuum"—a timeline associated with any given brand shock (Figure 7.2). Think of three key events—the brand shock itself,

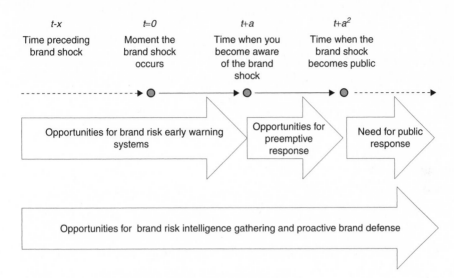

Figure 7.2 The brand-shock time continuum

the time when you become aware of the brand shock, and the time when the brand shock becomes public knowledge. In some cases, the three events are concurrent; in other cases, you see lag times between the three. Lag times create the opportunity to respond before things get completely out of hand.

The value of looking at these three events as part of a continuum is to recognize that you may need to consider two sets of responses: (1) What do you do once you become aware of a brand shock, but before there is widespread public knowledge of it? and (2) What do you do once the public starts to become aware of the brand shock?

As Amit, Tim, Gopal and I talked through the concept of brand shocks and the brand shock timeline, we also discussed how to characterize the types of responses that an organization could employ. Our primary question was, When should an organization hold its ground and vigorously defend itself, including going after the saboteurs, and when should it apologize, compensate affected parties, and focus its energies on remedial or corrective actions?

So what should you do when?

■■■■■ CONSIDER WHETHER—AND HOW FAR— YOU WANT TO PULL THE REPENTANCE, REMEDIATION, AND RECTIFICATION LEVERS IN RESPONDING TO BRAND SHOCKS

A Golden Oldie: The Tylenol Crisis

Johnson & Johnson's handling of what has become known as the "Tylenol Crisis" is often considered the gold standard of crisis management and crisis communications.

Tylenol is manufactured and marketed by McNeil Consumer Healthcare, a Division of McNEIL-PPC, Inc. In 1982 at the time of the incident, the name of that operating company was McNeil Consumer Products Company. At that time, Tylenol enjoyed high market share (37 percent), strong growth, and high profitability. Tylenol was also a major contributor to the financial success of its parent company, Johnson & Johnson.[6]

In 1982, seven people on Chicago's West Side died mysteriously. As Tamara Kaplan writes in "The Tylenol Crisis: How Effective Public Relations Saved Johnson & Johnson,"

> the cause of these strange and sudden deaths did not remain a mystery for long. The connection to Tylenol was discovered within days with the help of two off-duty firemen who were at home listening to their police radios. The two men, Philip Cappitelli and Richard Keyworth, were exchanging information about the deaths, when they realized that Tylenol was mentioned in two of the reports. The men made some assumptions and told their superiors that there was a possibility that the over-the-counter drug was the mysterious killer.[7]

What had in fact happened was that a person or persons unknown had "replaced Tylenol Extra-Strength capsules with cyanide-laced capsules, resealed the packages, and deposited them on the shelves of at least a half-dozen or so pharmacies and food stores in the Chicago area" where they were purchased and consumed, resulting in the seven deaths.[8]

When, as the result of a media inquiry, McNeil Consumer Products Company and its parent company, Johnson & Johnson, became aware of the possible connection between the deaths and

Tylenol, Johnson & Johnson chairman James Burke formed a strategy team charged with protecting consumers first, and saving the product second. The initial response was to ask consumers not to consume any type of Tylenol. Production and advertising for Tylenol were halted and then all Tylenol capsules were withdrawn from Chicago-area stores. After more contaminated capsules were discovered, McNeil Consumer Products Company ordered a nationwide withdrawal of all capsules and destroyed more than 31 million capsules, at a cost of more than $100 million.

In conjunction with the product withdrawals, McNeil Consumer Products Company set up toll-free numbers for consumers and the media, organized press conferences, and sent its chairman to appear on major news and talk shows. As a result of the tampering, McNeil Consumer Products Company introduced the tamper-evident packaging for Tylenol that persists today.[9]

The new packaging was just one part of the campaign—new advertising, a massive promotional campaign, extensive presentations to medical professionals, and proactive communications— that helped McNeil Consumer Products Company bounce back to pre-crisis sales levels within months of the incident.

In an opinion piece published in *USA Today* in 2004, Eric Dezenhall, the founder and CEO of an eponymous communications firm, describes the degree to which the Tylenol case dominates our discussions of crisis management. "The media love the story because it validates the canard that 'fessing up' is the best form of crisis management. Business schools worship the model because it's teachable and it had a happy ending for the manufacturer. Public relations firms use it to sell spin as the answer to industrial woes...The Tylenol crisis taught us what excellent companies do when confronted by saboteurs."[10]

The Tylenol case is clearly the example other companies should follow if they find themselves on the brink of losing everything. Even the Department of Defense uses it in a course on crisis communications.[11] The DoD identifies three common elements used by McNeil Consumer Products Company and other commercial organizations as part of a crisis response strategy and compares the behavior of McNeil Consumer Products Company with its typical response (see table 7.3).

Table 7.3 The three r's: Critical elements of a crisis response strategy

Crisis response strategy element	Description	Department of Defense's assessment of its typical response
Repentance	Asking for forgiveness	"The military will rarely use repentance due to fear of it being used to establish legal culpability. In fact it is DoD policy to train public affairs practitioners to never say they are sorry."
Remediation	Giving compensation to the victims of a crisis	"DoD will normally use remediation only if a court of law mandates compensation to victims of a crisis."
Rectification	Taking actions to prevent the recurrence of a crisis in the future	"The military...uses this rectification strategy very well. It is required by most units to produce an after-action review of a crisis to find out exactly what happened and to determine methods to prevent it from happening again."

Source: "Crisis Communication Strategies," Department of Defence Joint Course in Communication website, http://www.ou.edu/deptcomm/dodjcc/groups/OZCZ/Johnson%20$%20Johnson.htm.

Before you start building your playbook around the three responses in Table 7.3, it's important to understand that the Tylenol situation is only one example of a shock, one where the organization itself was the target of a criminal act. As Dezenhall writes in his 2004 *USA Today* piece, titled "Tylenol Can't Cure All Crises," "A company attacked by a criminal will be forgiven more quickly than one accused of being the criminal. Johnson & Johnson's actions were admirable, but logical. People were killed, so the company pulled the product from stores and encouraged consumers to throw it away."[12]

Nevertheless, McNeil Consumer Products Company's handling of its 1982 recall is often cited as the model for all companies to follow—including McNeil Consumer Healthcare itself, as in 2010 when, because of manufacturing problems, it faced potential product recalls in multiple business units.

THINK OF AN APOLOGY AS AN EXPRESSION OF REGRET. IT IS NOT ALWAYS AN ADMISSION OF GUILT OR THE FIRST STEP IN COMPENSATING VICTIMS

The Escalade Escapade

For our second case, let's go back to the public figure that first showed up in our introduction: Tiger Woods.

Before the Escalade escapade in November 2009, Tiger Woods was a highly compensated and highly competitive golfer who also enjoyed tremendous success as a corporate spokesperson for a diverse set of leading brands.

After the Escalade escapade, Tiger Woods got divorced, lost a number of lucrative endorsement contracts, and didn't fare too well on the professional golfing circuit. Humbled and humiliated might be the appropriate descriptors.

According to a USA Today/Gallup Poll, Woods' favorability rating dropped from 85 percent in June 2005 to 33 percent after the incident, and his unfavorability rating went from 8 percent to 57 percent. The managing editor of the poll noted that the drop was unprecedented and compared the 52 percentage-point plunge to a similar fall-off experienced by George W. Bush between 2001 and 2008.[13]

For the record, Woods apologized in a press conference in February 2010.[14] In fact, he apologized multiple times. "I had affairs. I was unfaithful. I cheated." Along with other news media, the *New York Times* noted the element of craft in Woods's confession, as is reflected in the title of its analysis: "Vulnerability in a Disciplined Performance."[15] His apologies spoke primarily to the rupture of trust that he had caused with his actions. "Every one of you has good reasons to be critical of me. I want to say to each of you simply and directly, I am deeply sorry for my irresponsible and selfish behavior...Parents used to point to me as a role model for their kids. I owe all those families a special apology. I want to say to them that I am truly sorry." He promised to clean up his act. "It's now up to me to make amends, and that starts by never repeating the mistakes I've made. It's up to me to start living a life of integrity."[16]

While some observers criticized Woods for coming across as stiff and scripted, others felt differently. *Wall Street Journal* commentator John Paul Newport, who watched the press conference with his wife and fifteen-year-old daughter, wrote that "we were all impressed by Mr. Woods's apparent sincerity...I know many doubters are calling this a scripted, insincere performance, but what do you expect from a young man who has just been through six weeks of humiliating therapy, and is probably deeply confused from looking at parts of himself he's always avoided?"[17]

You can also look at Woods's apology as an attempt at brand rehabilitation, where the brand in question was his own.

In a *New York Times* article titled "An Attempt to Revive the Lost Art of Apology,"[18] which was published after Woods's accident but prior to his public apology, Alina Tugend offers up hints as to the elements of a proper apology:

- Avoid defensive or self-congratulatory language. (She quotes an analysis of Eliot Spitzer's resignation that determined it was only 17 percent apology, with the rest being "about how great he was.")
- Do it in person.
- Focus on your counterpart or the target of the apology.
- Make it unambiguous (not "I want to apologize," which may sound like an intention rather than an actual apology).

Often there are concerns that an apology might be legally construed as an admission of guilt or an acknowledgment that you've done something wrong, but that's not necessarily the case. Tugend refers to a conversation with Jonathan Cohen, a law professor at the University of Florida who has written a number of articles on apologies, including "Legislating Apology: The Pros and Cons" and "Advising Clients to Apologize."[19] Cohen notes that many states have enacted "safe harbor" laws that allow people to offer "benevolent gestures expressing sympathy or a general sense of benevolence" without establishing fault and creating a legal liability.

In fact, according to the American Medical Association, "At least thirty states have enacted an 'I'm Sorry' law for health care providers...Generally these laws protect health care providers who express sympathy to a patient for an unanticipated outcome from having such statement used against the physician in a subsequent lawsuit."[20]

A simple example of what kind of apology is allowable under these laws is provided in *The Hospitalist*, published by the Society of Hospital Medicine.

> Dr. Smith is treating a 22-year-old patient, John Elway, for a fractured fibula. Dr. Smith sees no signs of neurological compromise while the patient is in a cast. After the cast is removed, it appears the patient has lost function in the leg because the cast was too tight. The patient was a star college athlete who was expected to be drafted into the NFL, but now likely won't be drafted. Dr. Smith tells the patient... "I want you to know how sorry I am this happened. I feel awful that you experienced this complication."[21]

There is some evidence that apologies help defuse the impact of a brand shock. As Elizabeth Bernstein writes in a *Wall Street Journal* article titled "I'm Very, Very, Very Sorry...Really?": "Apologies are so important that many hospitals train their staffs to say they are sorry to patients and their families following a medical mistake because they've found it deters malpractice lawsuits. Economists have shown that companies offering a mea culpa to disgruntled customers fare better than ones offering only financial compensation."[22]

WHEN THERE ARE BONA FIDE PROBLEMS, DEMONSTRATE A SENSE OF URGENCY, BUT MAKE SURE THAT YOU FIX IT RIGHT THE FIRST TIME

Sudden Acceleration

Finally, let's consider the case of Toyota and their seemingly problematic brakes.

For years, Toyota's approach to manufacturing set the bar for other manufacturers. Toyota has codified its approach in a set of guidelines it calls the "Toyota Production System," which it describes as "a production system steeped in the philosophy of the complete elimination of all waste and that imbues all aspects of production with this philosophy in pursuit of the most efficient production method."[23] Taiichi Ohno, one of the founders of the approach, provides details on TPS in his 1978 book *Toyota Production System: Beyond Large-Scale Production.*[24]

TPS is built on two concepts:

- Jikoda—"Quality must be built in during the manufacturing process!"
- Just-in-Time—"Making only 'what is needed, when it is needed, and in the amount needed!'"

I, like many other business writers and consultants, have used Toyota as a reference point when it comes to quality, pointing out its fanatical adherence to both fixing problems and asking workers to communicate awareness of these problems so that they are eliminated once and for all.

So, when acceleration problems with Toyota vehicles first starting being reported in late 2009, I, along with the same business writers and consultants who repeatedly used Toyota as a reference point for quality, was surprised.

In 2009 and 2010, Toyota recalled more than 8.5 million vehicles because of problems associated with braking and acceleration. The problems were initially attributed to accelerator pedals becoming jammed by loose floor mats or vehicle trim. Then, problems were attributed to sticky pedals that were slow to come up after the driver's foot was removed.

As the vehicles were recalled, Toyota suspended sale on eight models until the recalled vehicles could be repaired.

The *Time* magazine article faults Toyota for expanding too quickly, becoming too inflexible, believing its own press, and creating a culture where the delivery of bad news had become problematic. "Not only is Toyota producing more flawed cars than in the past, but an organization known for its unrivaled ability to suss out problems, fix them and turn them into advantages is looking clueless on all counts."[25]

In January 2010, Akio Toyoda, the grandson of the company founder, publicly apologized on television, telling consumers that he was "deeply sorry" and that "we think of our customers as a priority, and we guarantee their safety."[26]

Subsequently, Toyota published full-page apology ads in the national media; set up a landing page on its website (www.toyota. com/recall) that includes videos, recall details, and FAQs; replaced the faulty parts; and, in July 2010, announced changes in its car development processes to include more testing time and reduce the use of outsourced engineering. In August 2010, Toyota's chief quality officer for North America, Steve St. Angelo, indicated that his team was "looking under every rock and asking the question: Is there anything wrong or unusual about our pedals?"[27]

In August 2010, Toyota received very good news. The National Highway Traffic Safety Administration released its preliminary findings related to fifty-eight crashes blamed on the sudden acceleration of Toyotas. The NHTSA could find no new problems beyond those previously reported by Toyota and, in more than half of the cases examined, attributed the acceleration to "pedal misapplication" (i.e., the driver's hitting the accelerator instead of the brake).[28] These findings validated what Toyota had been saying all along.

By all appearances, Toyota seemed to follow the Johnson & Johnson playbook as characterized by DoD's write-up of the three R's—repentance, remediation, and rectification. Will it work, or are we missing something?

As Ken Belson wrote in an article published shortly after Toyoda's public apology, Toyota is not the first Japanese auto industry leader that has been "accused of negligence, causing car accidents and dragging its feet with investigators."[29] A decade ago, Bridgestone, the Japanese tire maker, recalled 6.5 million tires, and its executives were asked to testify in front of Congress, yet they returned to profitability within two years as a result of its diligent focus on problem remediation and brand rebuilding. Belson's point is that it's likely that Toyota can "follow the same arc as Bridgestone's."[30]

Belson writes that the option some companies use of trotting out a charismatic CEO after a brand shock, "much like David

G. Neeleman did at JetBlue after hundreds of its customers were stranded in planes in 2007," is probably not the right fit for Toyota, with its understated culture and historical tendency to deflect attention away from themselves.[31] Belson also writes that Toyota's long history of success may have left its crisis management skills rusty.

Finally, Belson writes that although Toyota's maniacal attention to detail and testing may have caused the cautious response that led to public criticism, this same maniacal attention to detail may allow it to get the recall right and avoid a relapse. "Its long record of building reliable cars is partly what has made this crisis so shocking," he said. "But it may also make a recovery plausible."[32]

REHEARSE YOUR RESPONSE

Let's move from cars to food.

In the past five years, we seem to have had an eruption of brand shocks related to food safety—spinach, peanuts, eggs, beef, pet food, and many products in between. The number of food recalls has more than doubled since 1999 and appears to be accelerating. From 2007 to 2008, food and beverage recalls increased by 60 percent. This is unfortunately becoming a more and more common occurrence as foods undergo more extensive processing and supply chains are extended.[33]

A number of our colleagues at Deloitte have worked with food manufacturers and food retailers on managing the recall process and have identified leading practices and practical suggestions that could apply to almost any brand shock. These are described in *Recall Execution Effectiveness: Collaborative Approaches to Improving Consumer Safety and Confidence*, a May 2010 study conducted by Deloitte on behalf of the Grocery Manufacturers Association, Food Marketing Institute, and GS1 US.

The study's recommendations emphasize minimizing the time from issue detection to action and minimizing the time required for execution. Both of these targets can be achieved through well-defined and standardized recall processes, and by rigorously training employees in these processes.

The report also suggests that organizations consider staging mock recalls to assess procedures and responsiveness. The key to the effectiveness of these mock recalls is to simulate the actual complexity and conditions that companies might actually encounter.

So consider spelling out processes that employees should follow once a brand shock occurs, providing the training for employees to execute these processes, and even running simulations that test your execution time and capabilities. Finally, think carefully about how others may need to be involved in your response and include them in both your plans and rehearsals.

IN THE END, IT'S ALL ABOUT MAINTAINING YOUR BRAND NARRATIVE

The word *narrative* has evolved from a purely literary term to one that can define any sequence of events and the message they send. As such, it's become a popular term in discussing political, military, and business cases. In a business context, the narrative is the story around which your employees rally and find inspiration.

The Counterinsurgency Field Manual explains the concept as follows: "The most important cultural form for counterinsurgents to understand is the narrative. A cultural narrative is a story recounted in the form of a causally linked set of events that explains an event in a group's history and expresses the values, character, or self-identity of the group. Narratives are the means through which ideologies are expressed and absorbed by members of a society." The authors go on to explain how Americans use the Boston Tea Party to explain why the Revolutionary War began, as well as to remind themselves of why they are fighting. They point out that "narratives may not conform to historical facts or they may drastically simplify facts to more clearly express basic cultural values."[34]

If you lose control of your company's narrative, you lose the hearts and minds of your customers. The reason the impact of the Tiger Woods incident was so devastating for his own personal brand, as well as for those that sponsored him, was that it threw into question the entire narrative that had been built around him.

When the narrative evaporated, so did brand loyalty and brand value.

In reports on the Johnson & Johnson Tylenol crisis, observers point out the role of the Johnson & Johnson credo in guiding their behavior, with its emphasis on "putting the needs and well-being of the people we serve *first*."[35] The credo provided the narrative backdrop for Johnson & Johnson's behavior during the crisis, and that behavior became another part of the narrative that has confirmed Johnson & Johnson's reputation for ethical behavior for so long.

When a brand shock occurs, it threatens the believability of your brand narrative: your response must include a reexamination of that narrative. When your brand suffers a shock, check for injuries. Update the narrative, if you need to, but let everyone know that you're okay. Make sure that you broadcast your commitment to the same elements that made your brand great in the first place.

However, there's a fine line between sticking with your brand narrative and sticking your head in the sand. Like our colleagues responsible for food recalls, we need to be extraordinarily efficient in understanding the issues, coming to a decision, and executing the plan. All of this needs to happen in an incredibly short period in a world where you get blamed for not acting swiftly and you get blamed even more when your initial response is incomplete.

Finally, the quote from *The Counterinsurgency Field Manual* at the beginning of this chapter is a good reminder that you need to carefully calibrate your response to a brand shock. Not every YouTube video that makes fun of your brand deserves a response, and inappropriately heavy-handed responses are often the basis for a viral brand shock.

KEY TAKEAWAYS

WHAT WE KNOW...	...AND WHAT YOU CAN DO
■ Think of a brand attack as an event, with the opportunity for pre- and post-event actions.	■ Keep a timeline in mind as you develop and execute your response to a brand shock.
■ Consider whether—and how far—you want to pull the repentance, remediation, and rectification levers in responding to brand shocks.	■ Executing the Johnson & Johnson Tylenol crisis playbook is not always the right strategy; at times, it may be appropriate to respond more aggressively.
■ Think of an apology as an expression of regret. It is not always an admission of guilt or the first step in compensating victims.	■ Well-executed apologies can defuse negative reactions rather than exacerbate them.
■ When there are bona fide problems, demonstrate a sense of urgency, but make sure that you fix it right the first time.	■ Don't let your urgency to respond to a situation overwhelm the need to get the facts right first; over time, the right response based on a comprehensive assessment of the issues trumps a quick response that requires rework.
■ Rehearse your response.	■ Practice is as essential to executing a response as a good plan is.
■ In the end, it's all about maintaining your brand narrative.	■ Keep your story out in front and tell it to everyone over and over again.

Chapter Eight

STEP FIVE

Learn and Adapt Your Brand Defenses

In COIN, the side that learns faster and adapts more rapidly—the bet-ter learning organization—usually wins. Counterinsurgencies have been called learning competitions. Thus, this publication identifies "Learn and Adapt" as a modern COIN imperative for U.S. forces.
> —The Counterinsurgency Field Manual

Early in their careers, most marketing professionals learn the impor-tance of persistence—and consistency. We learn that marketing campaigns benefit from sustained execution. Repeated changes in campaign strategy and design confuse customers, whereas repeated exposures to the same advertising, the same messaging, and the same campaign elements can create lasting positive impressions that extend well beyond the life of the campaign. When it comes to marketing, too much tinkering often leads to bad results.

By contrast, constant vigilance and constant adaptation are the hallmarks of brand counterinsurgency. As a brand counterinsur-gent, you know you can never fully anticipate all the dangers that lie ahead. No matter how well you prepare and how effective your early warning systems are, surprises will happen because insur-gents are, by definition, constantly improvising the next form of attack. The design of your brand defenses cannot be a "one and done" effort; you need to be prepared for multiple cycles of design, learn, redesign:

COIN design must be iterative. By their nature, COIN efforts require repeated assessments from different perspectives to see the various factors and relationships required for adequate understanding. Assessment and learning enable incremental improvements to the design. The aim is to rationalize the problem—to construct a logical explanation of observed events and subsequently construct the guiding logic that unravels the problem. The essence of this is the mechanism necessary to achieve success.[1]

The steps that we have discussed in the preceding chapters are foundational when it comes to learning and adapting—honing your assessment capabilities, engaging your employees, building and deploying your early warning systems, and repelling attacks. But the more effective you become, the more effective the insurgents will become. Hence, you need to formalize and institutionalize your processes for learning and adapting. The objective is to do the best that you can to stay one step ahead of the insurgents. The better and more purposeful your learning, the more you can compress the learning cycle and the more quickly you can adapt your brand defenses using the insights gained from analyzing each brand shock.

NEVER WASTE A CRISIS

If you're like me, your temptation when confronted with a crisis is to respond, fix the problem, and move on. Don't dwell on what's happened, look ahead, and, as our kindergarten teachers told us, don't cry over spilt milk. But for the brand counterinsurgent, a brand shock may present unique opportunities to both galvanize the organization and spur learning.

In November 2008, Rahm Emanuel, the chief of staff to the newly elected but not yet inaugurated president, Barack Obama, addressed a *Wall Street Journal* conference of chief executives. The economic situation was, at the time, grim. Emanuel's remarks suggested that the crisis could provide the impetus for action. "You never want a serious crisis to go to waste...This crisis provides the opportunity for us to do things that you could not do before."[2]

As Gerald Seib wrote in the *Wall Street Journal* shortly after the conference, "The thing about a crisis—and crisis doesn't seem too strong a word for the economic mess right now—is that it creates a sense of urgency. Actions that once appeared optional suddenly seem essential. Moves that might have been made at a leisurely pace are desired instantly."[3]

Emanuel was not the first or last member of the Obama administration to use this kind of language.

In March 2009, Secretary of State Hillary Clinton used a strikingly similar formulation in a speech at the European Parliament on rebuilding economies in a greener, less energy-intensive way. She said, "Never waste a good crisis...Don't waste it when it can have a very positive impact on climate change and energy security."[4] Shortly afterward, the president himself used his weekly radio address to discuss the opportunity created by a great crisis.[5]

Dr. Saj-nicole A. Joni, chief executive of Cambridge International Group, offered her perspectives on finding opportunities in a crisis in a November 2008 *Forbes* column titled, "Never Waste a Crisis":

> Great leaders know that significant opportunity lies in a world turned upside down...Does this crisis allow you to dramatically improve brand loyalty? Are there things your company can do that will make a difference to people caught in these difficult times? Might you redeploy marketing dollars to this? Might you tap the power of purpose in your employees' desire to help others, and make it clear what your brand stands for beyond the day-to-day business of consumption?[6]

Sometimes a setback provides an organization with the kick in the pants that it needs to move from complacency to action. The key is to figure out the right actions to take and incorporate them into your plans going forward. Your job as brand steward is to make sure that your organization does not follow its natural temptation to simply respond, fix, and move on.

"LEARN AND ADAPT" REQUIRES TAKING A HARD-NOSED LOOK AT WHAT REALLY HAPPENED

If you spend as much time on airplanes as we do, you can't really afford to waste too much energy worrying about airline accidents. Fortunately, we have the National Transportation Safety Board (NTSB), an independent Federal agency "charged by Congress with investigating every civil aviation accident in the United States and significant accidents in the other modes of transportation—railroad, highway, marine and pipeline—and issuing safety recommendations aimed at preventing future accidents."[7]

The NTSB opened its doors for business on April Fool's Day, 1967. Since then, it has become one of the world's leading accident investigation agencies, with investigations of more than 132,000 aviation accidents and more than 10,000 surface transportation accidents. It has issued more than 12,900 recommendations, pertaining to all modes of transportation, to more than 2,500 recipients. More than 82 percent of its recommendations have been adopted, resulting in many of the safety features that can be found in today's trains, planes, and automobiles.[8]

Since 1990, the NTSB has highlighted safety improvement opportunities on an annual "Most Wanted" list. Many of the items on the original list have been removed, since all of the necessary remediation has occurred.[9]

The NTSB is a relatively small agency, with less than five hundred employees. Its mission statement reads, "We identify and promote lessons learned from accident investigations to help make transportation safer"[10]—simple, clear, and, apparently, valuable, if you look at the statistical record.[11]

When you examine publicly available data on aviation accidents between 1990 and 2009, you see that despite significant increases

Table 8.1 Aviation accidents: 1990 vs. 2009

Year	Flight hours (millions)	Fatal accidents per 100,000 flight hours	Miles flown (millions)	Fatal accidents per 1,000,000 miles flown	Departures (millions)	Fatal accidents per 100,000 departures
1990	11.5	0.035	4.7	0.0009	7.8	0.051
2009	17.5	0.006	7.3	0.0001	10.2	0.010
2009 / 1990	152.2%	17.1%	155.3%	11.1%	130.8%	19.6%

Source: National Transportation Safety Board, http://www.ntsb.gov/aviation/Table6.htm.

in flight hours, miles flown, and departures, fatal accidents have decreased significantly (see table 8.1).

The NTSB believes that its success is a reflection of its focus (to determine the probable cause of the accident and to extract lessons learned that will prevent similar accidents in the future), its objectivity, and its rapid response rates, all of which result from a set of processes and tools that have been developed over the course of thousands of investigations.

The NTSB's operational core is the "Go Team." NTSB staff members are on call on a rotational basis for Go Team duty. When the call comes, the Go Team is deployed, under the leadership of an "investigator in charge." Typically, the Go Team membership is structured to address various areas of responsibility, including the operational history of the aircraft, the structure of the wreckage, the engine and systems, air traffic control communications, weather, human performance, and survival factors. The team stays on site as long as necessary before returning to NTSB headquarters to formulate its findings and safety recommendations.[12]

Now, imagine adapting the NTSB's approach in investigating transportation accidents to how you investigate brand shocks.

First, remember the timeline that we discussed in chapter 7? (See figure 8.1.)

So, the process needs to start as close as possible to $t+a$, the time when you become aware of the brand shock. Here is a suggested sequence of activities:

- **Log the incident**. Each time you become aware of a brand shock, it is logged.
- **Describe what happened**. The logging identifies exactly what happened, when it happened, and the consequences of the brand shock.

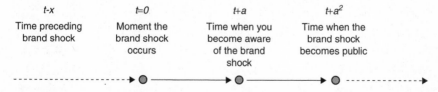

$t-x$	$t=0$	$t+a$	$t+a^2$
Time preceding brand shock	Moment the brand shock occurs	Time when you become aware of the brand shock	Time when the brand shock becomes public

Figure 8.1

Over time, organizations will be able to see whether the incidence of brand shocks is increasing or stabilizing, as well as whether the nature, intensity, or types of brand shocks are changing.

- **Assign an investigative team**. An individual with no direct responsibility for the affected area should be assigned to investigate, with the goal of a relatively rapid turnaround. As appropriate, additional individuals can contribute to the investigation.
- **Focus on cause and prevention rather than assigning blame**. The investigation's focus should be on determining the likely cause and extracting lessons to prevent similar incidents in the future.
- **Formulate the recommendation(s)**. A recommendation is created and forwarded to the individual with the authority to implement the recommendation.
- **Assign implementation responsibility**. The recommendation is reviewed and a determination is made whether to implement the recommendation.
- **Track implementation progress**. The status of the recommendation and the execution of the implementation are tracked.
- **Review your incident log regularly**. The log of incidents, as well as the tracking of recommendations and implementations, should be reviewed on a periodic basis. Perhaps some day, every organization's annual report will include a section on brand value and what they have done to either increase brand value or protect it. Measurement and tracking will be the focus of our next chapter.

If this seems like overkill, it may help to compare systematically tracking and investigating brand sabotage to the way companies systematically improve their manufacturing processes.

Imagine that you run a manufacturing plant. Every time you make a defective product, you fix it (or one of your employees fixes it before you even see it). Day after day, week after week, month after month, the defects never appear to your customers because you fix them before the products ever leave the plant.

At some point, you begin to realize that you're spending an awful lot of your time looking for defects and an awful lot of time fixing them. So you call in a group of experts, take a look at the defects, figure out what's causing them, eliminate the root cause, and move on.

Will this eliminate every defect? Not likely. Every time you make a change, whether it's adding a new product, using a new supplier, changing a formulation, fiddling with the temperature in the factory, or hiring new employees to work in the factory, you introduce the opportunity for new defects.

So, if you're smart, you implement a process for measurement and tracking, but you also treat the discovery of each defect as a golden opportunity for improvement. Determine the cause, extract lessons learned, and apply what you learn.

One of the primary advocates for applying "learn and adapt" approaches to manufacturing quality has been Toyota, as embodied in the Toyota Production System that we discussed in chapter 7. In fact, we believe that part of the reason the acceleration problems with Toyota vehicles received the attention that they did was because of Toyota's long track record of manufacturing quality based on its "learn and adapt" approach.

The intent of "learn and adapt" is not just to eliminate defects but to rethink an entire design approach. After the sudden acceleration problems that were first identified in the 1980s, the National Highway Traffic Safety Administration published the results of its probe in its 1989 "Silver Book." As we mentioned in chapter 7, the study found that startled drivers often hit the accelerator pedal instead of the brake, causing accidents. Many of the unintended acceleration events occurred in parked vehicles, so the design change developed by automobile manufacturers was the installation of systems that required drivers to depress the brake before shifting into gear. Unintended acceleration complaints dropped by 60 percent.[13]

"Taking Lessons from What Went Wrong," an article by William Broad that appeared in the July 20, 2010, Science section of the *New York Times*, reminds us to find opportunity in crises. "Disasters teach more than successes...[They] can become a spur to innovation... The sinking of the Titanic, the meltdown of the Chernobyl reaction in 1986, the collapse of the World Trade Center—all forced engineers to address what came to be seen as deadly flaws."[14]

The notion of accident investigation with a focus on identifying the root causes and fixing them works for aviation accidents. It works in manufacturing plants. It works with cars. It works with failures of engineered products. And it can work for brands.

A "LEARN AND ADAPT" APPROACH NEEDS TO START AT THE TOP

Leaders are increasingly responsible for creating environments in which individuals and organizations learn from their experiences and for establishing climates that tap the full ingenuity of subordinates. Open channels of discussion and debate are needed to encourage growth of a learning environment in which experience is rapidly shared and lessons adapted for new challenges. The speed with which leaders adapt the organization must outpace insurgents' efforts to identify and exploit weaknesses or develop countermeasures.

—The Counterinsurgency Field Manual

I had a chance to reflect on my own thinking about "learn and adapt" recently, and I realized you don't need to look far to see how easy it is to get complacent.

I sit on the board of a not-for-profit organization based in Chicago. Our organization is independent of, but affiliated with, a national organization, and consumers of our services sometimes confuse the two.

The national organization decided to terminate one of its employees, who had made public comments that it determined were inconsistent with its values and policies. The termination was widely covered in the press and resulted in numerous phone calls and emails to our local organization. Some callers and correspondents supported the termination; others condemned it. Many of the phone calls and emails implied that we were part and parcel of the decision, when in fact we were not. However, given our affiliation with the national organization, this brand shock may not be dissimilar to the effect the activities of a value chain partner might have, as we discussed in chapter 3.

My wife forwarded an email from a friend of hers about the termination. The friend was not aware of my membership on the board. Ellen had told her friend that I was on the board of the local organization, and her friend asked her what I thought about it all.

Here is what I realized: First, despite all of the thinking that I have been doing on the subject of brand resilience and brand shocks, I had never really thought about it in conjunction with this not-for-profit organization on whose board I served. Second, I realized that we, as a board, had never discussed the possibility of such an incident prior to its occurrence. Third, I realized that I had no idea of what our policies are regarding a situation of this nature. Fourth, I realized that our response, while thoughtful and considered, was still somewhat improvised.

In summary, I realized that we, as a board, have the responsibility to ensure that the organization is better prepared next time.

This experience reinforces the sentiments that I noted early in this chapter: when confronted with a crisis, our temptation is to respond, fix the problem, and move on. Don't dwell on what's happened; look ahead. My recent personal experience certainly confirms this general observation.

For the record, I'm confident that our organization will weather this storm. We got a small number of calls and emails and our CEO and senior staff members contacted each caller and emailer, most of whom reacted very favorably and expressed continued support. But I did make a point of sending an email to other board members suggesting that we should use this teachable moment to our advantage.

FOCUS YOUR "LEARN AND ADAPT" ENERGIES ON YOUR CUSTOMERS

Mr. Nobody took up residence at our home from the moment our children were able to speak until they left for college. I don't miss him.

I first learned of Mr. Nobody when my now adult children were toddlers. Like other children, they managed to cause minor mischief, ranging from damage to our furniture and walls to the non-lethal physical injuries that they inadvertently inflicted upon one another. More than one family vacation included visits to hospital emergency rooms.

However, they were never at fault. If asked to identify the responsible party, they inevitably replied, "Nobody." Even when confronted with irrefutable evidence of their guilt and the consequences of their action, it was hard to get the kids to "fess up." When they finally did, they inevitably argued that they didn't mean to do it, it wasn't their fault, or they were incited to do it (presumably by Mr. Nobody).

My wife and I tried to take preventive, as well as remedial, measures to protect our children and our valuables from Mr. Nobody. Unfortunately, too often, we allowed ourselves to think that we had dealt with Mr. Nobody once and for all with strong words and punishments, only to be disappointed when he reappeared and we once again experienced the consequences of his actions.

Mr. Nobody has moved to the workplaces of America. Consider this example, which we first alluded to in chapter 3: In the spring of 2009, Kristy and Michael, two presumably bored kitchen employees in a North Carolina outlet of a major pizza chain, Domino's Pizza, created videos of themselves on the job. Kristy and Michael then decided to post the videos to YouTube.

Unfortunately for the pizza chain, the videos involved a variety of unsanitary food handling practices that fueled the worst fears of consumers who patronize quick-service restaurants.

At this point, any prudent person might wonder what the two employees were thinking that led them to do what they did. Imagine the conversation between two employees.

> *Employee 1:* Let's make some really disgusting videos showing how we prepare sandwiches for delivery, involving all kinds of health code violations. By the way, let's make sure that we clearly identify our employer by name.
>
> *Employee 2:* We can even wear our uniforms.
>
> *Employee 1:* Yeah, that sounds cool. And how about, after we make these really disgusting videos, we post them to YouTube? I'm sure that the Man will really get a charge out of them.
>
> *Employee 2:* Right, dude. Sounds awesome. Let's do it! Let's show the Man.

In a few days, the videos went viral and were viewed more than a million times. One million viewings—more than many television commercials. Google and Twitter were rife with references to the videos.

A blogger who saw the videos alerted the company. The company contacted YouTube. The offending videos were removed. Kristy apologized to the company. While not quite blaming Mr. Nobody,

Kristy wrote an email explaining, "It was fake and I wish that everyone knew that!!!! I AM SOO SORRY!"[15]

Right, dude.

The impact of the videos was amazing. Not only did they get more than a million viewings on YouTube, but between Google, Twitter, magazine articles, blogs, and television news, millions more heard the story. It has become the quintessential example of how employee use (or abuse) of social media can sabotage a brand.

"We got blindsided by two idiots with a video camera and an awful idea," said a company spokesperson. "Even people who've been with us as loyal customers for 10, 15, 20 years are second-guessing their relationship with [us], and that's not fair."[16]

Initially, the chain decided not to respond aggressively. Then the chain quickly reversed itself, creating a Twitter account to address comments and creating a video of its chief executive. Naturally, it posted its video to YouTube.[17]

Many observers seized upon the incident as a teachable moment to demonstrate the potential harmful effects of social media and the need for taking a more proactive stance in managing them. Many of the recommendations echo those that we present in this book, including assessment of threats, employee engagement and training, early warning systems, rapid response to brand attacks, and using social media as a platform for brand advocacy. Some pundits were quick to wag their fingers at the company for not focusing enough on social media and reputation management.[18]

The chain has, in fact, adopted many of these recommendations. You can go to its website and find links to its Facebook page. You can follow the chain on Twitter. You can sign up for email and text offers. These are all marks of a savvy marketer that understands the power of social media.

But then our pizza chain went one better, and took a page out of its attackers' playbook.

In December 2009, right before two of its busiest days, it launched a newly reformulated pizza and a new ad campaign, "Oh Yes We Did," to promote the new pizza. In addition to television commercials, the chain's website featured a new web section called "Oh Yes We Did," which included a documentary video showing consumers what prompted the chain to make such a radical change. The site included live feeds from Twitter and Facebook, sharing what consumers think of the new pizza. The chain advertised the documentary on YouTube.[19]

If you look at the documentary video (available on http://www .pizzaturnaround.com, along with a number of other videos showing the impact of the campaign), you will see how the chain used social media to elicit customer feedback that led to the reformulation and to track customer reactions. The website proudly proclaims, "Domino's Pizza presents a documentary, 'The Pizza Turnaround,' starring actual Domino's employees, inspired by our harshest critics."[20]

The website also features videos from Domino's CEO on Gayle King's radio show, the Pizza Throwdown held on the social commerce site *Bazaar Voice*, and taste tests from local news shows, Jim Cramer's *Mad Money*, and *The Colbert Report*.

Did it work?

If the money counts, yes.

Between the end of December 2009, when the campaign was announced, and late March 2010, the chain's stock price went from below $9 per share to almost $14 per share, an increase in value significantly higher than any other quick-service restaurant during this same period. As of October 2010, Domino's revenue growth has continued to outpace other competitors in the category by a significant margin.[21]

If media critics count, yes.

In an article for *Adweek* titled "Domino's Delivers: Time for my mea culpa: I was wrong about this campaign," Barbara Lippert wrote, "When I wrote about the introductory phase...I found the 'Oh yes we did!' stuff head-scratchingly earnest, to the point of self-parody...I thought the whole corporate mea culpa and vow to improve was too big a risk to take...[but] I...didn't foresee how well the opening spot would lay the groundwork. The genius is in the follow-up, making great use of every stop along the way in the apology-redemption story arc."[22]

If popular culture counts, yes.

In January 2010, Robert Redford and other leaders of the Sundance Film Festival indicated that the festival needed a major overhaul. The lead sentence in the *Los Angeles Times* article on the announcement?

"Sundance Film Festival organizers pulled a Domino's Pizza on Thursday afternoon, saying that they'd failed in some respects over the last few years and vowing to improve."[23]

Starting with the response to the YouTube videos, the chain's CEO was front and center of its activities—clearly a case where the company's leadership is visible and leading by example.

This may be a textbook example of the admonition to "never waste a crisis" and a model for moving an organization from a victim of brand sabotage to a leader in using the same improvised tools that caused its troubles in the first place.

An article in the April 8, 2010, issue of the *Economist*, "Brand Rehab: A surprising number of companies spend some time in the clinic," appeared after Domino's resurgence and could easily have been inspired by it. The two rules that it suggests about how to bounce back as a brand read like they were taken straight from Domino's playbook.

> First, the boss needs to take charge. This means sidelining corporate cluck-cluckers such as lawyers (who worry that any admission of guilt will lead to lawsuits) or financial officers (who obsess about the bottom line). It also means putting the survival of the company above personal considerations... The second rule is that crisis-racked firms should redouble their focus on their customers... Companies have a habit of... talking endlessly about how they are fixing this or reorganizing that. But most effective decontaminators look at the world's from... [the customer's] point of view.[24]

INQUIRING MINDS WANT TO KNOW

Do you let your organization know about incidents of brand sabotage, how you responded to them, and what you plan to do differently as a result? Or do you keep things on the QT?

If you're a fan of open book management (OBM), the answer is probably yes to the former.

Open Book Management: The Coming Business Revolution is the title of a 1995 book authored by John Case. The book argues that by sharing information with employees, particularly sensitive information regarding financial performance, companies can get employees to think like owners and help align their activities and decisions with the objectives of the actual owners of the company.[25]

Despite lots of publicity at the time, including numerous glowing stories about one of the stars of the book, John Stack, the CEO of SRC Holdings (e.g., "Jack Stack's Story Is an Open Book," in the July 2001 issue of *strategy+business*[26]), open book management tended to be embraced mainly by smaller, entrepreneurial companies. Its application in larger, publicly traded companies tended to be limited to individual facilities or departments. Today, more than fifteen years after the book was first published, you don't hear much about open book management.

But the concept may be more relevant now than ever. A lot has happened in the past fifteen years, notably the widespread use of the Internet and the ubiquity of social media. Thus, we were intrigued to find references to Case and OBM in the recently issued book *Open Leadership: How Social Technology Can Transform the Way You Lead,* by social media guru Charlene Li. She writes, "a key difference today is that a new generation of workers is coming of age that believes that 'sharingness' is next to—or more important than—godliness. Moreover, the demand to be more open about how an organization makes decisions and operates is coming from people both inside *and outside* the organization."[27]

The premise of Li's book is that leaders need to be more open, transparent, and authentic, given the technologies and tools that are available today and the internal and external expectations that she describes above. As she says in her introduction, "The question isn't whether you will be transparent, authentic, and real, but rather, *how much* you will let go and be open in the face of new technologies... It is critical that your organization not enter into these new open relationships without guidelines. Simply opening up and devolving into chaos, or worse, 'letting nature take its natural course' are certain recipes for disaster."[28]

So, one of the questions that you will have to ask yourself is how open you want your "learn and adapt" process to be. Do you let the rank and file of your organization peer in at what happens during brand shocks and how you respond, or do you keep this information relatively secure, lest you expose your vulnerabilities and defenses?

As Li says, the question isn't "if," but "how much." You need clearly defined policies about what you share and in what level of detail.

In this context, it's interesting to revisit the book that we've used as a guide for our brand resilience journey. *The Counterinsurgency Field Manual* is a publicly available document. On its cover and in its table of contents, where you might normally expect to see a copyright notice, it says, "Distribution Restriction: Approved for public release; distribution is unlimited."[29] This means that anyone and everyone can download, print, and read the official manual that "establishes doctrine (fundamental principles) for military operations in a counterinsurgency (COIN) environment."[30] In fact, according to Lieutenant Colonel John A. Nagl's foreword to the University of Chicago's edition, "The field manual was widely reviewed, including by several *Jihadi* Web sites; copies have been found in Taliban training camps in Pakistan. It was downloaded more than 1.5 million times in the first month after its posting to the Fort Leavenworth and Marine Corps websites."[31]

So, here's the question. If the US Army and Marine Corps are willing to make their doctrine for military operations in a counterinsurgency environment public, how much information are you willing to share internally and externally about your experiences with brand sabotage?

KEY TAKEAWAYS

WHAT WE KNOW...	...AND WHAT YOU CAN DO
■ Never waste a crisis.	■ Sometimes a setback provides an organization with the kick in the pants it needs to move from complacency to action. Your job as brand steward is to make sure that your organization does not follow its natural temptation to simply respond, fix, and move on.
■ "Learn and adapt" requires taking a hard-nosed look at what really happened.	■ Every time you experience a brand shock, mobilize your "Go Team":
	❑ Log the incident.
	❑ Describe what happened.
	❑ Assign an investigative team.
	❑ Focus on cause and prevention rather than assigning blame.
	❑ Formulate the recommendation(s).
	❑ Assign responsibility for implementation.
	❑ Track implementation progress.
	❑ Review your incident log regularly.
■ A "learn and adapt" approach needs to start at the top.	■ As a board member or senior executive, make your expectations for "active action" reports clear.
■ Focus your "learn and adapt" energies on your customers.	■ In thinking through your adaptations, evaluate the changes from the customer's perspective.
■ Inquiring minds want to know.	■ Clarify your policies for communicating the changes that you implement in response to brand shocks, recognizing that expectations for transparency are high.

Chapter Nine

STEP SIX

Measure and Track Brand Resilience

Commanders and staffs revise their assessment and measures of effectiveness during the operation in order to facilitate redesign and stay abreast of the current situation. Sound assessment blends qualitative and quantitative analysis with the judgment and intuition of all leaders. Great care must be applied here, as COIN operations often involve complex societal issues that may not lend themselves to quantifiable measures of effectiveness. Moreover, bad assumptions and false data can undermine the validity of both assessments and the conclusions drawn from them. Data and metrics can inform a commander's assessment. However, they must not be allowed to dominate it in uncertain situations. Subjective and intuitive assessment must not be replaced by an exclusive focus on data or metrics. Commanders must exercise their professional judgment in determining the proper balance.

—The Counterinsurgency Field Manual

Traditionally, commanders use discrete quantitative and qualitative measurements to evaluate progress. However, the complex nature of COIN operations makes progress difficult to measure. Subjective assessment at all levels is essential to understand the diverse and complex nature of COIN problems. It is also needed to measure local success or failure against the overall operation's end state.

—The Counterinsurgency Field Manual

So far, we've discussed the processes for assessing brand risks, establishing your defenses, responding to brand shocks, and adapting your behavior and defenses based on lessons learned. Now it's time to see how to rate yourself. This chapter is all about measuring and tracking brand resilience.

Why measure?

- As Ronald Reagan said at the 1987 signing of the Intermediate-Range Nuclear Forces Treaty with the Soviet Union, "Trust, but verify."[1]
- Or, as Lou Gerstner, IBM's former CEO, wrote in his 2002 memoir *Who Says Elephants Can't Dance?:* "People do what you inspect, not what you expect."[2]
- Or, most important, as Yogi Berra, the baseball player, coach, and manager, reputedly said, "You've got to be very careful if you don't know where you're going, because you might not get there."[3]

The right measurement and tracking capabilities are crucial to understanding whether your efforts to manage brand risks are working. *The Counterinsurgency Field Manual,* which distinguishes between a measure of effectiveness and a measure of performance, offers up some useful definitions of measures.

- "A *measure of effectiveness* is a criterion used to assess changes in system behavior, capability, or operational environment that is tied to measuring the attainment of an end state, achievement of an objective...MOEs focus on the results or consequences of actions...[and] answer the question, Are we achieving results that move us toward the desired end state, or are additional or alternative actions required?"[4]
- By contrast, *measure of performance* answers the question, "Was the task or action performed as the commander intended?"[5]

This chapter discusses both types of measures in relation to tracking and monitoring brand resilience, as well as potential systems for this monitoring. We'll describe a variety of approaches companies are using today, and we'll argue that you've got to start somewhere, even if it's a relatively simplistic "How am I doing?" approach. You can, over time, migrate toward a more sophisticated approach that incorporates formal measures of brand value and impact analysis.

■■■■■ BUILDING BRAND RESILIENCE MEASUREMENT AND TRACKING CAPABILITIES CAN BE VIEWED AS AN EVOLUTIONARY PROCESS THAT STARTS WITH CAPTURING THE VOICE OF THE CUSTOMER

Measurement can take many forms, from casual inquiry to well-defined metrics. At one end of the spectrum, we have the organizational equivalent of Ed Koch, the former mayor of New York. Koch's trademark phrase (which became the title of a book of his collected sayings) was "How'm I doing?"[6] It was Koch's way of calibrating the sentiments of his constituents, and it proved an effective, if somewhat subjective, methodology. While Koch got grief from some quarters for what they considered a vacuous approach to feedback, it endeared him to many New Yorkers during his three terms as mayor, and established him as a politician who, unlike some of his predecessors, actually seemed to care what his constituents thought.

At the opposite end of the spectrum is the widely adopted CompStat policing approach. CompStat, which is shorthand for "computer statistics" or "comparative statistics," was first implemented in 1994 by then New York City police commissioner William Bratton to collect, analyze, and map crime and police performance data. The goal of CompStat is to hold police commanders accountable for crime levels in the geographic areas for which they are responsible.

CompStat has now been implemented by the police departments of most American cities because of the transformational effect it had in New York, where crime was significantly reduced. As Dr. Vincent Henry reported, in a paper titled "CompStat Management in the NYPD: Reducing Crime and Improving Quality of Life in New York City," "The total number of reported crimes for the seven major crime categories declined an unprecedented 65.99% in 2003 from the levels reported in 1993. Only 146,397 of these major crimes occurred in 2003, as compared to 430,460 in 1993, and the 2003 figures represent the lowest annual number of total complaints for the seven major crimes in well over three decades."[7]

What exactly is CompStat?

According to its proponents, CompStat a management philosophy, supported by an information system and a set of processes and discipline, with the objective of crime reduction through accountability. CompStat's effectiveness can be attributed to the meticulous tracking of crimes and the clear linkage of crimes to geographic locations. This tracking forms the basis for the rigorous management process described in Henry's paper.

> In an agency where isolation, "turf protection," and the hoarding of information previously reigned, the NYPD now holds weekly management meetings that bring together a broad spectrum of police officials to intensely review the computer-generated crime data and to strategize new ways to cut crime in specific locations. At these meetings, local commanders and middle managers are held highly accountable for their crime-fighting activities by executives who require them to report on steps they have taken to reduce crime as well as their plans to correct specific crime and quality of life conditions. Also essential to the CompStat process are continual follow-up and assessment of results. Finally, building on its Community Policing orientation, a variety of interested parties ranging from school safety officials to prosecutors is invited to attend and participate in order to help fashion a comprehensive and highly focused response in crime-ridden areas.[8]

The San Francisco Police Department identifies CompStat's four distinct principles:

Accurate and Timely Intelligence
...It is necessary to provide a vehicle where essential information can easily and effectively be shared with all levels of the organization.

Effective Tactics
...CompStat tactics encourage "thinking outside the box" and mandate that all resources, both internal and external, are considered in responding to a problem.

Rapid Deployment
...With CompStat, the police department is now armed with vital intelligence regarding emerging crime trends or patterns which allows for a strategic police response.

Relentless Follow-up and Assessment
...The review of the data presented and the performance of the command officers responsible for the existing crime issues assists those
same officers in future decision making when creating new crime
reduction strategies, allocating resources and deploying personnel in
their assigned areas.[9]

An article by Jon Shane in the April 2004 *FBI Law Enforcement
Bulletin* describes CompStat as "one of the most innovative, decep-
tively simple, and economical means to controlling crime and
disorder."[10] Shane's praise is widely echoed. As James Willis,
Stephen Mastrofski, and David Weisburd write in their 2003 Police
Foundation report "CompStat In Practice: An In-Depth Analysis
of Three Cities," "CompStat's creators and advocates present it as
a way to transform sluggish, unresponsive police organizations
into focused, efficient, and smart organizations." Transformational
elements that they identify include motivated employees, organizational nimbleness, sophisticated analytical capabilities, collaborative problem solving, and "decision making in an atmosphere that
has an elevated tolerance for risk and encourages new approaches
to persistent problems."[11]

The San Francisco Police Department, like many major police
departments that have implemented CompStat, reports crime statistics publicly. As a quick look at the numbers will show, CompStat's
results are impressive. (See table 9.1.)

Similar CompStat miracle stories are told by police departments
in Denver, Boston, Philadelphia, Miami, New Orleans, and Newark,

Table 9.1 San Francisco violent and nonviolent crime: 1995 vs. 2009

Year	Total violent crimes	Total non-violent crimes	Violent and non-violent total
1995	10,903	49,571	60,474
2009	5,960	34,607	40,567

*Source: San Francisco Police Department CompStat Reports 1995, 2009, http://
sf-police.org/index.aspx?page=3255*

New Jersey. Typically, in a city where CompStat has been implemented, the police department website includes a CompStat section, including the local Uniform Crime Reporting program statistics.

CompStat's critics and advocates agree that CompStat's success requires significant changes in behavior and processes, and it requires changes in the structure of police organizations. The information is the platform for these changes, but does not in and of itself ensure that a city will achieve the same results as those realized in cities with successful CompStat implementations.

So, when it comes to brand resilience, where do you want to be? At the "How am I doing?" end of the spectrum or the CompStat end?

Over the years, we've observed three levels of maturity in measuring and tracking brand resilience, ranging from emergent to cutting-edge. Organizations operating at the first level, "emergent", tend to regularly collect "voice of customer" (VOC) data through a variety of informal and formal mechanisms, ranging from posing as a customer (a.k.a. mystery shopping) to customer satisfaction or loyalty surveys. But for "emergent" organizations, brand value is not systematically measured and tracked (except possibly by third parties), and brand value metrics are certainly not a cornerstone of their performance management programs. Executives often spend time with customers and/or observe front-line operations, but without a specific agenda. Within these organizations, awareness of the potential for brand risk is uneven. Early warning systems are minimal or non-existent. In these organizations, the bulk of brand value-related discussions and decisions take place within the marketing function.

"Developing" organizations, which have more mature brand resilience measuring and tracking systems, regularly collect VOC data as well. They also have formal programs for measuring customer loyalty and may track metrics such as Net Promoter scores (NPS), a specific customer loyalty metric based on the work of Fred Reichheld and Bain & Company.[12] The concept was introduced in Reichheld's 2003 *Harvard Business Review* article "The One Number You Need to Grow"[13] and focuses on the question, "How likely is it that you would recommend our company to a friend or colleague?" In "developing" organizations, there is greater awareness about the importance of brand value, and there are programs to measure it but usually on an intermittent or episodic basis. These organizations do not generally use brand value as an integrated element in performance management. There is awareness of brand risks, and brand shocks may be tracked. Discussions and decisions about brand value may take place at the executive level rather than just within marketing.

"Cutting-edge" organizations regularly collect VOC data, use formal customer loyalty metrics, and link loyalty data to behavioral/consumption data. These organizations systematically measure and report on brand value (e.g., they include it in annual reports) not just among customers but employees as well. "Cutting-edge" organizations manage brand risks as part of their overall risk management programs. In these organizations, brand value and risk are regular items on the board's agenda, in addition to being the focus of discussions with the executive team and marketing department.

Level one: Emerging	Level two: Developing	Level three: Cutting edge
• Regular collection of voice of customer (VOC) data through a variety of informal and formal mechanisms • Executives may spend time interacting with customers and/or observing frontline operations • Brand value not systematically measured or tracked • Brand shocks not systematically tracked • Uneven awareness of potential for brand risk • Brand value discussions and decisions tend to be confined primarily to marketing department	• Regular collection of VOC data, including formal customer loyalty measures (e.g., Net Promoter) • Executives tend to be very customer-focused • Episodic or intermittent measurement of brand value • Greater awareness of brand risks • Brand shocks are identified and tracked • Brand-value-related discussions and decisions tend to be more frequent at the executive level	• Regular collection of VOC data, including formal customer loyalty measures and integration with behavioral and consumption data • Executives viewed as chief customer and brand officers • Systematic measurement and reporting of brand value, including employee brand clarity • Brand risk management is part of overall risk management program • Brand value and brand risks regularly part of the board agenda

◄───►

| "How am I doing?" | *Level of brand resilience measurement sophistication* | CompStat |

Figure 9.1   Spectrum or brand resilience measuring and tracking

GETTING INSIGHTS INTO WHAT HAPPENS ON THE FRONT LINES IS A GOOD PLACE TO START

Candid Camera may have been one of the earliest television reality shows. The show aired on various broadcast and cable networks for almost sixty years, beginning in 1948. The premise of *Candid Camera* was the use of a hidden camera to capture the reactions of ordinary people to extraordinary, even bizarre situations. The reactions of these ordinary people inevitably ranged from embarrassed to amused to outraged, and each scenario concluded with the disclosure of the hidden camera and the show's tagline "Smile! You're on *Candid Camera!*"[14]

The show, which actually originated on radio with a hidden microphone, inspired a number of other television shows, including British, Australian, and Canadian versions and Fox's *Totally Hidden Video.* And today, many of the videos that appear on YouTube are the spiritual, if not lineal, descendants of the segments that used to air weekly on *Candid Camera* broadcasts.

Flash forward to 2010 for CBS's new hit show *Undercover Boss*, the corporate equivalent of *Candid Camera.*

The show debuted on CBS immediately after the 2010 Super Bowl broadcast. As you may recall, this broadcast received the highest ratings of any television show at that time, with more than 100 million viewers. The first broadcast of *Undercover Boss* captured almost 39 million viewers in its own right and was, according to CBS's website, the "#1 new series of the 2009–2010 season, averaging 17.7 million viewers...the largest audience for a new series following the Super Bowl...the biggest new series premiere since 1987 and the most-watched premiere episode of any reality series."[15]

That's a pretty dramatic set of outcomes for a show that boils down to following a top executive out of the corner office on an undercover mission to see the inner workings of the company. As the show's website says, "While working alongside their employees, they see the effects that their decisions have on others, where the problems lie within their organizations and get an up-close look at both the good and the bad while discovering the unsung heroes who make their companies run."[16]

Executives from a diverse set of companies have appeared on the show, including 1-800-Flowers, 7-Eleven, Chicago Cubs, Chiquita,

Choice Hotels, Churchill Downs, DirecTV, Frontier Airlines, Great Wolf Resorts (the boss of which was the first female CEO to appear), GSI Commerce, Herschend Family Entertainment, Hooters, Lucky Strike Lanes, NASCAR, Roto-Rooter, and White Castle.

Maybe *Undercover Boss* involves a little more drama and less comedy than *Candid Camera,* but it uses the same rhetorical flourish with its end-of-segment "reveal," when the unwitting participants learn that there's more going on than they initially realized. Although the camera is never hidden in *Undercover Boss,* subterfuge (e.g., "we're doing a documentary on entry level jobs") is still required for the show to work.

If you go to the *Undercover Boss* website, you'll see discussion forums on such topics as "Do you think every business, both public and private, needs a reality check like this?" and "A Show With Rare Potential To Bring About Social Change." Viewers undoubtedly like the show because of its fundamentally redemptive nature: Highly compensated senior executive goes undercover, often in disguise; senior executive sees how hard the frontline employees work and how committed they are; senior executive realizes that frontline employees are key to the company's success; senior executive expresses gratitude to frontline employees, and vows to make big changes. Our favorite aspect of *Undercover Boss* is that the senior executive starts to recognize what it takes to deliver the brand to customers at the point of sale, and how fragile the brand can be in the midst of the pressures employees face on the job.

The insights that executives develop on *Undercover Boss,* and from executive frontline engagement programs in general, are not statistically valid or even necessarily representative, but they are a start when it comes to understanding the challenges in building a resilient brand and ensuring that employees clearly understand that brand.

SYSTEMATIC TRACKING OF BRAND VALUE SHOULD BECOME PART OF YOUR BRAND RESILIENCE MEASUREMENT PROGRAM

We turned to Benoit Garbe, a vice president at Millward Brown Optimor, on the topic of brand value measurement.[17]

Millward Brown Optimor is a strategic consultancy that is part of global marketing services giant WPP and provides, according to their website, "objective, fact-based advisory on how to ignite business growth through brands and optimize marketing strategies and investments." In chapter 1, we referred to two Millward Brown Optimor rankings and metrics: The BrandZ Top 100 Most Valuable Brands list ranks the world's most valuable brands according to their dollar value, and the TrustR metric measures the bond between consumers and brands based on their willingness to put their personal trust and credibility on the line.

Benoit gave us a high-level overview of Millward Brown Optimor's approach to brand valuation: "Our methodology consists of three steps: determining a company's intangible earnings by reviewing its financials, calculating the percentage of demand for a product or service that is attributable to its brand alone (a 'brand contribution' metric based on extensive consumer research), and finally, a forecast of a brand's long-term future performance." Benoit indicated that when he and his colleagues used this methodology "to examine a portfolio made up of thirty of the strongest brands (i.e., with the highest brand contribution) compared to the S&P 500 between April 2006 and April 2010, the result is staggering: $100 invested in the S&P 500 would have shown a decrease in value of 11.5 percent, while the same amount invested in a portfolio of the strongest brands would have increased by 18.5 percent during that time period."

According to Benoit, "in 1980, virtually the entire value of an S&P 500 company consisted of tangible assets—buildings, machines, inventory, etc. A 2010 study by Millward Brown Optimor found that today, these tangible assets account for only 30 to 40 percent of a business's value. The rest is intangible value, half of which—30 percent of total business value—is attributable to *brand*. For many companies, brand is their single largest business asset."

The key practice that Benoit shared with us is measuring the strength and clarity of the brand among *employees* as well as consumers. He told us that brand research companies have recently started evolving and adapting their sophisticated consumer-centric methodology to assess the strength and clarity of the brand among employees.

Companies have started adding new brand dimensions to their annual employee satisfaction surveys to identify gaps across countries, levels, and functions. From the C-suite to summer interns, companies need to understand whether and how their employees, be they in finance, customer service, or R&D, perceive the brand, and how these perceptions impact their decisions. Employees are the most powerful brand ambassadors a company can have—the best products and services in the world are largely the result of groups of passionate people who genuinely believe in their brand. Unless companies find a way to accurately assess employees' alignment with and commitment to their brands, they may be unknowingly sabotaging their most powerful business asset.

Armed with these insights, my colleague Hasim Surel and I examined a number of company websites and annual reports to see what organizations have to say about brand value. What we discovered is that communications about brands fall into three categories:

- Investments in branding (most common)
- Brand risk (frequent)
- Explicit brand value tracking, including measuring brand clarity among employees (very infrequent)

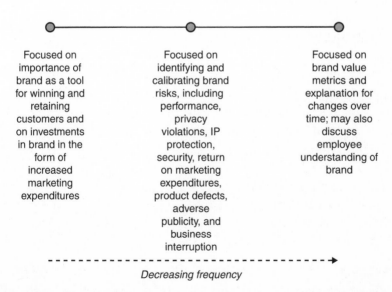

Figure 9.2 Organizational communications related to brand value

Investments in Branding

This one was easy for Hasim and me. Not surprisingly, many organizations talk about how powerful their brands are and about the franchises that they have built around these brands. In some cases, organizations describe in very specific terms the investments that they are making in their brands, primarily through increased marketing budgets. These discussions tend to be most common among companies that offer well-recognized and traditionally strong consumer brands and are trying to maintain, grow, and leverage these brands even further, such as Del Monte, the food and pet food manufacturer.

Del Monte

A reader of Del Monte's 2009 annual report will undoubtedly be impressed by the company's belief in the power of its brands and its willingness to make substantial investments in building and maintaining brand value.[18]

First, the annual report describes Del Monte's successful efforts at realigning its portfolio and its focus on "leveraging the branded strength of the portfolio and unlocking the potential of our strong brand equities . . . to gain market share and launch new products."

Then, the annual report goes on to discuss fairly hefty increases in marketing expenditures, which it describes as investments in its brands: a 50 percent increase in 2009, with an additional increase of 30 percent to 40 percent expected in fiscal 2010.

Finally, the annual report provides examples of how Del Monte is using the power of its brands to build success for its new product innovations. "In fiscal 2009 we added to our growing line of Del Monte Fruit Chillers frozen fruit sorbet products with Fruit Chillers Tubes, freeze-and-eat snacks that are kid-friendly and make it easy to have a healthy, tasty fruit-based dessert."

Brand Risk

The second area where we found discussions of brand value was in the "Risk Factors" section of annual filings. Here, Hasim and I needed to work a little harder to find examples, although we eventually did find a number of companies that seem to take the notion of brand shocks seriously, including Google and Target.

Google

Google, the organization whose name is often synonymous with "search," tops Millward Brown Optimor's brand value list, with $114 billion in value.

Google acknowledges its success in building an incredibly valuable brand without much in the way of the traditional marketing investments described by Del Monte. But it clearly recognizes and openly admits that it's because of its strong brand that it can expand its base of users, advertisers, network members, and business partners. It also notes that the importance of brand recognition will "increase due to the relatively low barriers to entry in the Internet market."[19]

In its 2009 annual report, Google devotes quite a bit of attention to the potential for the brand to be "negatively impacted" by a diverse set of factors. Its list includes many of the types of internal and external brand shocks that we discussed in chapters 3 and 4: service outages, other types of business interruption, product malfunctions, data privacy and security issues, failure to maintain its technology leadership position, inability to "continue to provide high-quality products and services," international operations (including governmental restrictions), intellectual property rights violation, "fraudulent clicks," and management of its hypergrowth.

Target

Target, a leading retailer, is another example of an organization that identifies brand risk as a key risk factor in its 2009 annual report. At the top of its list of brand risks is "our ability to remain relevant to our guests with a brand they trust."[20]

The annual report goes on to note the importance of preserving, growing, and leveraging the value of the Target brand, but notes that the value of the brand "is based in large part on perceptions of subjective qualities, and even isolated incidents that erode trust and confidence, particularly if they result in adverse publicity, governmental investigations or litigation."

Brand Value Tracking

Hasim and I had to work a lot harder to find examples in this category. Three of the organizations that caught our attention with their discussions about specific brand value metrics are BNP Paribas, Vodafone, and Philips.

BNP Paribas

Brand Finance is a global brand valuation consultancy that publishes annual rankings of brand value, much like the previously mentioned Millward Brown Optimor rankings.

In March 2008, BNP Paribas, a leading worldwide bank, issued a press release calling attention to Brand Finance's ranking of BNP Paribas in the top five worldwide banking brands in the retail banking segment, with a brand value of almost $9 billion.[21] In February 2010, BNP issued another press release announcing that it was ranked sixth in the global banking sector (not just the retail banking segment) in terms of brand value, just behind HSBC, Bank of America, Santander, Wells Fargo, and Citi—and that it was up two notches, from number 8 the prior year. This ranking corresponded to an increase in brand value from $9.4 billion in 2009 to $14.1 billion in 2010. The press release also noted that BNP Paribas is the number three brand in Europe and is number one in France.[22]

Vodafone

Vodafone, the mobile phone network operator, shows up as the tenth-ranked company on Millward Brown Optimor's BrandZ Top 100 list, with a brand value of $44.4 billion. Vodafone's 2010 annual report describes Vodafone's brand positioning around customer-centricity ("Power to you") and its focus on building "brand value by delivering a superior, consistent and differentiated customer experience."[23]

The annual report also describes Vodafone's practice of conducting brand health tracking "to measure the performance of the brand in each country and generate insights to manage the brand as effectively as possible." The report notes Vodaphone's "top ten position in a number of rankings of brands across all industries," specifically pointing to its ranking as the seventh-most-valuable brand in the world by Brand Finance.

Philips

Philips serves professional and consumer markets through three sectors: health care, lighting, and consumer lifestyle. Its 2009 annual report includes a chart showing year-to-year changes in brand value ($8.1 billion in 2009, according to Interbrand, another brand consultancy) and its forty-second-place ranking among the top one hundred global brands. Philips attributes an increase of 85 percent in its brand value over the preceding five years to its launch of a new brand promise ("Sense and Simplicity") and its success in translating this brand promise "into a positive customer experience designed around their needs."[24]

Philips's annual report also discusses two more areas where its practices put it close to or among leading companies. First, it describes how it has adopted Net Promoter scores (NPS) to measure customers' willingness to recommend Philips and its products and assess to what extent the company is meeting its "commitment to put people at the center of our thinking, to eliminate unnecessary complexity and to deliver the meaningful benefits of technology." Second, Philips describes its employee engagement survey, which includes questions regarding brand clarity and identification with the brand.

Finally, the Philips annual report includes brand risks in its discussions of risk factors. The first set of risks that it discusses have to do with the company's ability to capture profitable growth opportunities by leveraging its investment in its "Sense and Simplicity" brand campaign, "with a focus on simplifying the interaction with its customers, translating awareness into preference and improving its international brand recognition."

The second brand risk that Philips identifies is that its "brand image and reputation would be adversely impacted by non-compliance with the various [patient] data privacy and [medical] product security laws." It goes on to note that these risks "may arise with respect to remote access or monitoring of patient data or loss of data on customers' systems."

Frankly, we were surprised by how hard it was to find examples of annual reports that included explicit discussions about brand value metrics. Although the annual report is of course only one vehicle for organizations to share information, it is a central one. It seems extraordinary that this information is relatively hard to find, if we believe Millward Brown Optimor's assertion that 30 percent of total business value is attributable to brand.

BOARDS SHOULD PLAY A ROLE IN MEASURING AND TRACKING BRAND RESILIENCE

Our Deloitte colleagues who have made governance and risk management issues their life's work wax eloquent regarding the role of boards of directors.

They have published a number of books, articles, and whitepapers that discuss the concept of a Risk Intelligent Enterprise, all of which can be found on our website.[25] The premise of risk intelligence is that surviving and thriving in these uncertain and turbulent times requires calculated risk taking rather than risk avoidance. Risk intelligence is really about embedding risk capabilities throughout all levels of an organization and all core business processes so that the organization better understands and executes against the risk-reward tradeoffs. The result is improved resilience and agility.

Among the whitepapers created by the team are "Putting risk in the comfort zone: Nine principles for building the Risk Intelligent Enterprise"[26] and "Risk Intelligent governance: A practical guide for boards."[27] Many of the principles articulated in these whitepapers apply to brand risk management as well as to the broader set of risks that organizations face.

One of the key principles of risk intelligence is that the board should take a strong leadership role, with the objective of helping managers create a cohesive process in which risks and their effects are routinely identified, evaluated, and addressed. This role includes:

- Setting the expectations and tone for risk management
- Elevating risk as a priority
- Enabling the collection and dissemination of relevant metrics
- Initiating the communication and activities surrounding intelligent risk management

- Executing the risk-intelligent governance process by maintaining a disciplined, collaborative approach focused on process design, process monitoring, and accountability
- Fostering a culture that supports open discussion about uncertainties, encourages employees to express concerns, and makes it easy to elevate concerns to appropriate levels
- Helping management incorporate risk intelligence into strategy
- Helping define the risk "appetite"—that is, how much risk the brand can stomach

Ultimately, boards should insist that the organizations that they serve track measures of effectiveness and measures of performance. This means understanding both whether the right efforts are being made to manage brand risk and whether these efforts are producing the right outcomes. Unless the board makes this an organizational priority, they can't expect that anyone else will.

So here are some questions that any board member might want to ask regarding brand risk:

- Have we included brand risk in our overall risk intelligence program?
- Is brand risk management part of the board agenda?
- Do we regularly discuss brand risks, how management is handling brand risks, and brand risk scenarios?
- Are we helping to drive brand risk management and tracking activities, as well as processes to act upon this information?
- Have we ensured that brand risk management roles, responsibilities, and accountabilities are clearly defined and understood?

KEY TAKEAWAYS

WHAT WE KNOW...

- Building brand resilience measurement capabilities can be viewed as an evolutionary process that starts with capturing the voice of the customer.

- Getting insights into what happens on the front lines is a good place to start.

- Systematic tracking of brand value should become part of your brand resilience measurement and tracking program.

- Boards should play a role in measuring and tracking brand resilience.

...AND WHAT YOU CAN DO

- Assess where you stand today when it comes to
  - "voice of customer" data,
  - executive visibility into brand delivery,
  - brand value measurement,
  - tracking brand shocks,
  - executive group and board engagement in brand value discussions and decisions.

- If one is not already in place, consider a program for executives to gain firsthand visibility into what it takes to "deliver the brand."

- Start a program for measuring and tracking brand value. Consider incorporating measures of brand clarity and understanding into employee engagement surveys.

- Ask your chief risk officer to include brand risk management in the scope of his or her activities. At the board level:
  - Emphasize the importance of focusing on brand risks and ensure that management roles, responsibilities, and accountabilities for brand risk are clearly defined and understood.

KEY TAKEAWAYS CONTINUED

- Put brand risk on the board agenda.
- Regularly discuss brand risk scenarios and how management is handling brand risk.
- Promote measurement and tracking activities.

Chapter Ten

STEP SEVEN

Generate Popular Support for Your Brand Resilience Campaign

Insurgents and counterinsurgents seek to mobilize popular support for their cause. Both try to sustain that struggle while discouraging support for their adversaries.

—The Counterinsurgency Field Manual

Skillful counterinsurgents can deal a significant blow to an insurgency by appropriating its cause. Insurgents often exploit multiple causes, however, making counterinsurgents' challenges more difficult. In the end, any successful COIN operation must address the legitimate grievances insurgents use to generate popular support.

—The Counterinsurgency Field Manual

We have now arrived at the final set of activities associated with being a good brand counterinsurgent and the last in our seven-step brand resilience program: mobilizing popular support for your brand resilience efforts. There is no shortage of books, gurus, and service providers with strong points of view and ample advice on brand building, and many companies do an absolutely outstanding job with it. Given this, we have oriented much of the discussion in this book toward answering the question of what you can do to protect the fragile brands that are the source of so much value for organizations today—a question even organizations with the most respected and venerable brands must ask themselves.

However, this chapter will borrow some ideas from brand-building territory, since leveraging brand advocates is a key part of your overall counterinsurgency program. As useful as brand advocates can be for traditional brand building, they are even more crucial in supporting your brand resilience campaign.

BRAND RESILIENCE CAMPAIGNS THAT FAIL TO GAIN POPULAR SUPPORT, NO MATTER HOW ARTFUL, ARE UNLIKELY TO SUCCEED

If you need an example of a well-fought counterinsurgency effort that failed due to lack of popular support, take a close look at the conflict between France and colonial Algeria from 1954 to 1962. Algeria became a French military colony in the 1830s and became a part of France (an overseas department, technically) in the 1840s. The insurrection that began in 1954 with attacks by National Liberation Front guerillas on French military and civilian targets culminated in Algerian independence in 1962.

The 1966 Italian film *The Battle of Algiers* tells a good part of this story in a very graphic and compelling manner.[1] Though fictional, the film is based on actual events that took place between 1954 and 1960. Filmed in black and white, it has the look and feel of a newsreel or a documentary, though the characters are composites of real people and the details of events are altered slightly to support the overall narrative.

In the movie, as in reality, French paratroopers attempt to neutralize the insurgent National Liberation Front through assassinations, summary executions, torture, intimidation, and other violent tactics. While their efforts are initially successful, the French never gain the support of the masses; rather, the masses begin to actively support the insurgents. The movie ends with a series of demonstrations and riots that set the stage for Algerian independence.

The underlying theme of the film is that counterinsurgency efforts that rely purely on superior force are not sustainable. In fact, the film argues, superior force applied inappropriately can easily backfire and create even more support for insurgents and their causes.

The movie has become the cinematic version of a field manual on how not to run a counterinsurgency campaign. Although *The Counterinsurgency Field Manual* does not mention the movie in its body text, its annotated bibliography includes an entry for Alastair Horne's book *A Savage War of Peace*—"one of the best analyses of the approaches and problems on both sides during the war in Algeria"—that refers readers to the movie for more on the conflict, describing *The Battle of Algiers* as "troubling and instructive."[2]

In 2003, the Pentagon arranged for its senior officers to screen the film, as a way to stimulate dialogue about how to deal with insurgencies. Reportedly, the flyer announcing the screening included the following description: "Children shoot soldiers at point-blank range. Women plant bombs in cafes. Soon the entire Arab population builds to a mad fervor. Sound familiar?"[3]

According to an article by Michael Kaufman that appeared in the *New York Times* shortly after the screening, "The Pentagon's showing drew a more professionally detached audience of about 40 officers and civilian experts who were urged to consider and discuss the implicit issues at the core of the film—the problematic but alluring efficacy of brutal and repressive means in fighting clandestine terrorists in places like Algeria and Iraq. Or more specifically, the advantages and costs of resorting to torture and intimidation in seeking vital human intelligence about enemy plans."[4]

The following year, the movie was re-released to the general public. Based on what we read about the Pentagon screening, my wife and I added *The Battle of Algiers* to our queue of movies to watch. We found it incredibly powerful, in part because it is sufficiently nuanced to avoid romanticizing or demonizing either the Algerian insurgents or the French. I found myself agreeing wholeheartedly with Ann Hornaday's comment in the January 9, 2004, issue of the *Washington Post*: "The greatness of 'The Battle of Algiers' lies in its ability to embrace moral ambiguity without succumbing to it."[5]

If *The Battle of Algiers* shows the consequences of failing to gain popular support, what's the alternative?

BRAND ADVOCATES CAN SOMETIMES BE FOUND IN UNEXPECTED PLACES

Brand advocates provide an alternative to the *Battle of Algiers* dilemma. Let's start with a definition. An advocate, simply put, is an individual who speaks, pleads, or argues in favor of a cause or on another individual's behalf. So what do we mean by brand advocates?

Blackcoffee, a "brand expression" consultancy, defines brand advocates as individuals who preach the merits of a given brand with prompting, and distinguishes between brand advocates and brand enthusiasts, who require no such prompting.[6] While we understand their distinction, in an effort to keep things simple, we'll use "brand advocacy" to refer to both prompted and unprompted preaching. The Net Promoter methodology that we discussed in chapter 9 is one way to measure the support for your brand among current users. But since non-users and non-buyers may never show up in measures like Net Promoter, we will also apply Blackcoffee's maxim that brand enthusiasts need not be buyers, users, or even beneficiaries of the brand to be brand advocates.

Earlier, we introduced the terms "brand saboteurs" and "brand shocks." A brand advocate is the opposite of a brand saboteur and has the opposite effect on your business.

Level of support for your brand

Figure 10.1 How individuals interact with your brand

We also discussed the degree of intentionality associated with brand saboteurs. As we pointed out, the damage that some saboteurs do may be completely unintentional or the byproduct of other activities. (Remember our hapless restaurant workers from chapter 8?) The same can be said about brand advocates. They may wind up creating great value for a brand without intending to do so—we'll see an example in just a few moments. As with brand saboteurs, brand advocates' intentions may have little to do with their impact.

The 2010 midterm elections provided an unbelievably powerful example of how unintentional brand advocacy can work. Enter President Barack Obama and the Slurpee. A Slurpee, as you may know, is a frozen carbonated beverage that is available only at 7-Eleven stores. It has the consistency of a soda left in the freezer and taken out just before it was fully frozen.[7] Although the drink was accidentally invented in the 1950s by a Dairy Queen franchisee, it was licensed to 7-Eleven, and Bob Stanford, a 7-Eleven agency director, coined the name Slurpee in 1967, supposedly to describe the sound that you make while drinking one.

During the campaign leading up to the midterm elections, Obama described Republicans as standing around "sipping Slurpees" while he and Democrats were busy trying to fix the economy. His remark, a somewhat derisive reference, in our opinion, was widely repeated in print and broadcast media. Apparently, the Slurpee slam didn't sway the electorate. The election yielded less-than-favorable results for the Democrats and the president, including the loss of control of the House of Representatives and the loss of a significant number of seats in the Senate.

The day after the election, the idea of a "Slurpee Summit," bringing together the new Republican leadership with the president, surfaced at a presidential news conference. Then, in a moment that 7-Eleven executives may remember forever, the president referred to Slurpee as "a very delicious drink." Imagine your delight when the most powerful man in the country describes your product as "a very delicious drink." As Bruce Horovitz wrote in a *USA Today* article, titled "Obama's 'Slurpee Summit' joke makes icy drink hot," which appeared the following day, "President Obama has just given Slurpee something it could never buy: global street cred."[8]

That's unintentional brand advocacy in action, for sure! We can't imagine that the president spent a lot of time considering the commercial consequences of his remark. But 7-Eleven could not have asked for a better marketing platform. The company responded with immediate action. "We are not surprised by President Obama's comments about Slurpee, which is nonpartisan and has been bringing people together for more than 40 years," said Joe DePinto, 7-Eleven's president and CEO, in a press release. "We have made an offer to the White House to install Slurpee machines and to host a Slurpee Summit."[9] The company also launched the "Slurpee Unity Tour 2010," in which Slurpee trucks drove from Dallas to Washington, D.C., offering free samples.[10]

Horovitz quotes Margaret Chabris, a 7-Eleven spokesperson, in his article. "This is a rare opportunity for a brand. We don't want to be opportunistic, but nothing has ever been this big for Slurpee... If the president wants a Slurpee Summit, we're offering to cater it with red and blue Slurpees—and we'll even offer a purple Slurpee, since that's what you get when you bring red and blue together."[11]

The Battle of Algiers illustrates what happens when you fail to win popular support and the Slurpee incident exemplifies the positive impact of brand advocacy. The question for you is how to avoid the former like the plague and secure more of the latter.

NEVER TAKE A BRAND ADVOCATE FOR GRANTED—BRAND ADVOCATES CAN BE FICKLE, AND TODAY'S BRAND ADVOCATE COULD BE TOMORROW'S BRAND SABOTEUR

Brand advocates can turn on you, quickly, viciously, and unexpectedly. Sometimes it's benign neglect. The television talk show host who touts your book today is under no obligation to praise it tomorrow. The celebrity who patronizes your restaurant today may never show up again. Sometimes, it's more damaging. The reviewer who loved your last product and praised it lavishly on her website may hate your newest product and savage you on that very same website without hesitation. The "mommy blogger" who helped defend you against consumers who disliked your newly reformulated product joins the Greek chorus of critics when she dislikes the new packaging for another product. When it comes to brand advocates, memories can sometimes be short-lived.

HOWEVER, BRAND ADVOCATES CAN BE POWERFUL ADDITIONS TO YOUR COUNTERINSURGENCY ARSENAL

In early 2010, two of our colleagues, Pat Conroy and Anupam Narula, published a whitepaper examining the behavior of brand advocates. Their paper, titled "A new breed of brand advocates: Social networking redefines customer engagement," argues that "although many companies are actively engaging consumers through social media to shape their brands, there are some consumers who, while not being primarily targeted by companies, are nonetheless proactively offering and sharing their opinions. Consequently, there is a group of consumers that is shaping brands through advocacy and critiques, enabled by social media."[12]

The paper summarizes the results of a survey, conducted in August 2009, of more than 1,700 consumers across the United States, regarding their activities in three consumer-product categories: salty snacks, all-purpose household cleaners, and beer. The survey focused just on users of these categories, not the broader universe of brand advocates.

As a result of their analysis, they identified four characteristics of brand advocates:

- They have a favorite brand.
- They spend an above-average amount of money on the category (approximately twice as much as the average consumer).
- They allocate more than half of their spending in the category to their favorite brand.
- They engage with the brand more often than the average consumer (two to three times as much), in the following ways:
  - Recommending products and sharing them with other consumers (two to four times as often as the average consumer)
  - Seeking information and interacting
  - Providing input to the brand
  - Paying a premium or purchasing more products when they're on sale

Five percent of the respondents who purchased salty snacks and household cleaning solutions qualified as advocates, and 12 percent who purchased beer did so. Conroy and Narula determined that brand advocates are worth twice as much as the average consumer in terms of the revenue they generate for you, even without including the significant potential value of their advocacy. They estimate that increasing the number of advocates by 50 percent results in market share increases of 3 percent for household cleaners, 4 percent for salty snacks, and 9 percent for beer. To put that into perspective, a 1 percent market-share gain in the beer category in the United States is worth $990 million.

Clearly, having these brand advocates on your side when a brand shock takes place would be highly advantageous. As our colleagues ask at the end of their article, "The question is, how will you influence the influencers?"

INFLUENCING BRAND ADVOCATES IS HARD WORK

So, all you need to do is find these high-spending brand advocates and enlist them in your cause, right? Of course, this is easier said than done. As Marta Strickland notes, in an article titled "Five brand advocacy myths," "Brand advocacy is a term that is thrown around a lot within the social media spectrum. Conversations usually center on finding brand advocates who will serve as a social media lightning rod and generate an avalanche of user-generated content from a community based on their actions. Marketers are just as likely to find these mythical advocates as they are to track down Big Foot riding a unicorn."[13]

Perhaps organizations can take a page from the playbook of nongovernmental organizations. NGOs such as the United Nations Children's Fund (UNICEF), are accustomed to developing grassroots support for a cause. UNICEF's term for this activity is "social mobilization," which it defines as "a process that engages and motivates a wide range of partners and allies at national and local levels to raise awareness of and demand for a particular development objective through face-to-face dialogue. Members of institutions, community networks, civic and religious groups and others work in a coordinated way to reach specific groups of people for dialogue with planned messages."[14]

Some companies take the approach of aligning with a cause. If the alignment comes across as authentic, consumers who share that alignment will likely be staunch brand advocates when the chips are down. The challenge, as Jeremy Heimans and Alnoor Ladha point out in their article "The New Rules for Purpose-Driven Brands," is that "What was even five years ago a source of competitive advantage and differentiation for forward-thinking brands is now just the status- quo. The risk this creates is [that this] will leave consumers feeling jaded and desensitized—and less primed for outreach from well-intentioned brands."[15]

Heimans and Ladha argue that cause-related advocacy requires true enterprise-level commitment, with real and meaningful consumer engagement. They point to Dove's multiyear, multifaceted "Campaign for Real Beauty" as a leading and effective practice. The campaign, which was launched in 2004, focuses on helping women enjoy confidence in her own beauty. According to its website, "Dove educates and encourages the next generation to build a positive relationship with beauty. Through our online tools and workshops, we support women to act as mentors for girls growing up today. Together with our partners, we have touched the lives of millions of girls to date, equipping them with critical media literacy skills and self-esteem education to help them reach their full potential."[16]

Nike is another brand that takes corporate responsibility very seriously. Nike's website articulates its point of view that "[c]orporate responsibility must evolve from being seen as an unwanted cost to being recognized as an intrinsic part of a healthy business model, an investment that creates competitive advantage and helps a company achieve profitable, sustainable growth."[17] The website also contains a comprehensive 170-plus page report that describes Nike's corporate responsibility strategy, as well as its activities relative to workers and factories, the environment, communities, people and culture, and public policy and advocacy.[18]

One example of this commitment is the investments that Nike began making in 2005, through its foundation, in " 'The Girl Effect': the ability of adolescent girls in developing countries to bring unprecedented social and economic change to their families, communities and countries."[19] The focus is on providing education to these girls, given studies that have shown the beneficial effects of increased education on health and income.

A second challenge of enlisting brand advocates is more operational in nature: finding brand advocates and managing relationships with them over time. This will be addressed largely by advances in software technology. In our research, numerous small venture-backed companies are competing in this space, and more will certainly emerge in the next few years. It's interesting to observe the various spins that these companies put on their offerings, all of which seem to share common functionality, centered on identifying brand advocates, mobilizing these advocates, and tracking their activities. Many of these technology providers are members of the Word of Mouth Marketing Association (WOMMA), a "non-profit organization dedicated to advancing and advocating the discipline of credible word of mouth marketing, both offline and online."[20] WOMMA describes itself as "dedicated to building strong discipline within the word of mouth marketing industry...[and] helping to create a prosperous word of mouth marketing profession based on ethical leadership, measurable ROI, best practices, and a more honest and open relationship between marketers and consumers."[21]

Here are three examples of technology solutions, literally ranging from A to Z. We mean not to endorse any specific option but merely to offer examples of the solutions that are currently available.

Affinitive[22]

Affinitive, founded in 2002 by Bob Troia, "engages, empowers, and connects passionate consumers by giving them the tools to express their passion for the brands, products, services, and causes they love, thereby cultivating conversation, long-lasting loyalty, and sustained awareness."[23]

Affinitive's core technology is Enclave, which it describes as a "consumer engagement platform." Capabilities supported through Enclave include an affinity-based community/social networking platform (e.g., enhanced profiles, event management), research capabilities (e.g., polling, surveys), content management for consumer-generated content, viral and buzz marketing support, activity management (e.g., tracking participation in activities that foster loyalty), reporting, and CRM integration.

Affinitive's website features a long list of industry solutions, including automotive, consumer products, fashion and beauty, food and beverage, hospitality and travel, media and entertainment, mobile and telecom, publishing, retail, sports and leisure, and video games, as well as case studies of effective applications.

Mobilization Labs[24]

Another technology solution currently in the market is the Wildfire Platform from Mobilization Labs. Mobilization Labs brands itself as "The Science of People in Action." It does not currently show up on WOMMA's member list.

Mobilization Labs is an Atlanta-based company founded in 2005 by Caleb Clark and Joe Uhl. Mobilization Labs claims that

> we have pioneered a new genre of technology called social mobilization and productized this methodology into a software service known as the Wildfire platform...We were the first to introduce social mobilization technology...to the political market, using social networks and the internet to build support bases around candidates and their ideas. It has been used by gubernatorial, senatorial, and US Presidential campaigns across the country, and it has also spread far beyond politics. Wildfire powers many of today's grassroots-driven initiatives including platinum recording artists, large non-profit organizations, and Fortune 1000 companies.

Mobilization Labs describes its toolset using terms familiar to political campaigns and social movements—a personal impact engine "to measure and rank your supporters' impact and recognize and reward them for their contributions," a community "headquarters" where supporters can connect and engage, tools that allow supporters to recruit their teams, an activity tracker that tracks the actions of supporters, supporter profiles that help see who they are, who they know, and what they've done, real-time reporting and analytics dashboards, a mobilization tool that assigns tasks to supporters, and micro-targeted communications.

"Wildfire for Corporations" talks about creating loyal brand advocates through a series of processes—creating communities, moving supporters into action, and measuring progress, all with the goal of launching new products, recruiting new brand advocates, getting the right messaging out, and building the brand.

Zuberance[25]

Zuberance, a venture-backed firm founded in 2007 by Rob Fuggetta, a former partner in Silicon Valley marketing and communications firm Regis McKenna, won Forrester's 2009 Groundswell Award in the Energizing B2C category.

Zuberance's Advocate Platform is another example of a technology solution focused on mobilizing brand advocates. Zuberance describes brand advocates as "highly-satisfied customers and others who proactively recommend brands and products online and offline without being paid to do so." Fuggetta's whitepaper "What's a Brand Advocate Worth?"[26] argues that brand advocates are worth five times the average customer due to higher spend value and "advocacy" value. The paper includes a "Zuberance Brand Advocate Value Calculator."

Zuberance describes its Advocate Platform as "a hosted Word of Mouth marketing solution that makes it easy for companies to systematically: identify Brand Advocates by name and email address, mobilize Brand Advocates to spread positive Word of Mouth and help generate sales, and track Brand Advocate marketing programs and results in real-time plus capture unique, actionable Advocate insights."

The platform includes:

- Advocate apps that make it easy for advocates to create and publish reviews, testimonials, answers to prospects' questions, plus share promotional offers with their social networks
- Marketer tools that enable marketers to create, launch, and manage advocate marketing programs and campaigns
- An advocacy engine that enables marketers to reliably scale and track effectiveness of advocate marketing programs
- Advocate insights that enable marketers to capture unique, actionable insights about advocates

Given our current fascination with brand sabotage, we found it interesting that none of the brand advocacy technologies that we looked at explicitly discuss using these tools to activate the "volunteer army" on behalf of a company that has experienced a brand shock. For the most part, the capabilities described by the websites of the various vendors focus on what you can do to build the brand rather than defend the brand, although it's fairly intuitive that these same capabilities might be employed to support a brand resilience campaign. We suspect this is the result of the same brand sabotage myopia that pervades many corporate marketing functions—which is why we're writing this book!

But regardless of what the consultants say, clearly some marketers are figuring out how to activate this volunteer army. If you remember the Pampers story from chapter 4, you may also remember that one of the tactics employed by Proctor & Gamble was to enlist "mommy bloggers" to tell P&G's side of the story regarding the true causes of the diaper rash attributed to the reformulated product. We will soon see much more of this tactic: using the brand community and brand advocates to help get the word out in response to brand shocks, like digital smoke signals.

The other opportunity for brands may lie in helping their advocates identify what's really going on, and identify potential solutions to the brand shocks. The October 2008 issue of the *Harvard Business Review* contains an article, "The Contribution Revolution: Letting Volunteers Build Your Business," by Scott Cook, Intuit's cofounder. In it, Cook talks about his own personal revelation that if you're not spending time thinking of "ways that people outside the company could volunteer their time, energy, and expertise to make life better for [your] customers…you risk missing the boat on a sea change that's transforming business." Cook goes on to talk about how the leading companies are consciously creating "user contribution systems" for "aggregating and leveraging people's contributions or behaviors in ways that are useful to other people."[27]

When it comes to "user contribution systems" for brand resilience, we offer up two suggestions. First, get your brand advocates to participate in your early warning systems, as described in chapter 6. Leverage their distributed presence to help you identify issues and potential brand shocks in the marketplace early in the cycle. Think of them as volunteer forest rangers in your fight to detect and control the devastating fires that could, if left unaddressed, engulf and consume your brand. Second, use your brand advocates to suggest solutions to these problems as they arise. One example of an organization that has done an effective job of tapping into the knowledge of its community of customers, partners, employees, and experts, is SAP and its SAP Community Network, or SCN (www.sdn.sap.com). SAP describes SCN as "SAP's professional social network. It provides trusted connections to our dynamic community…[and] delivers an unparalleled depth and breadth of knowledge, insight and rich content about SAP solutions and services, in a collaborative environment that encourages innovation and sharing of best-run business practices."[28]

SCN currently has more than 2 million members. The currency of the network is recognition points—no trips to Hawaii or lavish dinners, just badges that acknowledge one's contributions on SCN and the opportunity to establish oneself as an expert. This may not sound like a lot, but it works, and appears to work well—questions posed to this volunteer army are answered in a matter of moments, thanks to the efforts of SCN members.

It works for Wikipedia, it works for SCN, and it can work for you.

KEY TAKEAWAYS

WHAT WE KNOW...	...AND WHAT YOU CAN DO
■ Brand resilience campaigns that fail to gain popular support, no matter how artful, are unlikely to succeed.	■ Build a plan for gaining popular support into your brand resilience program.
■ Brand advocates can sometimes be found in unexpected places.	■ Make efforts to systematically identify brand advocates and associated allies.
■ Never take a brand advocate for granted—brand advocates can be fickle, and today's brand advocate could be tomorrow's brand saboteur.	■ Pay particular attention to any grievances your brand advocates may have so that you don't inadvertently convert them to brand saboteurs.
■ However, brand advocates can be powerful additions to your counterinsurgency arsenal.	■ Start developing a plan for calling on your brand advocates to help you respond to brand shocks, including playing a role in your early warning system and developing solutions to bona fide problems.

PART THREE

A GLANCE AHEAD

Chapter Eleven

LOOKING BACKWARD, LOOKING FORWARD

A counterinsurgency campaign is...a mix of offensive, defensive, and stability operations conducted along multiple lines of operations. It requires Soldiers and Marines to employ a mix of familiar combat tasks and skills...It requires leaders at all levels to adjust their approach constantly. They should ensure that their Soldiers and Marines are ready to be greeted with either a handshake or a hand grenade while taking on missions...Conducting an effective counterinsurgency campaign requires a flexible, adaptive force led by agile, well-informed, culturally astute leaders.
—The Counterinsurgency Field Manual

In this book, we've asked you to take a journey with us, one we hope will shake up your thinking about building and maintaining strong brands.

We are now close to the end of this journey. So let's take this time to review what we've learned—what it takes to be effective with your brand resilience efforts today, and what's likely to change over the next few years in the brand resilience landscape.

We introduced the book with the story of Tiger Woods and his unfortunate encounter with a fire hydrant over the 2009 Thanksgiving weekend. This seemingly minor car accident set off a chain-reaction of events that led a number of market-leading brands to abandon Woods as their marketing avatar.

Whatever the personal consequence, the economic consequences of Woods's accident were significant enough to bring the issue of brand sabotage into sharp focus. Woods's "Escalade Escapade" is just the tip of the iceberg in a world fraught with brand risk.

In chapter 1, we explored the growth of brand value in recent history, as well as the fragility of brands. The paradox that increased value means increased fragility makes the protection of these brands critical.

In chapter 2, we offered up a new vision of marketing as warfare—marketing as counterinsurgency. Using the insights developed by the Army and Marine Corps *Counterinsurgency Field Manual*, we developed a seven-step program for managing brand risk and recovery (Figure 11.1), starting with an assessment of the internal and external risks.

In chapters 3 and 4, we discussed the actual risks that your brand might face, both the internal risks, from employees, executives, and value chain partners, and the external risks, from customers, reviewers, gadflies and ideologues, and competitors. One of the key points we made in these chapters is that brand risks are inherent in doing business. If you operate a business, you will have brand risks. The only way to avoid brand risks is to stop operating. The goal, therefore, is not to eliminate brand risks, but to develop the capabilities to manage these risks intelligently. The second key point we made, implicit in the first, is that brand risks are not purely by-products of social media. Brand risks existed long before Twitter,

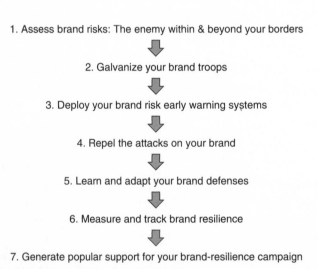

1. Assess brand risks: The enemy within & beyond your borders

2. Galvanize your brand troops

3. Deploy your brand risk early warning systems

4. Repel the attacks on your brand

5. Learn and adapt your brand defenses

6. Measure and track brand resilience

7. Generate popular support for your brand-resilience campaign

Figure 11.1   Brand resilience: A seven-step program for managing brand risk and recovery

Facebook, and the like were even twinkles in the eyes of their inventors. Social media do not cause brand risk but can certainly amplify it. By the same token, social media can enhance awareness within the organization of brand risks.

In chapter 5, we talked about the importance of enlisting your employees in your brand resilience efforts. We suggested that the three critical ingredients for effectively engaging your brand troops are a clear mission, a purposeful outreach program, and a strategy for employee ownership of the mission.

Chapter 6 introduced the concept of a brand resilience early warning system as a way to help you gain early visibility into insurgent activities. We talked about the challenges that many organizations have in recognizing that their brands are under attack, and we explored the opportunities for crowdsourcing your intelligence efforts, just as the US Geological Survey is trying to do with earthquake detection. We also covered options for acquiring early warning system capabilities through third-party solutions.

Chapter 7 covered how you can respond once you're actually under attack. We described the brand attack as an event, which we called a "brand shock," with the opportunity for pre- and post-event actions. We called this series of events and actions the "brand shock time continuum" and suggested that there may be a lag between when you first become aware of a brand shock and when awareness spreads to the public. In this chapter, we identified the three levers for responding to brand shocks—repentance, remediation, and rectification—and when to pull these levers. We also stressed the importance of maintaining your brand narrative throughout the entire sequence of events, from brand shock to post-event actions.

Chapter 8 dealt with developing your capabilities to learn from each brand shock and adapting your defenses accordingly. We argued that the "learn and adapt" model requires a hard-nosed look at what really happened, analogous to the way the National Transportation Safety Board investigates every civil aviation accident in the United States. We stressed the need for strong executive leadership to demonstrate the "learn and adapt" strategy. We also stressed the importance of aligning the changes you make, based on your internal analyses of brand shocks, with what really matters to customers.

Chapter 9 focused on measuring and tracking the effectiveness of your brand resilience activities to avoid falling into the trap identified by baseball legend Yogi Berra: "You've got to be very careful if you don't know where you're going, because you might not get there." We talked about the ways companies adapt their measurement capabilities over time, usually beginning with qualitative assessments before developing the kind of rigor and discipline involved in the CompStat approach used by most major metropolitan police departments. We looked at recent annual reports from large companies and made comparisons among annual reports that exhibit each of three main focuses: brand building, calibrating brand risks, and tracking measurements of brand value, including employee brand understanding.

Chapter 10 tackled the challenge of generating popular support for your brand resilience campaign. We talked about what happens to counterinsurgency campaigns that fail to generate popular support. We also discussed the concept of brand advocates and how brand advocates can play a role in supporting brands. We provided examples of both unintentional and intentional brand advocates and shared an analysis developed by our colleagues on the value of brand advocates. We concluded with a discussion about approaches for gaining the support of brand advocates, as well as the emerging technology tools that try to tap in to the passion and energy of brand advocates.

We introduced each chapter with excerpts from *The Counterinsurgency Field Manual* because we believe that the counterinsurgency metaphor is a powerful and compelling one for thinking about the threats that brands face and the challenges of responding. *The Counterinsurgency Field Manual* also offers valuable insight into the importance of evolving your brand defense strategies: counterinsurgency is a learning competition, and "the side that learns faster and adapts more rapidly—the better learning organization—usually wins."

In addition to a "learn and adapt" mindset, what else will it take to increase the likelihood of effective brand resilience efforts?

Here is our list of key success factors for brand resilience:

1. **Manage your brand resilience efforts programmatically.**
   Develop formal brand resilience plans. Define your brand resilience processes. Assign brand resilience roles and responsibilities. Establish and track brand resilience metrics.

Just acknowledging that brand risk is an issue and announcing your intentions to deal with it are insufficient. An article by Elizabeth Lux on brand value, which appeared in the October 6, 2010 issue of the *Wall Street Journal*, makes this point. Lux argues that "while it is relatively easy to talk about reputation risk in the abstract, it is far harder to protect against it in practice. A recent survey conducted by Airmic, the association for insurance and risk managers, frames the conundrum well. Of those who took part in the poll, 80% claimed that reputational risk is their top concern. However, only 43% believed that they have formal and well-managed plans in place to tackle it."[1]

2. **Make sure that your brand resilience program doesn't become just another employee chore.**
Embed brand resilience capabilities into your risk management and brand management programs. Inculcate the need for brand resilience in the minds of your employees. Include brand resilience on the agenda for board meetings.

If brands are as valuable as the experts claim, isn't it essential to link your brand resilience efforts with all of your operations and governance processes?

3. **Open up your brand resilience program.**
Get help internally and externally. Communicate accomplishments, but make sure that you also communicate challenges. Cast the net broadly to find solutions to brand shocks.

4. **Avoid the temptation to view brand sabotage as just a social media problem.**
Brand resilience is not just about managing the adverse impact of social media. If you concentrate all of your brand resilience efforts on social media, you'll be unprepared for a broad range of potentially much more devastating brand shocks.

5. **Assume that tomorrow's brand shocks will look different from today's.**
Learn and adapt, but recognize that insurgents are also learning and adapting. The sooner you learn to defend yourself from one type of brand shock, insurgents will adapt and launch entirely different types of attacks.

WHAT WILL CHANGE IN THE FUTURE?

It's unlikely that incidents of brand sabotage will decrease. My expectation is that we will see more and more incidents over the coming three to five years, largely facilitated by high-speed mobile networks capable of rapidly disseminating high-definition video and data.

Several areas will likely continue to be problematic for companies as they work to reduce the potential for brand sabotage. Here are four you will likely be dealing with for the foreseeable future:

- The management of extended supply chains, particularly, product safety and sustainability. Expect to see more reports of unsafe and contaminated products and on non-sustainable or unpopular practices on the part of suppliers.
- The idea of privacy, mostly as it pertains to collecting, managing, and sharing customer and prospect data. A particularly prickly area will be location-based information, which is currently seen as the Holy Grail by many marketers. In 2010, the *Wall Street Journal* ran a major, nine-part investigative series on privacy, the first part of which was titled, "The Web's New Gold Mine: Your Secrets." This article described the results of a survey that the newspaper had conducted about the broad array of cookies and other surveillance technology that companies are deploying on Internet users (with or without their knowledge). One of the findings of the study was that "the nation's 50 top websites on average installed 64 pieces of tracking technology onto the computers of visitors, usually with no warning. A dozen sites each installed more than a hundred."[2] Expect to see more reports of companies violating either explicit or implicit expectations regarding privacy. Expect to see calls for greater legislative controls, as well as attempts by corporations to thwart regulation through self-policing activities and standards.
- The scrutiny of employee behavior, ranging from frontline employees to senior executives. Expect to see preemptive measures on the part of organizations, including a much greater emphasis on codes of conduct and training.
- The disclosure of highly confidential information. In 2010, WikiLeaks reminded us how it feels when information that you thought was confidential is broadly released. Expect additional leaks of embarrassing and brand-damaging information and plans that you never intended to disclose publicly.

ON THE FLIP SIDE, HOW WILL ORGANIZATIONS RESPOND?

Here's our list of tools and strategies you can expect to see companies deploy in defense of their brands:

- Greater use of technology solutions to detect incidents of brand sabotage. In chapter 6, we described some of the tools that are currently available. Our best guess is that many of these solutions will be incorporated into existing technology platforms. Wouldn't monitoring capabilities be an obvious extension of Google's current search capabilities?
- Increased focus on the development of programs and the adoption of technologies designed to identify, mobilize, and track the activities of brand advocates
- More frequent mentions of brand value and brand risk in company communications, such as annual reports, including formal tracking of brand value metrics
- More frequent appearance of brand-related discussions on board agendas
- More frequent inclusion of brand risk in overall risk management programs and priorities
- More rigorous policies and processes related to the creation and handling of confidential information about your brand

One of the scary elements of brand sabotage is that the digital trail will be more and more difficult to erase. Brand shocks that might have faded away quickly in earlier times are now likely to persist for a long time to come.

A FINAL WORD

We have been thinking about the topics of brand sabotage and brand resilience for almost two years. When we initially started talking to our colleagues and acquaintances about these topics, we received glimmers of recognition and some head-nodding, but no real traction.

It took us a little while to clarify our definition and gather a few illustrative examples. Most of our initial examples were related to social media in one way or another, and our listeners often jumped to the conclusion that that's what brand sabotage and brand resilience are all about. This was particularly true for colleagues and acquaintances who were too young to remember many of the older examples, such as the 1982 Tylenol scare.

Tiger Woods's accident really crystallized the issue for me, inasmuch as the impact was swifter and more significant than anything else in recent memory. Suddenly, we had an accessible example that almost everyone could relate to, golf fan or not, because of Tiger Woods's ubiquity in advertising. One day, it was hard to avoid ads with his image. Three months later, it was hard to find one.

Other incidents that took place subsequent to the Tiger Woods accident hammered home our point about brand sabotage. Contaminated food. Product defects and recalls. The ouster of corporate and political leaders who behaved badly. WikiLeaks, or what the *Wall Street Journal* described as "wilding on the web."[3] We no longer needed to spend as much time explaining the concept of brand sabotage as we had a year earlier. People got it because they started to see powerful examples happening every day.

That's why so many of the examples in this book are literally ripped from the headlines. Every day as we perused the *New York Times* or the *Wall Street Journal*, we inevitably found more instances to prove our point. Our pile of clippings grew larger and larger. It became harder and harder to avoid seeing brand sabotage everywhere we turned.

When we first started to write this book, our focus was very much on the phenomenon of brand sabotage. But with the encouragement of many colleagues and friends, we realized that in order for the book to be useful in the unpredictable years ahead, it must also focus on what companies can do to respond. We convinced ourselves, and we hope now you as well, that the phenomenon is very real, but also very manageable.

We started the book with the story of Tiger Woods's accident and its aftermath. The irony of the accident as a brand debacle is perfectly captured by the tag line of the professional services firm that had featured Woods in its advertising for so long—seven words that capture the essence of this book's message with respect to brand sabotage: "It's what you do next that counts."

FURTHER READING

Branding is not a new topic. The market is filled with books and publications on brand building that complement *Brand Resilience*'s focus on managing brand risk and recovery.

David Aaker is a prolific and highly regarded author widely acknowledged as a thought leader in the area of branding. An emeritus professor at the Haas School of Business at the University of California—Berkeley and vice chairman of Prophet, Aaker has authored fourteen books and more than one hundred articles related to marketing and branding. Some of his better-known brand-related books are *Managing Brand Equity* (Free Press, 1991), *Building Strong Brands* (Free Press, 1995), *Brand Portfolio Strategy* (Free Press, 2004), and *From Fargo to the World of Brands* (Iceni, 2005). Aaker's most recent book, *Brand Leadership* (coauthored with Erich Joachimsthaler) discusses the elements of brand leadership, including defining and elaborating a brand identity; designing the brand's architecture to achieve clarity, synergy, and leverage; building a brand beyond the obvious route of advertising by incorporating such aspects as sponsorship and the role of the Internet; and organizing the entire company around global brand leadership.

Marty Neumeier, who contributed the foreword to this book, is another prolific author and thought leader on the subject of branding. Marty, a designer by trade and inclination, focuses on bridging the gap between brand strategy and brand execution. Marty's books include *The Brand Gap: How to Bridge the Distance Between Business Strategy and Design* (New Riders Press, 2003), *The Dictionary of Brand* (AIGA Center for Brand Experience, 2004), and *Zag: The Number One Strategy of High-Performance Brands* (Peachpit Press, 2006). In *Brand Gap*, Marty explains brand building through five disciplines of differentiation, collaboration, innovation, validation, and cultivation. The book is quick and compelling in its attempts to render some practicality to the theory of brand management.

Allen Adamson has authored a pair of books (both published by Palgrave Macmillan, the publisher of this book) on branding that you may find beneficial. With the mantra "Simple trumps everything," Adamson boils down his twenty-five-plus years of experience in brand development to provide six steps to understanding what makes a good brand in *BrandSimple: How the Best Brands Keep it Simple and Succeed* (2007). In *BrandDigital: Simple Ways Top Brands Succeed in the Digital World* (2009), Adamson explores the new digital branding landscape, and its plethora of choices and new terminology, citing corporations such as Nike, Procter & Gamble, and Unilever to demonstrate how the best marketers are using digital tools to build and manage their brands.

The Brand Bubble, by John Gerzema and Ed Lebar (Jossey-Bass, 2008), discusses how brands have increased in value despite ebbing consumer interest and trust, raising the specter of commoditization. Gerzema and Lebar go on to discuss how certain brands achieve "energized differentiation" and provide extensive advice on how to conduct energy audits and reenergize moribund ideas.

Other books to consider on branding include:

- A pair by Al Ries and Jack Trout (coauthors of *Marketing Warfare*, which we discussed in chapter 2): *The 22 Immutable Laws of Marketing: Violate Them at Your Own Risk!* (Harper Business, 1994) and *Positioning: The Battle for Your Mind* (McGraw-Hill, 2000)
- *A New Brand World: Eight Principles for Achieving Brand Leadership in the 21st Century* (Penguin, 2003) by Scott Bedbury and Stephen Fenichell
- *Emotional Branding: The New Paradigm for Connecting Brands to People* (Allworth Press, 2010) by Marc Gobé
- *How Brands Become Icons: The Principles of Cultural Branding* (Harvard Business Press, 2004) by Douglas Holt
- *Kellogg on Branding: The Marketing Faculty of the Kellogg School of Management* (Wiley, 2005), edited by Tim Calkins and Alice Tybout
- *Married to the Brand: Why Consumers Bond with Some Brands for Life* (Gallup Press, 2005) by William McEwen
- *Strategic Brand Management: Building, Measuring, and Managing Brand Equity*, third edition (Prentice-Hall, 2007), by Kevin Lane Keller. This is the one of the more widely used academic textbooks for strategic brand management in the marketing programs of top business schools.
- *Strategic Brand Management: Creating and Sustaining Brand Equity Long Term* (Kogan Page, 1997) by Jean-Noel Kapferer

- *Why Johnny Can't Brand: Rediscovering the Lost Art of the Big Idea* (N. W. Widener, 2010) by Bill Schley and Carl Nichols Jr.
- *Brand Risk: Adding Risk Literacy to Brand Management* (Gower Publishing Company, 2008), by David Abrahams, covers the topic of brand risk management from the perspective of a risk management professional. Although Abrahams touches on some of the subjects covered in *Brand Resilience*, the focus is more technical and financial in nature.

A number of articles cover the topic of brand sabotage. Recent examples include Dan Schwabel, "5 Ways to Avoid Sabotaging Your Personal Brand Online," *Mashable / Business*, February 11, 2010, and Laura Lake, "Protect Your Brand From Employee Sabotage With A Social Media Policy," About.com: Marketing, July 5, 2010. Two of the earlier examples that we found were a pair of articles by professors Elaine Wallace and Leslie de Chernatony. The two authored an article in 2008 in *The Service Industries Journal* ("Classifying, identifying and managing the service brand saboteur") and an article titled "Exploring Brand Sabotage in Retail Banking" in 2009 in the *Journal of Product & Brand Management*, Vol. 18, Issue 3. Both articles focus on managers' and employees' views about service brand sabotage at the front line in retail banking.

Finally, if you want to do a deeper dive into extreme risk management, we suggest a compendium entitled, *Learning from Catastrophes: Strategies for Reaction and Response* (Pearson Prentice Hall, 2009), by Wharton professors Howard Kunreuther and Michael Useem. The 2009 publication date notwithstanding, *strategy + leadership* includes the book in its "2010 Best Business Books," with the following comments, "For any executive worried that his or her organization might be overtaken by low-probability, high consequence events, like a credit default swap implosion or a deepwater drilling fiasco, *Learning from Catastrophes: Strategies for Reaction and Response* could be the first step toward sleeping better at night.... The book's lessons include how to balance prevention and mitigation, and how to understand the difference between crisis response and true recovery."[1]

NOTES

ACKNOWLEDGMENTS

1. Deloitte refers to one or more of Deloitte Touche Tohmatsu Limited, a UK private company limited by guarantee, and its network of member firms, each of which is a legally separate and independent entity. Please see www.deloitte.com/about for a detailed description of the legal structure of Deloitte Touche Tohmatsu Limited and its member firms.

INTRODUCTION—IT'S WHAT YOU DO NEXT THAT COUNTS

1. John Paul Newport, "Looking Back: Year of the Tiger: The 2009 Golf Season Was Exciting and Eventful, Even before Everything Turned Upside Down," *The Wall Street Journal*, December 19, 2009, http://online.wsj.com/article/SB1000142405274870423810457460243172545073 4.html.
2. "Clubhouse Blues," uploaded to YouTube by lorymole2 on March 1, 2010, http://www.youtube.com/watch?v=ObfyXKx7eJc.
3. "Howard Stern Show Discusses Tiger Woods," uploaded to YouTube by AtheistsThinkMore, on December 14, 2009, http://www.youtube.com/watch?v=cgNRPgj_EnU.
4. Frank Rich, "Tiger Woods, Person of the Year," *The New York Times*, December 19, 2009, http://www.nytimes.com/2009/12/20/opinion/20rich.html.
5. Suzanne Vranica, "Tag Heuer Dials Back Woods," *The Wall Street Journal*, December 18, 2009, http://online.wsj.com/article/SB10001424052748703523504574604341424976878.html.
6. Emily Steel, "After Ditching Tiger, Accenture Tries New Game," *The Wall Street Journal*, January 14, 2010, http://online.wsj.com/article/SB10001424052748704675104575001243066822622.html.
7. Ken Belson and Richard Sandomir, "Insuring Endorsements against Athletes' Scandals," *The New York Times*, January 31, 2010, http://www.nytimes.com/2010/02/01/sports/01insurance.html.

8. Matthew Futterman and Douglas A. Blackmon, "PGA Tour Begins to Pay a Price for Tiger Woods's Transgressions," *The Wall Street Journal*, January 25, 2010, http://online.wsj.com/article/SB100014240527487036 99204575017550261245506.html.

9. Larry Dorman, "For Return, Woods Picks Place He's at Ease," *The New York Times*, March 16, 2010, http://www.nytimes.com/2010/03/17/sports/golf/17tiger.html.

10. "CNN: Tiger Woods' Full Apology," uploaded to YouTube by CNN on February 19, 2010, http://www.youtube.com/watch?v=Xs8nseNP4s0.

11. Jason Gay, "Maybe We All Need Rehab," *The Wall Street Journal*, February 20, 2010, http://online.wsj.com/article/SB10001424052748703 787304575075472168189584.html.

12. A study on the economic value of celebrity endorsements released by Carnegie Mellon University's Tepper School of Business in December 2010 indicated that Woods's sponsor Nike did not suffer the same level of sales declines as non-Woods sponsors, and Nike's profit was greater with Woods than without him. For additional detail on the study, see Kevin Chung, Timothy Derdenger, and Kannan Srinivasan, "Economic Value of Celebrity Endorsement: Tiger Woods' Impact on Sales of Nike Golf Balls," Tepper School of Business, Carnegie Mellon University, December 2, 2010, http://www.andrew.cmu.edu/user/derdenge/TWExecutiveSummary.pdf. Additional commentary can be found in E. J. Schultz, "Study: Standing by Tiger Helped Nike's Bottom Line," *Advertising Age*, December 2, 2010, http://adage.com/article?article_id=147431.

13. "Protecting & Strengthening Your Brand Across the Social Web," Business Development Institute, March 24, 2010, http://smallbiz technology.com/archive/2010/03/managing-your-reputation-prote .html.

14. Peter Verrengia, "It's What You Do Next That Counts, Tiger," ReputationPoint, November 30, 2009, http://reputationpoint.com/?p=324.

ONE—A BRAND NEW DAY

1. Jonathan Copulsky and Philippe Lebard, "Looking for Financial Relief in Tough Times? Try Brand Licensing," *Advertising Age*, July 14, 2009, http://adage.com/cmostrategy/article?article_id=137906.

2. Brett Pulley, "Fox, ESPN to Bid on Olympics Rights as NBC Faces Loss," *Bloomberg*, February 2, 2010, http://www.bloomberg.com/apps/news?pid=newsarchive&sid=aL.qWMf085zI; see also Michael

Hiestand, "Other '14 Events May Spoil Soichi Ratings," *USA Today*, August 27, 2010, http://www.usatoday.com/printedition/sports/20100827/hiestand27_st.art.htm.

3. Eric Wilson, "Kim Kardashian Inc.," *The New York Times*, November 17, 2010, http://www.nytimes.com/2010/11/18/fashion/18KIM.html; Katherine Rosman, "As Seen on TV: Brand Bethenny," *The Wall Street Journal*, November 24, 2010, http://online.wsj.com/article/SB10001424052748704369304575632673263667274.html.

4. Trump website, http://www.trump.com/.

5. Amy Chozick, "Desirée Rogers' Brand Obama," *The Wall Street Journal*, April 30, 2009, http://magazine.wsj.com/features/the-big-interview/desiree-rogers/.

6. Peter Baker, "Obama Social Secretary Ran into Sharp Elbows," *The New York Times*, March 11, 2010, http://www.nytimes.com/2010/03/12/us/politics/12rogers.html.

7. A number of articles appeared in the spring of 2010 discussing "Brand Palin," including: Timothy Egan, "The Palin Brand," *The New York Times*, May 26, 2010, http://opinionator.blogs.nytimes.com/2010/05/26/the-palin-brand/; Gabriel Sherman, "The Revolution Will Be Commercialized," *New York*, April 25, 2010, http://nymag.com/news/politics/65628/; Andrew Malcolm, "The Palin Brand: How an Ex-Alaska Governor Amassed $12 Million in 1 Year, Plus Lots of Political Capital," *The Los Angeles Times*, April 27, 2010, http://latimesblogs.latimes.com/washington/2010/04/sarah-palin-alaska-governor-12-million-political-capital-comeback.html; and David Carr, "How Palin Became a Brand," *The New York Times*, April 4, 2010, http://www.nytimes.com/2010/04/05/business/media/05carr.html.

8. Sarah Palin, *Going Rogue* (New York: HarperCollins, 2009).

9. Steven Stern, "Brooklyn: The Brand," *The New York Times*, December 14, 2010, http://www.nytimes.com/2010/12/15/dining/15brooklyn.html.

10. Wendy Wasserstein, "Pride and Platinum," *The New York Times Magazine*, February 10, 2002, http://www.nytimes.com/2002/02/10/magazine/style-pride-and-platinum.html.

11. Editorial, "Carlos the Brand," *The Wall Street Journal*, January 31, 2010, http://online.wsj.com/article/SB10001424052748703906204575027264127967140.html.

12. Barco Uniforms website, http://medical.barcouniforms.com/medical/catalog.asp?br=GR&cat=554&orig=554.

13. Rob Walker, "Branding Operation," *The New York Times Magazine*, October 3, 2010, http://www.nytimes.com/2010/10/03/magazine/03fob-consumed-t.html.

14. WorldLingo.com, "Bass Brewery," http://www.worldlingo.com/ma/enwiki/en/Bass_Brewery.

15. Tom Peters, "The Brand Called You," *Fast Company*, August 31, 1997, http://www.fastcompany.com/magazine/10/brandyou.html; Tom Peters, *The Brand You 50* (New York: Knopf, 1999).

16. Jennifer Mendelsohn, "Honey, Don't Bother Mommy. I'm Too Busy Building My Brand," *The New York Times*, March 12, 2010, http://www.nytimes.com/2010/03/14/fashion/14moms.html.

17. Genesower, "How to Build Your Personal Brand," *Playing in Traffic*, March 14, 2010, http://samsonmedia.net/blog/2010/03/how-to-build-your-personal-brand/.

18. "LeBrand: It Is Good to Be King James," Interbrand corporate website, http://www.interbrand.com/en/Interbrand-offices/Interbrand-New-York/Personal-Brand-Val-Lebron.aspx.

19. "BrandZ: Top 100 Most Valuable Global Brands 2010," Millward Brown corporate website, http://www.millwardbrown.com/Libraries/Optimor_BrandZ_Files/2010_BrandZ_Top100_Report.sflb.ashx.

20. Ibid.

21. Apple Inc., Form 10-Q, filed January 25, 2010, http://phx.corporate-ir.net/phoenix.zhtml?c=107357&p=irol-SECText&TEXT=aHR0cDovL2lyLmludC53ZXN0bGF3YnVzaW5lc3MuY29tL2RvY3VtZW50L3YxLzAwMDExOTMxMjUtMTAtMDEyMDg1L3htbtbA%3d%3d.

22. Copulsky and Lebard, "Looking for Financial Relief."

23. *Fortune*, "100 Best Companies to Work For," http://money.cnn.com/magazines/fortune/bestcompanies/2010/.

24. Jerry Useem, "Apple: America's Best Retailer," *Fortune*, March 8, 2007, http://money.cnn.com/magazines/fortune/fortune_archive/2007/03/19/8402321/index.htm.

25. "Gunsmoke," *Wapedia*, undated, http://wapedia.mobi/en/Gunsmoke; "Gunsmoke," *Mahalo*, undated, http://www.mahalo.com/gunsmoke-tv-show.

26. An article by Shira Ovide and Suzanne Vranica, " 'Lost' Finale Finds a Base, But Not Too Many Others," in the May 25, 2010, edition of the *Wall Street Journal* contains a table that vividly illustrates the splintering of television viewership. The *Gunsmoke* finale (March 31, 1975) had 30.9 million viewers, while the *Lost* finale (May 23, 2010) had 13.5 million viewers.

27. Watercooler changed its name to Kabam in August 2010 (see http://www.insidesocialgames.com/2010/08/03/watercooler-changes-name-kabam-deeper-social-games/); you can visit Kabam at http://www.kabam.com/.

28. James Hibbard, "Super Bowl Sets TV Ratings Record," *The Hollywood Reporter*, February 8, 2010, http://www.hollywoodreporter.com/news/super-bowl-sets-tv-ratings-20388.

29. Mike Linton, "Why Do Chief Marketing Officers Have a Short Shelf Life?" *Forbes,* May 15, 2009, http://www.forbes.com/2009/05/15/cmo-turnover-dilemma-cmo-network-dilemma.html.

30. International Organization for Standards 8402-1986, http://www.iso.org/iso/iso_catalogue/catalogue_ics/catalogue_detail_ics.htm?csnumber=15570. See, for example, "quality," *BusinessDictionary.com*, http://www.businessdictionary.com/definition/quality.html.

31. Consumers Union website, http://www.consumersunion.org/.

32. Alistair Davidson and Jonathan Copulsky, "Managing Webmavens: Relationships with Sophisticated Customers Via the Internet Can Transform Marketing and Speed Innovation," *Strategy & Leadership*, Vol. 34, Issue 3, 2006, http://www.emeraldinsight.com/journals.htm?articleid=1558343&show=abstract.

33. "Deloitte's State of the Media Democracy Survey Fourth Edition U.S. Release: December 2009," http://www.deloitte.com/view/en_US/us/Industries/Media-Entertainment/article/eb265fbf87595210VgnVCM100000ba42f00aRCRD.htm

34. The American Customer Satisfaction Index website, http://www.theacsi.org/.

35. Paul A. Argenti, James Lytton-Hitchens, and Richard Verity, "The Good, the Bad, and the Trustworthy," *strategy + business*, Issue 61, Fall 2010.

36. http://www.millwardbrown.com/Libraries/MB_News_Files/TrustR_MillwardBrown.sflb.ashx.

37. YouGov.com, http://www.yougov.com/frontpage/home.

38. The ad was placed by Motorola on behalf of its Droid X handset. See, for example, Raven Lovecraft, "Motorola Puts Ad in *New York Times* to Strike Back at Apple," TG Daily.com, July 28, 2010, http://www.tgdaily.com/mobility-brief/50849-motorola-puts-ad-in-new-york-times-to-strike-back-at-apple.

39. 2010 Edelman Trust Barometer, http://www.edelman.com/trust/2010/.

TWO—MARKETING AS WARFARE

1. Philip Kotler and Ravi Singh, "Marketing Warfare in the 1980s," *Journal Of Business Strategy*, Winter 1981, 30–41.

2. Bill Parks, Steven W. Pharr, and Bradley D. Lockeman, "A Marketer's Guide to Clausewitz: Lessons for Winning Market Share," *Business Horizons*, July–August 1994, 68–73.

3. Al Ries and Jack Trout, *Marketing Warfare* (New York: Plume, 1986).

4. Pat Conroy and Anupam Narula, "The Battle for Brands in a World of Private Labels," *The Deloitte Review,* Issue 7, 2010, http://www.deloitte .com/view/en_US/us/Insights/Browse-by-Content-Type/deloitte -review/6e46e86d189a9210VgnVCM100000ba42f00aRCRD.htm.

5. Ellen Byron, "P&G Chief Wages Offensive against Rivals, Risks Profits," *The Wall Street Journal,* August 19, 2010, http://online.wsj.com/ article/SB10001424052748703292704575393422328833674.html.

6. "Organization," The Official Homepage of the Unites States Army, http://www.army.mil/info/organization/.

7. Numerous suppliers offer campaign management software. For one example, see Aprimo's website, http://www.aprimo.com/Solutions_ B2B_.aspx?id=280. This example and other examples included in this book are provided for illustrative purposes only and do not constitute endorsement of the products or services described.

8. Credit for inventing the concept of the "four Ps" of marketing most likely belongs to E. Jerome McCarthy, a professor at Michigan State University. For an overview of the concept, see William Perreault, Jr., Joseph Cannon, and E. Jerome McCarthy, *Basic Marketing: A Marketing Strategy Planning Approach,* 17th edition (New York: McGraw-Hill/ Irwin), 2008.

9. Aric Rindfleisch, "Marketing as Warfare: Reassessing a Dominant Metaphor," *Business Horizons,* September–October 1996, http:// research3.bus.wisc.edu/mod/resource/view.php?id=1882 or http:// findarticles.com/p/articles/mi_m1038/is_n5_v39/ai_18736458/.

10. This book references *The Counterinsurgency Field Manual* extensively. This publication is also known as *FM 3-24* and *MCWP 3-33.5. FM 3-24* was released by the Department of the Army in December 2006 and is publicly available at http://www.fas.org/irp/doddir/army/fm3-24.pdf. The document is approved for public release, with unlimited distribution. *FM 3-24* is also available in a printed and bound edition for purchase through the University of Chicago Press at http://www.press. uchicago.edu/presssite/metadata.epl?mode=synopsis&bookkey=263154. The University of Chicago Press edition of *FM 3-24* includes additional materials, and the University of Chicago Press has agreed to donate a portion of the proceeds from this book to the Fisher House Foundation, a private-public partnership that supports the families of America's injured servicemen. All quotes from *FM 3-24* that are used in this book are taken from the publicly available downloadable version.

11. "Synopsis," *The U.S. Army/Marine Corps Counterinsurgency Field Manual,* The University of Chicago Press website, http://www.press .uchicago.edu/presssite/metadata.epl?mode=synopsis&bookkey=263154.

12. Ibid.
13. *FM 3-24*, Introduction.
14. Ibid.
15. Ibid.
16. *FM 3-24*, 1–157.
17. Ibid., 1–155.
18. Ibid., 1–152.
19. Paul Rogers, "Star Had Sued Valley Mogul to Keep Photograph Off Site," *Mercury News*, June 24, 2003. "Barbra Streisand Sues to Suppress Free Speech Protection for Widely Acclaimed Website," California Coastline website, http://www.californiacoastline.org/streisand/lawsuit.html.
20. Ibid.
21. "Sweet Success for Kit Kat Campaign: You Asked, Nestlé Has Answered," Greenpeace International website, May 17, 2010, http://www.greenpeace.org/international/en/news/features/Sweet-success-for-Kit-Kat-campaign/.
22. Xeni Jardin, "Ralph Lauren Opens New Outlet Store in the Uncanny Valley," Boing Boing website, September 29, 2009, http://www.boingboing.net/2009/09/29/ralph-lauren-opens-n.html.
23. Cory Doctorow, "The Criticism that Ralph Lauren Doesn't Want You to See!" Boing Boing website, October 6, 2009, http://boingboing.net/2009/10/06/the-criticism-that-r.html.
24. *FM 3-24*, 1–152.

THREE—STEP ONE, PART ONE

1. Frederick Funston, Stephen Wagner, and Henry Ristuccia, "Risk Intelligent Decision-Making: Ten Essential Skills for Surviving and Thriving in Uncertainty," *The Deloitte Review*, Issue 7, 2010, http://www.deloitte.com/view/en_US/us/Insights/Browse-by-Content-Type/deloitte-review/49bc61b284ea9210VgnVCM100000ba42f00aRCRD.htm.
2. "National Transportation Safety Board Operating Plan," National Transportation Safety Board website, www.ntsb.gov/abt_ntsb/Plans/FY10-Operating-Plan.pdf.
3. *FM 3-24*, 1–155.
4. Nassim Nicholas Taleb, *The Black Swan: The Impact of the Highly Improbable* (New York: Random House, 2007).
5. Chris Anderson, "Guest Review," posted to Amazon website, undated, http://www.amazon.com/Black-Swan-Impact-Highly-Improbable/dp/1400063515.

6. "Sabotage," *The Encyclopaedia Britannica,* http://www.britannica.com/EBchecked/topic/515124/sabotage.

7. Ben Zimmer, "The Language of Spilling Secrets, from Ancient Rome to WikiLeaks," *The New York Times Magazine,* August 20, 2010, http://www.nytimes.com/2010/08/22/magazine/22FOB-onlanguage-t.html?_r=1&ref=on_language.

8. Egil Krogh, "The Break-In That History Forgot," *The New York Times,* June 30, 2007, http://www.nytimes.com/2007/06/30/opinion/30krogh.html?_r=2&scp=2&sq=lewis%20fielding&st=cse.

9. Ibid.

10. Brian Chen, "Apple's Answer to Antennagate: Free iPhone 4 Cases," *Wired,* July 16, 2010, http://www.wired.com/gadgetlab/tag/antenna-gate/.

11. Wilson Rothman, "Apple Gives Free Bumpers to All iPhone 4 Owners," MSNBC, July 16, 2010, http://www.msnbc.msn.com/id/38263228/.

12. WikiLeaks website, http://wikileaks.org/.

13. Zimmer, "The Language of Spilling Secrets."

14. Paul Farhi and Ellen Nakashima, "Is WikiLeaks the Pentagon Papers, Part 2?" *The Washington Post,* July 27, 2010, http://www.washingtonpost.com/wp-dyn/content/article/2010/07/26/AR2010072605410.html.

15. L. Gordon Crovitz, "WikiLeaks and National Security," *The Wall Street Journal,* June 14, 2010, http://online.wsj.com/article/SB10001424052748703509404575301770502099014.html.

16. Edecio Martinez, "Steven Slater, JetBlue Flight Attendant, Curses Passenger, Grabs a Brew and Slides into Trouble," *48 Hours* website, August 10, 2010, http://www.cbsnews.com/8301-504083_162-20013138-504083.html?tag=mncol;lst;5.

17. Hilary Potkewitz, "Stressed JetBlue Attendant Not Flying Solo," *Crain's New York Business,* August 10, 2010, http://www.crainsnewyork.com/apps/pbcs.dll/article?AID=/20100810/FREE/100819968&utm_source=feedburner&utm_medium=feed&utm_campaign=Feed:+crainsnewyork.

18. The Ritz-Carlton has elevated the notion of employee empowerment to a fine art through rigorous training and consistent culture. The Ritz-Carlton's Malcolm Baldrige National Quality Award 1999 Application Summary describes the empowerment process and is publicly available at http://corporate.ritzcarlton.com/NR/rdonlyres/22E2CEC9-62A4-4EA2-9C3C-51628265E10E/0/rcappsum.pdf. Although it is more than ten years old, it still makes for good reading.

19. *FM 3-24*, Introduction.
20. Ibid., 1–157.
21. Rod Powers, "Punitive Articles of the UCMJ: Article 133—Conduct Unbecoming an Officer and a Gentleman," *About.com*, http://usmilitary.about.com/od/punitivearticles/a/mcm133.htm.
22. John Hofmeister, "Why We Hate the Oil Companies," *strategy + business*, Issue 59, May 3, 2010, http://www.strategy-business.com/article/10207?gko=d0e17.
23. Ibid.
24. Ibid.
25. Jonathan Copulsky and Philippe Lebard, "Looking for Financial Relief in Tough Times? Try Brand Licensing," *Advertising Age*, July 14, 2009, http://adage.com/cmostrategy/article?article_id=137906.
26. "Westin Heavenly Bed," Nordstrom website, http://shop.nordstrom.com/c/westin-heavenly-bed/home-accessories%3Fmarketingslots=2?origin=brandindex.
27. "Beyond Chocolate," Godiva Chocolatier website, http://www.godiva.com/beyond_chocolate/liqueur.aspx.
28. Copulsky and Lebard, "Looking for Financial Relief."
29. Brad Stone, "What's in a Name? For Apple, iPad Said More than Intended," *The New York Times*, January 28, 2010, http://www.nytimes.com/2010/01/29/technology/29name.html.
30. Suzanne Vranica and Amir Efrati, "Apple Tablet Draws Jeers, Legal Rumblings over iPad Name," *The Wall Street Journal*, January 30, 2010, http://online.wsj.com/article/SB10001424052748704194504575031532455016738.html.
31. Emily Steel, "Nestlé Takes a Beating on Social-Media Sites," *The Wall Street Journal*, March 29, 2010, http://online.wsj.com/article/SB10001424052702304434404575149883850508158.html.
32. Betsy McKay, "Food Dangers Get Closer Look," *The Wall Street Journal*, December 16, 2010, http://online.wsj.com/article/SB10001424052748704098304576021970089519118.html.
33. Pat Conroy and Anupam Narula, "The Battle for Brands in a World of Private Labels," *The Deloitte Review*, Issue 7, 2010, http://www.deloitte.com/view/en_US/us/Insights/Browse-by-Content-Type/deloitte-review/6e46e86d189a9210VgnVCM100000ba42f00aRCRD.htm.
34. "Criteo's Personalized Retargeting Solution," Criteo corporate website, http://www.criteo.com/us/retargeting/how-targeted-advertising-works.
35. Shopkick corporate website, http://www.shopkick.com/.

36. Paul H. Rubin, "Ten Fallacies about Web Privacy," *The Wall Street Journal*, August 30, 2010, http://online.wsj.com/article/SB100014240527 48704147804575455192488549362.html.

37. Courtney Banks, "Web Surfers Troubled by Tracking, Poll Says," *The Wall Street Journal*, December 21, 2010, http://blogs.wsj.com/digits/2010/12/21/web-surfers-troubled-by-tracking-poll-says/.

38. "FTC Testifies on Do Not Track Legislation," FTC website, posted December 2, 2010, http://www.ftc.gov/opa/2010/12/dnttestimony .shtm.

39. Funston, Wagner, and Ristuccia, "Risk Intelligent Decision-Making."

FOUR—STEP ONE, PART TWO

1. Francois Gossieaux and Ed Moran, *The Hyper-Social Organization: Eclipse Your Competition by Leveraging Social Media* (New York: McGraw-Hill, 2010), 323.

2. Weather regularly causes problems for airlines and politicians. In Chicago, the unexpected snowstorm of 1979 allowed mayoral candidate Jane Byrne to proclaim that Chicago was no longer "the city that worked" and defeat incumbent Michael Bilandic in the primary election. Byrne went on to win the general election, becoming Chicago's first female mayor. "Byrne's Victory: True Grit and Heavy Snow," *Illinois Issues*, May 8, 1979, Illinois Periodicals Online, http://www.lib .niu.edu/1979/ii790508.html.

3. Barbara "tire mire" Mikkelson, "Return to Spender," Snopes.com, January 3, 2007, http://www.snopes.com/business/consumer/nordstrom.asp.

4. Bernie Marcus, Arthur Blank, and Bob Andelman, *Built from Scratch* (New York: Crown Business Press, 1999).

5. A collection of David Segal's "The Haggler" columns from the *New York Times* can be found at http://topics.nytimes.com/top/news/business/columns/the_haggler/index.html?scp=1-spot&sq=The%20 Haggler&st=cse.

6. "Fatal Attraction Trailer," posted to YouTube by thornbrd, November 26, 2006, http://www.youtube.com/watch?v=IYpeKbHKVbU.

7. For more examples of how social media is being used to shame people, see Laura M. Olson, "The New Court of Shame Is Online," *The New York Times*, December 23, 2010, http://www.nytimes.com/2010/12/26/fashion/26shaming.html.

8. The description of this incident is based on publically available information, including both published articles and official government

documents, all of which are identified in the endnotes that follow. Two articles, in particular, are worth noting: Ellen Byron, "Diaper Gripes Grow Louder for P&G," *The Wall Street Journal*, May 14, 2010, http://online.wsj.com/article/SB100014240527487046352045752425212 17158484.html, and Kathy Shwiff and Anjali Cordeiro, "Regulators: Rash Is Not Caused by New Diapers," *The Wall Street Journal*, September 3, 2010, http://online.wsj.com/article/SB2000142405274870420680457 5467841765933692.html.

9. Jeff Plungis, "Procter & Gamble Diaper Complaints Can't Be Verified, U.S. Government Says," *Bloomberg*, September 2, 2010, http://www .bloomberg.com/news/2010—09-02/pampers-diaper-rash-reports -can-t-be-verified-u-s-safety-regulator-says.html.

10. Byron, "Diaper Gripes."

11. Truman Lewis, "Pampers Parents Liars? That's P&G's Response to Complaining Parents," ConsumerAffairs.com, May 7, 2010, http:// www.consumeraffairs.com/news04/2010/05/pampers_problems2 .html.

12. Byron, "Diaper Gripes."

13. "No Specific Cause Found Yet Linking Dry Max Diapers to Diaper Rash," U.S. Consumer Product Safety Commission website, http:// www.cpsc.gov/cpscpub/prerel/prhtml10/10331.html.

14. Another company that generated lots of web buzz was the Gap, when it introduced its new logo in 2010. After hearing a lot of negative chatter, the company decided not to change its logo after all. Rob Walker raised the question of whether negative publicity can actually help a brand in his article "Good News, Bad News," *The New York Times Magazine*, October 29, 2010, http://www.nytimes .com/2010/10/31/magazine/31fob-consumed-t.html. Walker's article focuses on the study "Positive Effects of Negative Publicity: When Negative Reviews Increase Sales," by marketing professors Jonah Berger, Alan T. Sorensen, and Scott J. Rasmussen, regarding the impact of negative publicity, http://marketing.wharton.upenn .edu/documents/research/Negative_Publicity.pdf. The authors conclude that "although companies and individuals often try to quiet negative publicity, our findings indicate that in some cases, it can actually have positive effects." In some cases, the value of the awareness generated by the negative publicity more than offsets the damage done by the negative comments.

15. According to an October 7, 2010, *Wall Street Journal* article titled "A Big Jump in Gripes about Airline Service," "Consumer complaints filed with the Department of Transportation [in 2010] are up a hefty 32%, to

8,797 from 6,676, compared with last year," http://online.wsj.com/article/SB10001424052748703735804575536134256657378.html.

16. Ibid.

17. Suzanne Vranica, "Snack Attack: Chip Eaters Make Noise about a Crunchy Bag," *The Wall Street Journal*, August 18, 2010, http://online .wsj.com/article/SB10001424052748703960004575427150103293906 .html.

18. "Our Compostable Bag Is Still Here," Sun Chips corporate website, http://www.sunchips.com/healthier_planet.shtml?s=content_ compostable_packaging. Based on Frito-Lay's announcement in October 2010 to reduce the use of its compostable packaging, the verbiage on the website has shifted slightly.

19. Suzanne Vranica, "Sun Chips Bag to Lose Its Crunch," *The Wall Street Journal*, October 6, 2010, http://online.wsj.com/article/SB100014240527 48703843804575534182403878708.html.

20. Sarah Parsons, "More Noise about SunChips Ditching Compostable Bags," change.org, October 20, 2010, https://news.change.org/stories/ more-noise-about-sunchips-ditching-compostable-bags.

21. Syms corporate website, http://www.syms.com/.

22. Gossieaux and Moran, *The Hypersocial Organization*, 155.

23. More and more high-end retailers, such as Saks Fifth Avenue and Nordstrom, "are opening their websites—and the brands they sell—to the slings and arrows of public opinion." Rachel Dodes, "Luxe Lowdown: Tony Sites Begin to Invite Buyer Reviews," *The Wall Street Journal*, October 18, 2010.

24. http://www.epinions.com/.

25. http://www.pissedconsumer.com/.

26. http://www.yelp.com/.

27. Biography of Angie Hicks, Angie's List corporate website, http:// www.angiehicksbowman.com/.

28. This speech is available widely on the Internet. One source is AmericanRhetoric.com, http://www.americanrhetoric.com/speeches/ teddyrooseveltmuckrake.htm.

29. "Corvair Handling and Stability," Corvair Society of America (CORSA) website, http://www.corvaircorsa.com/handling01.html; the actual reports (PB211015 and PB211014) are available for purchase at the National Technical Information Service's website, http://www.ntis.gov/.

30. For more suggestions, see James Surowiecki, "The Business-Movie Business," *The New Yorker*, October 11, 2010, http://www.newyorker .com/talk/financial/2010/10/11/101011ta_talk_surowiecki.

31. Stephen Miller, "He Used a Soapbox to Warn about Toys," *The Wall Street Journal*, September 8, 2010, http://online.wsj.com/article/SB1000 14240527487037200045754780080957980778.html.

32. Joe Bel Bruno, "Goldman Lists New 'Risk': Bad Press," *The Wall Street Journal*, March 1, 2010, http://online.wsj.com/article/SB100014240527 48704754604575095313135203110.html; a copy of the 2009 annual report can be found at http://www2.goldmansachs.com/our-firm/investors/financials/current/annual-reports/2009-complete-annual .pdf.

33. Thomas Kaplan, "Goldman Tries Rehab through Advertising," *The New York Times*, September 30, 2010, http://query.nytimes.com/gst/fullpage.html?res=9401E1DA1F39F933A0575AC0A9669D8B63.

34. Mark Leibovich, "Scamps, Saboteurs and the Occasional Criminal," *The New York Times*, January 31, 2010, http://www.nytimes.com/2010/01/31/weekinreview/31leibovich.html.

35. Jonathan Copulsky, "Suddenly, Brands Like Me. They Really Like Me," *Brandweek*, September 28, 2009.

36. The complete report of the 9/11 Commission is available for free on the Internet at http://govinfo.library.unt.edu/911/report/911Report.pdf. All quotations used in this book are taken from this version of the report.

37. Ibid, 344.

38. Ibid, 344.

39. Searcy Denncy Law Firm, www.thegulfcoastoilspill.com.

FIVE—STEP TWO

1. Frederick Funston, Stephen Wagner, and Henry Ristuccia, "Risk Intelligent Decision-Making: Ten Essential Skills for Surviving and Thriving in Uncertainty," *The Deloitte Review*, Issue 7, 2010, http://www .deloitte.com/view/en_US/us/Insights/Browse-by-Content-Type/deloitte-review/49bc61b284ea9210VgnVCM100000ba42f00aRCRD.htm.

2. Information about the Forest Service and Smokey Bear can be found at the USFS website, http://www.fs.fed.us/, and at http://www .smokeybear.com/.

3. "Assessing Progress towards an Integrated Risk and Cost Fire Management Strategy," 2007 U.S. Forest Service and Department of Interior Large Wildfire Cost Review, April 24, 2008, http://www.fs .fed.us/fire/publications/ilwc-panel/report-2007.pdf.

4. Norman Mclean, *Young Men and Fire* (Chicago: University of Chicago Press, 1993).

5. Timothy Egan, *The Big Burn* (New York: Houghton Mifflin Harcourt, 2009).

6. Richard Earle, *The Art of Cause Marketing: How to Use Advertising to Change Personal Behavior and Public Policy* (Chicago: McGraw-Hill, 2002), 61.

7. The entire series of surveys (2007–2010) is available for download at http://www.deloitte.com/view/en_US/us/About/Ethics-Independence/8aa3cb51ed812210VgnVCM100000ba42f00aRCRD.htm.

8. These results are consistent with individuals interviewed as part of "Life Sciences Professionals Social Networks Survey Findings," Deloitte Research, July 2010, in which only half of surveyed respondents say they have a social-networks policy and 43 percent had no guidelines for managing adverse events that may appear on a social network. The summary of these findings can be found in "To Friend or Not: New Insights about Social Networks in the Life Sciences Industry," Deloitte Research, 2010, http://www.deloitte.com/us/lssocialnetworks.

9. Interview with Tony Hsieh, CEO of Zappos.com by Victoria Brown, May 27, 2010, Big Think, http://bigthink.com/ideas/20673.

10. "Our Credo," Johnson & Johnson website, http://www.jnj.com/wps/wcm/connect/c7933f004f5563df9e22be1bb31559c7/our-credo.pdf?MOD=AJPERES.

11. "IBM Social Computing Guidelines," IBM website, www.ibm.com/blogs/zz/en/guidelines.html.

12. Dallas Lawrence, "6 Terrific Examples of Social Media Policies for Employees," Ragan.com, March 1, 2010, http://www.ragan.com/Main/Articles/40774.aspx.

13. Fred Burton and Scott Stewart, "Threats, Situational Awareness, and Perspective," *Stratfor Global Intelligence*, August 22, 2007, http://www.stratfor.com/threats_situational_awareness_and_perspective.

14. FM 3–24, 4–22.

15. "Online Social Media Principles," The Coca-Cola Company website, http://www.thecoca-colacompany.com/socialmedia/.

16. Cathy Benko and Molly Anderson, *The Corporate Lattice* (Boston: Harvard Business Press, 2010), 100, 102–103, 107, http://www.thecorporatelattice.com/.

SIX—STEP THREE

1. *FM 3-24*, Introduction.

2. Ibid., 1–155.

3. Jeff Howe, "The Rise of Crowdsourcing," *Wired*, Issue 14.06, June 2006, http://www.wired.com/wired/archive/14.06/crowds.html.

4. Jeff Howe, *Crowdsourcing: Why the Power of the Crowd Is Driving the Future of Business* (New York: Crown Business, 2008).

5. "Crowdsourcing: A Definition," Crowdsourcing website, http://www.crowdsourcing.com/.

6. US Geological Survey Twitter Earthquake Detection page, http://twitter.com/usgsted.

7. Timothy B. Hurst, "USGS Develops Twitter-Based Earthquake Detection System," *Ecopolitology*, January 7, 2010, http://ecopolitology.org/2010/01/07/usgs-develops-twitter-based-earthquake-detection-system/.

8. "About USGS," USGS website, http://www.usgs.gov/aboutusgs/.

9. "Earthquake Hazards—A National Threat," USGS Publications Warehouse.

10. Robert Scoble, "Twittering the Earthquake in China," Scobleizer blog, May 12, 2008, http://scobleizer.com/2008/05/12/quake-in-china/.

11. Rory Cellan-Jones, "Twitter and the Chinese Earthquake," BBC News dot.life, May 12, 2008, http://www.bbc.co.uk/blogs/technology/2008/05/twitter_and_the_china_earthqua.html.

12. "U.S. Geological Survey: Twitter Earthquake Detector (TED)," Department of Interior Recovery Investments website, September 9, 2010, http://recovery.doi.gov/press/us-geological-survey-twitter-earthquake-detector-ted/.

13. Hurst, "USGS Develops Twitter-Based."

14. "Shaking and Tweeting: The USGS Twitter Earthquake Detection Program," interview with Paul Earle and Michelle Guy hosted by Marisa Lubeck and posted on December 14, 2009 to USGS website, http://www.usgs.gov/corecast/details.asp?ep=113.

15. Another example of using Twitter to hone in on patterns is provided in "Geeks, Tweets, and Cash," *Deloitte Review*, Issue 7, 2010, http://www.deloitte.com/assets/Dcom-UnitedStates/Local%20Assets/Documents/Deloitte%20Review/Deloitte%20Review%20-%20Summer%202010/us_DeloitteReview_RileyCrane_0710.pdf. The article consists of an interview with Riley Crane of MIT Media Lab and the leader of the MIT Red Balloon Challenge Team that won the DARPA Network Challenge. "In December 2009, by using social networks and tools, a group of researchers at the Massachusetts Institute of Technology edged out about 4,300 other teams in a Pentagon-sponsored contest to correctly identify the location of 10 red balloons distributed around the United States." Riley discusses how his team

used "what we call a 'viral collaborative incentive program,' which mobilized crowds and helped the crowds and us to perform activities very efficiently and effectively to solve this big problem."

16. Ushahidi website, www.ushahidi.com/.

17. "Media Room & News," Humanity United website, http://www .humanityunited.org/pages/media/page:1.

18. "About Us," Ushahidi website, http://www.ushahidi.com/about.

19. Ibid.

20. Anand Giridharadas, "Africa's Gift to Silicon Valley: How to Track a Crisis," *The New York Times*, March 13, 2010, http://www.nytimes .com/2010/03/14/weekinreview/14giridharadas.html.

21. Adam Ostrow, "Inside Gatorade's Social Media Command Center," *Mashable*, June 15, 2010, http://mashable.com/2010/06/15/gatorade -social-media-mission-control/.

22. Ibid.

23. Ibid.

24. "Gatorade Mission Control," YouTube video posted by PepsiCoVideo, June 15, 2010, http://www.youtube.com/watch?v=InrOvEE2v38.

25. "The Press: Clipping Business," *Time*, May 30, 1932, http://www.time .com/time/magazine/article/0,9171,769604,00.html.

26. Ibid.

27. Julia Angwin and Steve Stecklow, " 'Scrapers' Dig Deep for Data on Web," *The Wall Street Journal*, October 12, 2010, http://online.wsj.com/ article/SB10001424052748703358504575544381288117888.html.

28. "Dow Jones Insight Overview," Dow Jones website, http://www .dowjones.com/product-djinsight.asp.

29. Ibid.

30. "Products: BuzzMetrics Services," Nielsen website, http://www .nielsen-online.com/products_buzz.jsp?section=pro_buzz.

31. About Us," NM Incite website, http://www.nmincite.com/?page_ id=311.

32. Ibid.

33. "About ListenLogic," ListenLogic website, http://www.listenlogic .com/about/index.php.

34. "Our Products," Listen Logic website, http://www.listenlogic.com/ products/index.php.

35. Ibid.

36. "Our Services," Listen Logic website, http://www.listenlogic.com/ services/index.php.

37. Ibid.

38. "Our Clients," ListenLogic website, http://www.listenlogic.com/ about/clients.php.

39. Reputation Defender website, http://www.reputationdefender .com/.

40. "The Press: Clipping Business."

41. "Klout: The Standard for Influence," Klout website, http://klout .com/.

42. Edward Tufte website, http://www.edwardtufte.com/tufte/.

SEVEN—STEP FOUR

1. Larry Weber, *Sticks & Stones: How Digital Business Reputations Are Created Over Time and Lost in a Click*, (Hoboken, NJ: Wiley, 2009).

2. Harlan Ullman and James Wade Jr., et al., *Shock & Awe: Achieving Rapid Dominance*, National Defense University Institute for National Strategic Studies, 1996, http://www.dodccrp.org/files/Ullman_ Shock.pdf.

3. Malcolm Gladwell, "Small Change: Why the Revolution Will Not Be Tweeted," *The New Yorker*, October 4, 2010, http://www.newyorker .com/reporting/2010/10/04/101004fa_fact_gladwell.

4. Ibid.

5. Ibid.

6. "Crisis Communications Strategies," Department of Defense Joint Course in Communication website, http://www.ou.edu/deptcomm/ dodjcc/groups/02C2/Johnson%20&%20Johnson.htm.

7. Tamara Kaplan, "The Tylenol Crisis: How Effective Public Relations Saved Johnson & Johnson," Aerobiological Engineering website, http://www.aerobiologicalengineering.com/wxk116/TylenolMurders/ crisis.html.

8. "Crisis Communications Strategies."

9. Tamper-evident packaging is designed to show any evidence of tampering. Additional details on Tylenol's tamper-evident packaging can be found at "Storage & Package Safety," Tylenol website, http://www .tylenol.com/product_detail.jhtml;jsessionid=ZC5JLDGKPKOCCCQP CCECUYYKB2IIWNSC?id=tylenol/pain/prod_ss.inc&prod= subpss&_requestid=1393901#.

10. Eric Dezenhall, "Tylenol Can't Cure All Crises," *USA Today*, March 19, 2004, http://www.usatoday.com/news/opinion/editorials/2004-03-17 -dezenhall_x.htm.

11. "Crisis Communications Strategies."

12. Dezenhall, "Tylenol."

13. Michael McCarthy, "Poll: Tiger's Favorability Showing Record Decline," *USA Today*, December 14, 2009, http://www.usatoday.com/ sports/golf/2009-12-14-tiger-woods-gallup-poll_N.htm.

14. A video of the press conference can be viewed at "NBC Video: Woods Apologizes," *The New York Times* video website, http://video.nytimes .com/video/2010/02/19/multimedia/1247467097314/nbc-video -woods-apologizes.html.

15. Alessandra Stanley, "Vulnerability in a Disciplined Performance," *The New York Times*, February 19, 2010, http://www.nytimes.com/ 2010/02/20/sports/golf/20watch.html.

16. "NBC Video: Woods Apologizes."

17. John Paul Newport, "Character and Decency Are What Count," *The Wall Street Journal*, February 20, 2010, http://online.wsj.com/article/SB 10001424052748703787304575075473080462374.html?mod=googlewsj.

18. Alina Tugend, "An Attempt to Revive the Lost Art of Apology," *The New York Times*, January 29, 2010, http://www.nytimes.com/2010/01/ 30/your-money/30shortcuts.html.

19. A list of Professor Cohen's publications can be found at http://www .law.ufl.edu/faculty/cohen/.

20. "I'm Sorry Laws: Summary of State Laws," American Medical Association (AMA) Advocacy Resource Center, February 2008, http:// www.ama-assn.org/ama1/pub/upload/mm/378/sorry-laws.pdf.

21. Patrick T. O'Rourke and Kari M. Hershey, "The Power of 'Sorry' " *The Hospitalist*, October 2007, http://www.the-hospitalist.org/details/ article/233905/The_Power_of_Sorry.html.

22. Elizabeth Bernstein, "I'm Very, Very, Very Sorry ... Really?" *The Wall Street Journal*, October 18, 2010, http://online.wsj.com/article/SB1000 14240527023044105045755600938840004442.html. Jennifer K. Robbennolt, a faculty member at the University of Illinois College of Law, has published several articles analyzing how apologies aid the resolution of a variety of legal cases, including wrongful firings, injury cases, and malpractice lawsuits. See "Robbennolt on Apologies and Legal Negotiation," Legal Informatics Blog, http:// legalinformatics.wordpress.com/2010/06/03/robbennolt-on -apologies-and-legal-negotiation/.

23. "Toyota Production System," Toyota website, http://www2.toyota .co.jp/en/vision/production_system/.

24. Taiichi Ohno, *Toyota Production System: Beyond Large-Scale Production*, (Portland, OR: Productivity Press, 1988).

25. Ibid.

26. Brian Ross, "Toyota CEO Apologizes to His Customers: 'I Am Deeply Sorry'," ABC News: The Blotter website, January 29, 2010, http:// abcnews.go.com/Blotter/toyota-ceo-apologizes-deeply/story? id=9700622.

27. Mike Ramsey, "Toyota Rethinks Pedal Design," *The Wall Street Journal*, August 17, 2010, http://online.wsj.com/article/SB1000142405274 87048686045754333351566752616.html?mod=WSJ_auto_LeadStory Collection.

28. Mike Ramsey and Josh Mitchell, "U.S. Study Points to Driver Error in Many Toyota Crashes," *The Wall Street Journal*, August 11, 2010, http://online.wsj.com/article/SB1000142405274870416490457542160316704696 6.html.

29. Ken Belson, "Toyota's Wrecked Image Needs the Right Bodywork," *The New York Times*, February 13, 2010, http://www.nytimes.com/2010/02/14/weekinreview/14belson.html.

30. Ibid.

31. Ibid.

32. Ibid.

33. Joint study conducted by Deloitte on behalf of the Grocery Manufacturers Association (GMA), Food Marketing Institute (FMI), and GS1 US, *Recall Execution Effectiveness: Collaborative Approaches to Improving Consumer Safety and Confidence*, May 2010, http://www.deloitte.com/assets/Dcom-UnitedStates/Local%20Assets/Documents/Consumer%20Business/US_CP_Joint%20Industry%20Recall%20Execution%20Effectiveness%20Report_052810.pdf.

34. *FM 3-24*, 3–50.

35. "Our Credo Values," Johnson & Johnson website, http://www.jnj.com/connect/about-jnj/jnj-credo/.

EIGHT—STEP FIVE

1. *FM 3-24*, 4–8.

2. Gerald Seib, "In Crisis, Opportunity for Obama," *The Wall Street Journal*, November 21, 2008, http://online.wsj.com/article/SB12272 1278056345271.html.

3. Ibid.

4. Katharine Q. Seelye, "A Different Emanuel for One Church," *The New York Times*, March 17, 2009, http://thecaucus.blogs.nytimes.com/2009/03/17/a-different-emanuel-for-one-church/.

5. Paul Steinhauser, "Ending Economic Crisis Won't Be Easy," CNNMoney.com, March 7, 2009, http://money.cnn.com/2009/03/07/news/economy/obama_saturday/index.htm.

6. Saj-nicole A. Joni, "Never Waste a Crisis," Forbes.com, November 24, 2008, http://www.forbes.com/2008/11/24/global-crisis-management -lead-management-cx_snj_1124joni.html.

7. "About the NTSB: History and Mission," NTSB website, http://www.ntsb.gov/abt_ntsb/history.htm.

8. Ibid.

9. "Most Wanted List: Transportation Safety Improvements," NTSB website, http://www.ntsb.gov/Recs/mostwanted/index.htm.

10. "National Transportation Safety Board Strategic Plan, Fiscal Years 2010 through 2015," November 30, 2009, NTSB website, https://www.ntsb.gov/Abt_NTSB/Plans/Strategic-Plan_2010-2015.pdf.

11. In December 2010, the NTSB chairman, Deborah Hersman, outlined an expanded role for NTSB beyond the investigation of specific accidents. This new role would include "a higher priority on collecting and studying industry-wide data about what prompted recent dangerous incidents." Andy Pasztor, "Air Safety Board Adds Prevention Role," *The Wall Street Journal*, December 27, 2010, http://online.wsj.com/article/SB20001424052970203568000457604404340675798 6.html.

12. "About the NTSB: The Investigative Process," NTSB website, http://www.ntsb.gov/abt_ntsb/invest.htm.

13. Richard Boyd, "Known Vehicle Causes of Unintended Acceleration," June 30, 2010, Office of Defects Investigation, National Highway Traffic Safety Administration, http://onlinepubs.trb.org/onlinepubs/ua/100630DOTSlidesBoyd.pdf; Mike Ramsey, "Toyota Rethinks Pedal Design," *The Wall Street Journal*, August 17, 2010, http://online.wsj.com/article/SB10001424052748704868604575433351566752616.html.

14. William Broad, "Taking Lessons from What Went Wrong," *The New York Times*, July 19, 2010, http://www.nytimes.com/2010/07/20/science/20lesson.html.

15. Chris Walters, "Consumerist Sleuths Tracks Down Offending Domino's Store," *The Consumerist*, April 14, 2009, http://consumerist.com/2009/04/consumerist-sleuths-track-down-offending-dominos-store.html; Stephanie Clifford, "Video Prank at Domino's Taints Brand," *The New York Times*, April 15, 2009, http://www.nytimes.com/2009/04/16/business/media/16dominos.html.

16. Ibid.

17. "Dominos CEO Response to YouTube Nastiness," Mukaumedia website, April 17, 2009, http://www.mukaumedia.co.uk/dominos-ceo-response-youtube-nastiness/.

18. Taulbee Jackson, "Domino's Loses 10% of Its Value in One Week," *Social Media Risk*, March 15, 2010, http://socialmediarisk.com/2010/03/dominos-loses-10-of-its-value-in-one-week/.

19. "Oh Yes We Did," Domino's Pizza website, http://www.pizzaturnaround.com/.

20. Ibid.
21. Miriam Reiner, "Domino's Pizza Heats Up on Earnings Beat," *The Street*, October 19, 2010, http://www.thestreet.com/story/10892960/dominos-pizza-heats-up-on-earnings-beat.html; "Domino's Pizza Inc." *The Street*, http://www.thestreet.com/quote/DPZ.html.
22. Barbara Lippert, "Domino's Delivers: Time for My Mea Culpa," *Adweek*, May 23, 2010, http://www.adweek.com/aw/content_display/creative/critique/e3idbde8a913c88374231ddc13b7ff852cd.
23. Stephen Zeitchik, "Sundance 2010: Festival Says It Wants to Change," *The Los Angeles Times*, January 21, 2010, http://latimesblogs.latimes.com/movies/2010/01/sundance-2010-festival-sats-it-needs-to-change.html.
24. Schumpeter, "Brand Rehab," *The Economist*, April 8, 2010, http://www.economist.com/node/15866025?story_id=15866025.
25. John Case, *Open-Book Management: The Coming Business Revolution* (New York: HarperBusiness, 1995).
26. Art Kleiner, "Jack Stack's Story Is an Open Book," *strategy + business*, July 1, 2001, http://www.strategy-business.com/article/20088?gko=5d060.
27. Charlene Li, *Open Leadership: How Social Technology Can Transform the Way You Lead* (San Francisco: Jossey-Bass, 2010), 23.
28. Ibid., xiii-xiv.
29. *FM 3-24*, cover.
30. Ibid., preface.
31. John A. Nagl, "The Evolution and Importance of Army/Marine Corps Field Manual 3-24, Counterinsurgency," *The Counterinsurgency Field Manual* (Chicago: University of Chicago Press, 2007), http://www.press.uchicago.edu/Misc/Chicago/841519foreword.html.

NINE—STEP SIX

1. President Reagan uttered this phrase at a news conference, citing this as an old Russian proverb, and provided the Russian version first. For a video clip of the news conference, go to "Trust but Verify," posted to YouTube by "theconservativewill" on March 7, 2008, http://www.youtube.com/watch?v=As6y5eI01XE&safety_mode=true&persist_safety_mode=1.
2. Louis V. Gerstner Jr., *Who Says Elephants Can't Dance?*, (New York: HarperCollins, 2002). IBM's website contains a review of Gerstner's book, written by Dennis Elenburg, IBM technical representative. You can find the review at "Book Review—Who Says Elephants Can't Dance?" IBM website, May 15, 2003, http://www.ibm.com/developerworks/rational/library/2071.html.

3. Yogi Berra with Dave Kaplan, *What Time Is It? You Mean Now? Advice for Life from the Zennest Master of Them All*, (New York: Simon & Schuster, 2002), 39.

4. *FM 3-24*, 5–94.

5. Ibid., 5–95.

6. Edward Koch, *How'm I Doing?: The Wit and Wisdom of Ed Koch*, (Scarsdale, NY: Lion Books, 1981).

7. Vincent E. Henry, "CompStat Management in the NYPD: Reducing Crime and Improving Quality of Life in New York City," The United Nations Asia and Far East Institute for the Prevention of Crime and the Treatment of Offenders, 129th International Senior Seminar Visiting Experts' Papers, http://www.unafei.or.jp/english/pdf/PDF_rms/no68/07_Dr.%20Henry-1_p100-116.pdf.

8. Ibid.

9. "SFPD CompStat," San Francisco Police Department website, http://sf-police.org/index.aspx?page=3254.

10. Jon M. Shane, "CompStat Process," *FBI Law Enforcement Bulletin*, April 2004, http://www2.fbi.gov/publications/leb/2004/april04leb.pdf.

11. James Willis, Stephen Mastrofski, and David Weisburd, "CompStat in Practice: An In-Depth Analysis of Three Cities," Police Foundation, 2003, http://www.policefoundation.org/pdf/compstatinpractice.pdf.

12. Netpromoter.com is the official website for the Net Promoter community and is managed by Satmetrix, http://www.netpromoter.com.

13. Frederick F. Reichheld, "The One Number You Need to Grow," *Harvard Business Review*, December 2003, http://hbr.org/2003/12/the-one-number-you-need-to-grow/ar/1; see also, Patrick Demoucelle, "One Number to Grow," Bain and Company results, March-April 2005, http://www.bain.com/bainweb/PDFs/cms/Public/Belgium_Results_One_number_to_grow.pdf, and Frederick F. Reichheld and James Allen, "One Number to Grow," Results Brief Newsletter, February 24, 2004, http://www.bain.com/bainweb/publications/publications_detail.asp?id=15302&menu_url=publications_results.asp.

14. Candid Camera website, http://www.candidcamera.com/.

15. "Undercover Boss," CBS website, http://www.cbs.com/primetime/undercover_boss/.

16. Ibid.

17. The comments that follow were the results of emails and commentary provided by Benoit Garbe during October–November 2010 and are quoted with his permission.

18. Del Monte Foods 2009 Annual Report, http://media.corporate-ir.net/media_files/irol/86/86259/AR2009/Del_Monte_2009_Annual_Report_entire.pdf.

19. Google 2009 Annual Report, http://investor.google.com/pdf/2009_google_annual_report.pdf.

20. Target 2009 Annual Report, http://media.corporate-ir.net/media_files/irol/65/65828/AP_Hi.pdf

21. "BNP Paribas Ranked 6th Most Valuable International Banking Brand by BrandFinance," July 3, 2009, BrandFinance website, http://www.brandfinance.com/news/press_releases/bnp-paribas-ranked-6th-most-valuable-international-banking-brand-by-brandfinance.

22. Ibid.

23. Vodafone 2010 Annual Report, http://www.vodafone.com/content/index/investors/reports/annual_report.html.

24. Philips 2009 Annual Report, http://www.annualreport2009.philips.com/.

25. "The Risk Intelligent Enterprise: Principles of Risk Intelligence," Deloitte website, July 14, 2010, http://www.deloitte.com/view/en_US/us/Services/featured-services/governance-risk-management/7169a68c4d101210VgnVCM100000ba42f00aRCRD.htm.

26. "Putting Risk in the Comfort Zone: Nine Principles for Building the Risk Intelligent Enterprise," Deloitte website, August 31, 2010, http://www.deloitte.com/view/en_US/us/Services/audit-enterprise-risk-services/governance-regulatory-risk-strategies/Enterprise-Risk-Management/6b929c9096ffd110VgnVCM100000ba42f00aRCRD.htm.

27. "Risk Intelligent Governance: A Practical Guide for Boards," Deloitte website, September 23, 2010, http://www.deloitte.com/view/en_US/us/Services/additional-services/governance-risk-management/86cad27dc6e23210VgnVCM100000ba42f00aRCRD.htm.

TEN—STEP SEVEN

1. "The Battle of Algiers," directed by Gillo Pontecorvo, written by Gillo Pontecorvo and Franco Solinas, released in Italy on September 8, 1966 and in the United States on September 20, 1967. Originally distributed by Rizzoli (now RCS MediaGroup S.p.A.); now distributed by Rialto Pictures. In French and Arabic. For additional information, see "The Battle of Algiers", Rialto Pictures website, http://www.rialtopictures.com/battle.html.

2. *FM 3-24*, Annotated Bibliography.

3. Michael T. Kaufman, "The World: Film Studies; What Does the Pentagon See in 'Battle of Algiers'?" *The New York Times*, September 7, 2003, http://www.nytimes.com/2003/09/07/weekinreview/the -world-film-studies-what-does-the-pentagon-see-in-battle-of -algiers.html.

4. Ibid.

5. Ann Hornaday, "'Battle of Algiers': A Revolution in Film," *The Washington Post*, January 9, 2004, http://www.washingtonpost.com/ wp-dyn/articles/A2099-2004Jan8.html.

6. "Define: Brand Enthusiast," Blackcoffee website, http://www .blackcoffee.com/brand-related/brand-terms/B/brand-enthusiast.

7. Slurpee website, http://www.slurpee.com/.

8. Bruce Horovitz, "Obama's 'Slurpee Summit' Joke Makes Icy Drink Hot," *USA Today*, November 4, 2010, http://www.usatoday.com/ money/industries/food/2010-11-04-slurpee04_ST_N.htm.

9. "7-Eleven® Slurpee® Trucks Take to the Road to Capitol Hill and Bring Slurpee Summit to the People," 7-Eleven website, http://corp.7 -eleven.com/Newsroom/2010NewsReleases/7ElevenBringsSlurpee SummittothePeople/tabid/446/Default.aspx.

10. Slurpee website, http://www.slurpee.com/.

11. Horovitz, "Obama's 'Slurpee Summit.'"

12. Pat Conroy and Anupam Narula, "A New Breed of Brand Advocates: Social Networking Redefines Customer Engagement," Deloitte 2010, http://www.deloitte.com/assets/Dcom-UnitedStates/Local%20 Assets/Documents/Consumer%20Business/US_CP_BrandAdvocates Study_020910.pdf.

13. Marta Strickland, "Five Brand Advocacy Myths," *Direct Marketing News*, February 5, 2010, http://www.dmnews.com/direct-by-design -blog/section/1241/.

14. "Communication for Development: Social Mobilization," UNICEF website, http://www.unicef.org/cbsc/index_42347.html.

15. Jeremy Heimans and Alnoor Ladha, "The New Rules for Purpose-Driven Brands," *Advertising Age*, October 14, 2010, http://adage.com/ goodworks/post?article_id=146452.

16. "Campaign for Real Beauty," Dove website, http://www.dove.us/#/ cfrb/.

17. "Nike Responsibility," Nike website, http://www.nikebiz.com/ responsibility/.

18. "Nike, Inc. Corporate Responsibility Report FY 07 08 09," Nike website, http://www.nikebiz.com/crreport/content/pdf/documents/en -US/full-report.pdf.

19. "Nike Foundation and Buffetts Join to Invest $100 Million in Girls," Nike website, May 27, 2008, http://www.nikefoundation.org/files/The_Girl_Effect_News_Release.pdf.
20. "About WOMMA," WOMMA website, http://womma.org/about/.
21. "About Us," Affinit!ve website, http://www.beaffinitive.com/about/.
22. Ibid.
23. Ibid.
24. Mobilization Labs website, http://www.mobilizationlabs.com/.
25. Zuberance website, http://www.zuberance.com/.
26. Available for download at http://www.zuberance.com/whitepaper.php.
27. Scott Cook, "The Contribution Revolution: Letting Volunteers Build Your Business," Harvard Business Review, October 2008, http://hbr.org/2008/10/the-contribution-revolution/ar/1.
28. "About Us," SAP Community Network website, http://www.sdn.sap.com/irj/scn/about.

ELEVEN—LOOKING BACKWARD, LOOKING FORWARD

1. Elizabeth Lux, "Brand Value," The Wall Street Journal, October 6, 2010, http://online.wsj.com/article/SB10001424052748704206804575467690964993952.html.
2. Julia Angwin, "The Web's New Gold Mine: Your Secrets," The Wall Street Journal, July 30, 2010, http://online.wsj.com/article/SB10001424052748703940904575395073512989404.html.
3. Editorial, "Wilding on the Web," The Wall Street Journal, December 10, 2010, http://online.wsj.com/article/SB10001424052748703766704576009713110732514.html.

FURTHER READING

1. Walter Kiechel III, "Leadership: Highlights in a Low Year," in "2010 Best Business Books," strategy + business, Issue 61, Winter 2010, 80. Also available as Reprint 10409 and accessible at http://www.strategy-business.com/media/file/sb61_10409.pdf.

INDEX